GOD and the Editor

# GOD
## AND THE
# EDITOR

My Search for Meaning at

## The New York Times

## Robert H. Phelps

Syracuse University Press

For a listing of books published and distributed by Syracuse University Press,
visit our Web site at SyracuseUniversityPress.syr.edu.

ISBN-13: 978-08156-0914-8      ISBN-10: 0-8156-0914-0

**Library of Congress Cataloging-in-Publication Data**
Phelps, Robert H.
God and the editor : my search for meaning at the New York Times /
Robert H. Phelps. — 1st ed.
p. cm.
Includes bibliographical references and index.
ISBN 978-0-8156-0914-8 (cloth : alk. paper)
1. Phelps, Robert H.   2. Journalists—United States—Biography.   I. Title.
PN4874.P475A3 2009
070.92—dc22
[B]
2008053116

*For Betty, who made*
*all the difference*

Photo by Deborah Smiley.

**Robert H. Phelps** learned editing basics at the *Providence Journal-Bulletin* before the *New York Times* hired him as a copyeditor. In 1965 he became news editor of the *Times* Washington bureau. He retired in 1974 and signed on with the *Boston Globe,* where he led coverage of school desegregation, for which the *Globe* won a Pulitzer Prize. Phelps is coauthor of *Libel: Rights, Risks, Responsibilities* and editor of *Witness to History,* the memoirs of Ambassador Charles E. Bohlen. For ten years he edited *Nieman Reports,* the journalism quarterly at Harvard University. Born July 19, 1919, in Erie, Pennsylvania, Phelps received a BA from the University of Michigan and an MS from the Graduate School of Journalism at Columbia University. A widower, he lives in Lincoln, Massachusetts.

# Contents

PART THREE • **The *Boston Globe***

# Illustrations

# Preface

**In the summer of 2003,** the online economics columnist David Warsh suggested that I write my memoirs. This did not seem like a good idea to me. I had held positions of responsibility as an editor at the *New York Times* for nearly twenty years and had even done some reporting, but most of my work was as an editor, a shadowy figure in the backfield, blocking for, cheering on, and sometimes scolding star reporters and top editors. Those were the journalists who wrote memoirs.

Warsh persisted, arguing that I had been involved in some of the big news stories of the second half of the twentieth century. He knew, from our conversations, that I had things to say about how reporters learned only half the lesson of the Pentagon Papers, why the *Times* played catch-up to the *Washington Post* on the Watergate scandal but, contrary to popular belief, eventually surpassed the *Post* on that seminal story, how the *Times* left out a key element of the riots at the 1968 Democratic convention in Chicago, how top *Times* editors forgot basic rules in headlining stories of John F. Kennedy's election and assassination. Warsh knew, too, of my mixed appraisals of such luminaries as A. M. Rosenthal, James B. Reston, Tom Wicker, Max Frankel, and E. Clifton Daniel and of my admiration of Seymour Hersh, Neil Sheehan, and Bill Beecher, three unlike scoop artists. Moreover, I had led the *Boston Globe's* coverage of school desegregation, for which it won the 1975 Pulitzer Prize for community service, and had sought to raise standards at that high-flying, if sometimes irresponsible, paper. Finally, I had attempted to guide young journalists like David Rosenbaum at the *Times* and Eileen McNamara at the *Globe* only to find that they guided me.

So I decided to write the book. After the usual delaying tactics— selecting a new chair easy on my bad back, moving furniture to make a comfortable place to write, buying a new computer and learning how to use new software, searching old files of letters and memos, and sucking my thumb over how to start—I took the easy way out by starting in Erie, Pennsylvania, where I was born and reared.

As I moved along I realized that journalism was only one path in my life. What Warsh and most others did not know was that from my youth and throughout my career I had quietly but persistently sought spiritual truth. The Hound of Heaven did not chase me, I hunted it, with little enlightenment. In fact, for most of my life journalism became, in effect, my religion. Then, in May 2003, Betty, my wife of fifty-six years, died and some remarkable things happened. Or did they? The reader will have to judge how much *God and the Editor* contributes to history and journalism and whether my spiritual journey was authentic.

# Acknowledgments

**How fortunate** for author and reader that so many writers, editors, advisers, critics, cheerleaders, counselors, gofers, naysayers, and nitpickers helped shape this book. David Warsh led the charge, sacrificing time, that most precious of gifts, from his online economics column to guide every step of the way. Two who also sacrificed quality time to critique more than one draft and offer sage advice were William Robbins, a former colleague at the *New York Times,* now retired in Texas, and Thomas F. Mulvoy Jr., former colleague at the *Boston Globe,* also retired, who successfully mothers as well as fathers four boys.

Phillip Querido, a friend from student days at the Columbia Graduate School of Journalism, kibitzed from Sao Paulo, Brazil, as did Dana Little, my former assistant in Washington, and her husband, Morgan Gilbert, from San Miguel de Allende, Mexico, thus making this an international project. Special thanks go to Deborah Smiley for numerous suggestions for changes and especially for her picture of my wife on the dedication page. Two who pointed out misjudgments and mistakes in the drafts were Cleve Mathews, who sat side by side with me through many a stormy day in Washington, and Eileen McNamara, who created her own stormy days as a Pulitzer Prize–winning *Boston Globe* columnist.

At the risk of leaving some people out, here are others who aided and abetted: James Naughton, former Washington colleague, now retired from the Poynter Institute; Richard Cheney—no, not that one, this is an old navy buddy and public relations whiz; John Crewdson, who somehow skipped the chores of internship at the *New York Times* to rise directly to stardom; Seymour Hersh, the investigator; Hank Klibanoff, managing editor/news of the *Atlanta Journal-Constitution;* Stephen Mielke, archivist of the Woodward-Bernstein papers at the Ransom Research Center at the University of Texas at Austin; Murray Seeger, whose copy I chopped up in New York, and Nadine Rebovich, who, from her desk at the Town of Lincoln library, searched doggedly around the country for old newspaper files.

When all is sent to the printer, however, everything depends on the publisher. My heartfelt thanks and admiration to Julie DuSablon, who edited the manuscript, to Mary Selden Evans, the executive editor of Syracuse University Press, to her skilled and caring assistant, Marcia Hough, to Lynn Hoppel and Lisa Renee Kuerbis for patience in creating the dust jacket, to Mona Hamlin in marketing, and to Kay Steinmetz for a sure hand in seeing me home.

PART ONE • **From Jesus to Journalism**

# 1. The Bible (Somewhat Revised) Told Me Who I Was

**In 1937,** when I was seventeen, I learned that I was not who I thought I was. I started to write "Howard" on a form the school sent home asking the name my parents wanted on my diploma. It was the only name I had known; my family and my friends called me Howard; that was the name registered in school. When I showed the form to my mother she smiled and said, "You know, your real name is Robert."[1]

She wasn't quite right, as I learned later, but I was surprised and delighted, and not just because it was a step toward enlightenment valuable for anyone of any age, let alone a spoiled kid reared in a World War I housing project during the Great Depression. I had long sensed a sissy quality in the name Howard, perhaps because I never measured up physically to my two brothers, perhaps because I played the violin. Well, let's not overstate the case—I took violin lessons, an endeavor that didn't fit in with the blue-collared, sports-minded residents of Ferncliff, the housing project where we lived, on the western edge of Erie, Pennsylvania, a chronically depressed Great Lakes industrial city.

Violin lessons fit in with my mother's idea of what a frail boy might study to keep him from the factories where most of the Ferncliff boys went after high school. I was born a blue baby and childhood diseases kept me crib-bound for the first year. I did take one step out of infancy; I threw myself from bed rather than lie in my wet diapers. With a little more spunk I would have walked before I was two years old.

A few years later the right side of my face nearly doubled in size. Diagnosing the illness as a form of tuberculosis (whatever the illness, puzzled doctors in those days often called it TB before they had viruses to blame),

2. My mother, Ruth Edwina Fox Phelps, barefoot grape picker, eighth-grade dropout, bride at sixteen, unpublished writer of romances, Democratic committeewoman.

Dr. Joseph Stackhouse, the family physician, lanced the swelling, cutting under my right eye. When the swelling subsided the puncture left a scar under my chin, which, twenty-nine nephews and nieces were told decades later, Japanese soldiers inflicted in hand-to-hand fighting in World War II.

Surprising everyone, I was well enough at eight to become a "junior merchant," the description newspaper publishers used for child labor, delivering forty or fifty copies of the *Erie Daily Times* afternoons in our neighborhood. In the spring I came down with pneumonia—not just regular pneumonia, but, as my mother boasted to neighbors, double pneumonia, meaning in both lungs. My parents gave up their bed for me. Week after week I sank lower and lower. One night my father, on the midnight

3. My father, Harry Vernon Phelps, abandoned by parents at eight, sixth-grade dropout, Wells-Fargo messenger, painter, leader of wartime General Electric strike.

watch, crept downstairs and whispered to my mother, sleeping on the sofa, "He's gone."

I was not dead. It was my first, and perhaps my greatest, act of deception. With antibiotics not yet available, Dr. Stackhouse turned to the miracle drug of the ages, whiskey. A few thimblefuls of Prohibition-era booze, purchased with a prescription at Jackson's Drug Store, revived my ravaged body. My father celebrated by drinking the rest. Pop felt great immediately; I took much longer to recover.

The few months as a paperboy provided me with sufficient evidence to cite over the years that I began my journalism career at the very bottom.

I took violin lessons for six or seven years, practicing two hours a day, but lacked the supple fingers and, more importantly, the ear for music necessary for success. To me, perfect pitch was a called third strike. With superb bowing and the skillful piano accompaniment of William Nelson, a member of my class at Strong Vincent High School, I did win the 1937 Erie County violin championship for high school students. In the competition for the Western Pennsylvania title, I placed last of the three contestants.

Finally facing up to the question, I asked my teacher, Howard Schilken, what I could hope to achieve. He said I could become what he was, a symphony orchestra player and a high school music teacher. Could I become a soloist? "What's wrong with playing in a symphony orchestra?" he responded. Everything, to the ambitious youth I had become, filled with dreams of reaching the top, unwilling to settle for less than perfection. I did not take another violin lesson.

I wrote a letter of inquiry to Harvard University, citing my high grades and asking if I could go there although I could not pay the tuition. The answer came back: go to a good state university. While the Depression had eased, my parents still lacked the money even for a cheap state college. To cut costs to the minimum, I stayed at home, carried my lunch, and walked to Cathedral College, a new two-year college sponsored by the Erie Roman Catholic diocese.

While Catholic education was known in those days for teaching by rote, my English teacher, the youthful John Waldron, helped me to think critically. He taught me how to ask questions as I read, a skill that proved invaluable the rest of my life, especially as an editor. A Catholic University graduate who had initially intended to become a priest, he led me into poetry beyond the level of America's most beloved, like Joyce Kilmer's "Trees" and Rudyard Kipling's "If." With classes of eight or ten students, Waldron had time for a great deal of personal attention.

At the beginning of freshman English he gave the class a spelling test. When I failed it he said I should learn the rules. "But spellers are born, not made," I protested. He took me in hand and showed me the rules. At the end of the semester he squeezed his eyes shut, wrinkled his freckled brow, shook his head, and sadly agreed that, as far as I was concerned, spellers

were born, not made. My spelling deficiency was a sure indication, unde-
tected at the time, that I was going to be a journalist.

Waldron was the first of a half-dozen men who saw not only my
shortcomings but also my possibilities for growth. Without their encour-
agement and help I would have foundered along the way as I struggled
to find my place in journalism. In each case these teachers went beyond
their role of merely correcting my mistakes to point the way to an ethical
life. Not one of those influential mentors ever suggested ways to make
more money.

It was at this little junior college that my respect for Catholicism
developed. Waldron was a principal reason. So was Dr. Joseph Wehrle,
the founder and president of the school. He lived with a big long-haired
dog in a single room in an old mansion that housed the administrative
offices and all the classrooms. In this room, furnished only with a brass
bedstead, a desk, and a few chairs, he counseled students, puffing on cig-
arettes and running his large hands through his tousled blond hair—or
his dog's. His simple, dedicated life impressed me. Father Wehrle was
greatly responsible for building the school into what is now the thriving
Gannon University.

In one of our many conversations, I told Waldron that the Catholic
Church would never convert me; he countered that it had never tried. I
was wary of religion because in my early teens I was "saved" at a revival
meeting at the Delaware Avenue Baptist Church in my neighborhood. The
pastor, the Rev. Thomas D. Edwards, had invited an evangelist to preach
every night for a week. I played the violin and grandmotherly Emily
Vaughn played the piano. Each night ended with the evangelist urging
the congregation to go forward to accept Jesus as savior. I sat in my chair,
unmoved. The last night of the revival the evangelist told a story of a service he had conducted in another town. He had noticed that every night a
man sat in the last row, but never went forward, not even after hearing the
message for nearly a week.

On leaving the church, the evangelist saw the man sitting on a park
bench, desolate, his head in his hands. Asked what was wrong, the man
said that each night a voice behind him had told him to go forward, but he
had resisted. On that last night the voice had said, "It's now or never." The

man turned around; there was no one there. He rose, hesitated, and sat down. His last chance had passed; he knew that he would never be saved. The evangelist told the man he was right; he was doomed. Don't be like that man, the evangelist admonished the Delaware Avenue congregation, it may be now or never for you.

We were playing a hymn with each verse ending, "almost persuaded, almost, not quite." As we finished, Emily Vaughn went forward, as she had every night. Something hit me inside. It was not a voice; it was not transcendence. There was no joy, no rapture, no feeling of being a new person. It was, perhaps, a guilty feeling that Emily Vaughn, a saintly woman, believed she had to be saved while I didn't. I put down my violin and went forward, standing with her and a few others, our heads bowed. When the service was over Pastor Edwards and the evangelist congratulated us, but I spoiled the victory. "Wait a minute," I said. "I'm not convinced about a lot of things."

"Like what?"

"Well, that it is wrong to dance or play cards or drink wine," all Phelps family pleasures.

"Well, let us kneel down now and pray that you see that they are wrong."

"No," I insisted, "but I will pray that if they are wrong I will see that."

Irritated, Pastor Edwards muttered, "Oh, all right," and we knelt and prayed.

The news got home before I did. My mother smiled. I was ashamed.

A few Sundays later, as a group of us kids were playing stickball under a street light, Pastor Edwards drove by in his Model T Ford. "I haven't seen you at church," he said. "No, and you won't," I replied. "You tricked me."

I never went back to Delaware Avenue Baptist Church. From then on I was wary of committing myself to any religion and doubly wary of evangelicals. But religion still interested me. When Jehovah Witnesses knocked on our door I invited them in, listened to their earnest spiel about Jesus's appearance on World War I battlefields, read their booklet, "Where Are the Dead?" and even at that youthful age marveled at their gullibility.

My secular upbringing provides no explanation for this early interest in religion. My parents were born Methodists and sent their first child, John, to Sunday school at a nearby Christian Science Church. They yanked him out when he rejected a simple bandage for a scrape on a knee in a playground accident, insisting that prayer would heal the wound. In fact, my mother and father did not go to any church until my final high school years and did not urge their four kids to do so. Even then Mom and Pop opted for the fuzzy-minded Unitarians, a decision that cast doubt on their Christianity among our Baptist and Roman Catholic neighbors, who professed more rigorous beliefs.

Mom kissed us when we went to bed but did not teach us to kneel and pray, as depicted in Norman Rockwell paintings, not even the childish, "Now I lay me down to sleep, I pray the Lord my soul to keep." Although a parchment copy of the Ten Commandments was tacked on my parents' bedroom door, we did not have a Bible in the house. At meals we all dived into our food without benefit of grace except when my father's great uncle Albion paid his annual fall visit. On those occasions Pop would turn to his elderly kinsman—Albion must have been only in his late forties, but he wore a beard!—and asked him to give the blessing. Uncle Albion, a true camp-meeting Methodist, bowed his head and was off on a thank-you so long and so earnest that no Supreme Being worthy of the capitalized title could reject it. My sister Margaret and I heard only the beginning. Just as Uncle Albion was warming up, one of us began to giggle, the other would quickly follow, and Mom would sternly order us to leave the table.

When my parents joined the Erie Unitarian Church I went along and kept going every week, mostly because I fell in love there with Lucy Jane Marlow (she did not know it), but also because the Unitarians claimed my hero president, Thomas Jefferson, as one of their own. A folder I picked up at church quoted Jefferson as saying: "I trust that there is not a young man now living in the United States who will not die a Unitarian." That double negative tripped me up for a moment, but I was sharp enough to see that no source was named for the quotation. Did Jefferson actually say that? (It was not until journalism school that I learned I could not survive without "allegedly.") Like Jefferson, I praised the Unitarians but kept my distance. It's only fair to note that American Unitarians hadn't organized into churches at that time; there are lots of them now.

The Unitarians opened up a new way of looking at religion, the Bible as social gospel. The emphasis shifted from Jesus the man-God who died to save our sins, as preached by most Protestants, to Jesus the reformer who sought to help the poor, the weak, the neglected.

This kind of religion fit comfortably into the constant talk of politics at the Phelps dinner table. My mother was the Democratic committee-woman in our neighborhood; my father was vice president of the union at the General Electric Erie plant. We were stout defenders of President Franklin D. Roosevelt and gobbled up information about the New Deal wherever we could find it. I learned to go beyond the comics in the *Erie Daily Times* to read about exciting changes in government and society.

Glaring under his bushy eyebrows on page one, John L. Lewis, president of the United Mine Workers, thundered to coal operators: "You lie in your beards and you lie in your bowels." (Years later, when I met Lewis, his soft hands appalled me.)

The liberal Drew Pearson was our favorite political columnist, because he always seemed to tell the inside story. The loveable Will Rogers, another favorite, was always good for a laugh. Newspapers were exciting.

Radio was coming into its own, too. Opposed by newspaper publishers, Roosevelt talked directly to the people in his fireside chats, the Phelps family crowding around our $125 Crosley table radio. I hung on to Westbrook van Voorhis's voice on *Time* magazine's weekly radio program as he intoned, "As it must to all men, death came this week to—" (whoever had died) and, after a short obituary, boomed out "Time marches on!"

My spine tingled in reading Emperor Haile Selassie's plea for help in fighting the Italian invasion of Ethiopia: "I say prophetically and without bitterness, unless the West comes to the aid of the East, the West is doomed." Hitler's harangues in German, which, of course I didn't understand, held me with their power, and when H. V. Kaltenborn, one of the first radio commentators, analyzed their significance in his German accent, I was experiencing history.

Given this context and the urgings of Joe Gray, a friend, I decided to study journalism when I transferred to the University of Michigan in 1939 for my final two years in college. I wanted to write about events and change the world.

And yet, beyond politics and history, words also had a deeper, personal impact. In his opening prayer in his weekly radio broadcasts from the Shrine of the Little Flower in Royal Oak, Michigan, the Rev. Charles E. Coughlin mesmerized me: "O Word of God incarnate, O wisdom from on high, O truth unchanged, unchanging, O light in our dark sky."[2]

Those words appealed to my heart. To me, Father Coughlin was praying about eternal truths far more important and far more personal but often conflicting with my political leanings. His prayer threatened to supplant my favorite, if apocryphal, Unitarian prayer, which appealed to my head: "O God, if there is a God, save my soul, if I have a soul."

At the University of Michigan the conflict deepened. My head defeated but did not knock out my spiritual longings. When I opened the text of my first psychology book I was "shocked"—that's the word I used in writing to my parents—to see a long section questioning Christianity. Contradictions in the Bible, scientific evidence rebutting as myths Old Testament stories such as the creation of the world, and opposing claims by other religions added up to a powerful doubt of Christianity.

By the next spring I was calling myself an agnostic, but, true to form, I was skeptical of agnosticism. As the Harvard psychologist and philosopher William James wrote, there is a "will to believe." For a course in religion I critiqued the Ann Arbor Unitarian Church as lacking in spirituality, a defect that I found in some, but not all, Unitarian churches wherever I have lived. Not until my wife died did I resolve the seeming contradiction between myth and spirituality.

In Ann Arbor I discovered that the journalism department was based on the concept that students should spend most of their time getting a broad background in the social sciences instead of concentrating on the techniques of news gathering and writing. The concept was, and still is, sound, but if I had entered Michigan as a freshman I would have learned early that foresighted journalism students worked at the well-regarded *Michigan Daily*, the student newspaper, which provided on-the-job training while allowing time for general studies. Generally those who wanted to start out on small papers studied at the journalism department and those who wanted to jump right into big-time journalism worked on the *Michigan Daily*.

With my naïveté, I doubt that I could have held a job on the *Michigan Daily*. My protected life at home, a social life limited to boys in our housing project, and the lack of a wider exchange of ideas with students at Cathedral College seriously handicapped me. A richer background would have given me the same start that more privileged students enjoyed.

The journalism department with its three professors offered the best education for me. John Brumm, grandfatherly and serious, headed the department, but Assistant Professor Wesley Maurer was the driving spirit. Although his only journalism credentials were that he had worked on a small paper in the Hocking Valley in Ohio, he taught with a confidence buttressed by his Socialist views. Maurer eventually headed the department and stayed on for many years. Donald Hamilton Haines, a tweedy, mustachioed fiction writer, taught magazine writing.

At the first meeting of the newswriting class I asked Maurer whether the lead paragraph of stories should be a summary. He cut off the class snickers—other students had learned the answer in high school—by responding, "That's a discerning question." I hung on to those few words of praise because I needed them to sustain me as I strived to master journalistic writing. My papers were awkward and unorganized, because in my pre-Michigan days I had not followed the first rule of writing: write every day. If I had spent as much time writing as I had practicing the violin, I wouldn't have been so tongue-tied at the typewriter in Ann Arbor. I struggled over every paper. It is a wonder that no one told me to forget journalism. There were many disquieting signals.

I received a 5, the lowest mark, on my first news story. Not sensing any improvement in the next two months I asked Professor Maurer near the close of my first semester whether I should stay in journalism. He said yes, but expressed no enthusiasm. To my surprise, he gave me a B in newswriting; to my disappointment a law school professor gave me a C in Law of the Press. Both were below my usual As in high school and Cathedral College. In a letter home I doubted whether I could handle the second semester's advanced newswriting class.

In April Maurer warned me of "dire consequences" in June unless I wrote more news articles. I explained that with two outside jobs I had trouble finding the time. He obligingly adjusted my classes. A few weeks later he said I was coming along slowly, not to worry, to keep plugging.

The second semester my newswriting mark dropped to a C and the professors selected me for only a minor role in putting out a clipsheet of articles students wrote and edited. The clipsheet was sent to Michigan newspapers and many weeklies used it for fillers. It was the best the department offered in published material, a puny contrast to the student-run *Michigan Daily*.

In the end, I could count only a few minor successes in those two years at the journalism school. Other students had tittered at my naïveté. I was embarrassed by the laughter that followed the reading of a story I had written that used "ejaculated" as a synonym for "said."

The article I wrote with the most impact was based on an interview with a professor who said that government, in building roads and schools and providing police and fire protection and other services, gave taxpayers more for their money than business did in selling products to consumers. Editorial writers at some Michigan newspapers who read the article in the clipsheet denounced it as another example of socialism emanating from wooly heads at Ann Arbor.

Brumm did like my essay on religious beliefs. It said that true religion consisted of helping people. Brumm wrote on it, "Better than a creed."

Less certain as a success was a lead I wrote on an article on poverty. A product of my class-consciousness and my devotion to the sound of words, it led with the opening lines of Edwin Markham's "Man With the Hoe":

Bowed by the weight of centuries he leans
Upon his hoe and gazes on the ground,
The emptiness of ages in his face,
And on his back the burden of the world.

Brumm read it to the class and asked, "Is this good or is the author wallowing in it?" The class thought I was wallowing but I was pleased because I thought he really liked it.

The other "success" was a headline I wrote on a brief feature story I had written for the clipsheet. It concerned couples who took out marriage licenses but never married: "Altar-Struck Couples Alter Struck Hearts." I still think that is good because it isn't just a play on words; the pun works both ways, as it should. That tiny sign was the first indication that I might make it as an editor.

With my Cathedral College grades knocked down to Cs and my only As in philosophy, political science, and psychology, I was graduated without honors from Michigan on June 22, 1941, the day Hitler invaded the Soviet Union. At a party for the journalism graduates at his home, Professor Maurer advised me to get a job at a small newspaper. "Everyone will write to the Chicago and Detroit papers," he said, "but you would be better off going to a small paper, where you will learn a lot more."

Professor Maurer obviously did not see great possibilities for me. In truth, two years in Ann Arbor had shaken my belief in myself. I doubted I could be a journalist, much as I had doubted I was a musician. A new world beckoned, but where was it summoning me?

# 2. Sex, Pacifism, and the Cub Reporter

**When I returned home** I wrote a form letter that I sent to a half dozen small papers in Michigan. Demonstrating my continued interest in religion, I emphasized knowledge of church affairs I did not possess. Cribbing from a headline in *Time* magazine, I began: "In Europe, only the cross has not bowed to the swastika" and went on to say that newspapers did not cover religion adequately.

Since postwar revelations about tepid church reaction to Hitler, I now know how shortsighted I was to accept *Time*'s conclusion of widespread church resistance to him. But my point was accurate. Newspapers and the media in general didn't do a good job in covering religion. They have improved but there is a long way to go. Although my academic knowledge of religion was limited to two courses I had taken, I boldly suggested that I could show them how to write about the subject. A few editors invited me for interviews. Concerned that I might be misleading them, I begged off, saying I faced a military draft call. The Selective Service system was calling up men soon after they graduated from college. It was a test I feared.

I worried whether I should declare myself a conscientious objector. From Ann Arbor I had written my parents:

> I wonder if I must suffer for my stand. I wouldn't be so afraid of prison
> as I would be the treatment I would get from my friends who fail to see
> my side of the picture. I think they would renounce all connections with
> me as friends did to conscientious objectors in World War I.

I opposed American intervention in the war against the Axis. For me pacifism was a moral imperative. War was wrong even against Hitler.

Pacifism represented true religion in practice. It offered a purity of belief I had not found in churches. I applied for exemption from the draft as a conscientious objector.

Not belonging to any church, I cited moral grounds. The film *All Quiet on the Western Front*, about World War I, and its star, Lew Ayres, a pacifist himself, had inspired me, but I realized the draft board wouldn't recognize a Hollywood picture and actor as legitimate influences. I cited Leo Tolstoy and Mahatma Gandhi. That statement was a stretch. I had read *War and Peace* and some comments about Tolstoy's pacifism but had not delved deeply into his beliefs. My sole acquaintance with Gandhi came from news stories and movie newsreels about his nonviolent campaign to free India from British rule.

In Ann Arbor, I lacked the time to get active in the debate that was roiling the campus over whether the United States should intervene. While I shied from America First, the principal antiwar organization, which was supported by the aviator hero Charles A. Lindbergh, I was greatly influenced by Harry Elmer Barnes, a historian who lectured at Columbia University, Smith College, and other colleges. He was also a Scripps-Howard columnist.

A revisionist, Barnes placed blame for World War I not just on Germany, but also on France and Russia. I attended his campus lecture at Rackham Hall in May 1940 as Hitler pursued his blitzkrieg through the Netherlands and Belgium into France. Barnes said that the war in Europe was between the new thieves, Germany and Italy, who wanted colonies seized the previous century by the old thieves, England and France. Because the United States was a former British colony, it had no stake in the war's outcome. His speech made sense to me and I joined in the enthusiastic applause.

The draft board quickly rejected my request for exemption because I was not a member of a traditionally pacifist church, like the Society of Friends, the Quakers.

While waiting for orders to appear for a physical examination, I wrote a letter applying for a reporting job on small dailies in Western Pennsylvania whose cities' names began with "A." Before I could get to the "Bs" I received a call from the *Daily Citizen* in Ambridge, offering me a job.

Ambridge, named for the American Bridge Company, then a subsidiary of U.S. Steel, was a blue-collar town of about 25,000, many of Eastern European lineage, just north of Pittsburgh on the Ohio River. I went down and took the job.

At $20 a week I was the only full-time reporter. With my credentials I was overpaid. My first day on the job, August 4, 1941, I made page one with a one-sentence story about a panhandler sent to jail for fifteen days. Harrison E. Salisbury, who decades later changed my career, wrote the lead article, a UP war roundup leading with Hitler's army closing in on Kiev.

My immediate boss was Arthur T. Thompson, the editor, a boorish man in his sixties who had been fired from a small paper in Central Pennsylvania and was filling in the years before he died. He seldom touched my copy or that of the city editor, Percy H. "Doc" Dougherty. A town character, Dougherty, ever flashing his yellowed and blackened teeth, lived at the paper, sleeping in his clothes at his desk every night, waking when printers arrived in the morning with his coffee. He worked the telephone, calling sources regarding city council meetings, school board sessions, and tips and articles in other papers. Scribbling his articles in pencil on half sheets of copy paper, he would toss them to Thompson, who would write the headlines. When the workday was over Doc would head for a bar and drink beer into the night, as his rotund belly attested. Then he returned to the paper and nodded off at the desk. He did not attend the public sessions he wrote about, depending on friends he cultivated over decades to fill him in. The sour odor of beer, cigars, and undigested food wafted about him.

Thompson found me a room in the house where he lived. Our landlady shuffled around in a bathrobe and bedroom slippers. Her taciturn husband clerked in a steel mill. Their daughter, Deanie, a telephone operator, was pretty, chubby, and sexually attractive. Deanie told me about troubles with her boyfriend and with a gas station mechanic with whom she was having an affair.

One day she showed me a small diamond engagement ring that her boyfriend had given her. Knowing about her affair with the mechanic, I wrote a column of local personal items, which I didn't do very often, and included a mention of an anonymous telephone operator's engagement. Stealing from a syndicated advice-to-the-lovelorn column, I noted that just because a man had put a ring on the telephone operator's trembling finger didn't mean they would get married.

That night Deanie burst into my room while I was sleeping, shouting that I had made a fool of her because she was the only telephone operator in town with a new engagement ring. I succeeded in calming her and she suddenly became amorous. She took off her clothes and slid her Renoir body into my bed, surprised that I was naked. "You're so thin," she said, stroking me. "Do you have any protection?" I didn't and she slid her voluptuous self right out.

I was learning to use the power of the press for personal advantage, a weakness that took me years to overcome. I did not consider the item a violation of Deanie's privacy; my motive was only to tease, a skill I had developed as a child with my tart tongue because people laughed at my barbs. I dismissed Deanie's protest because she seemed to enjoy the publicity and her eagerness to sleep with me showed how clever I was. If any professor at the University of Michigan taught journalism students in classes I attended about Supreme Court Justice Louis Brandeis's decades of advocacy of the right of privacy the subject went right over my head. At the *Ambridge Citizen*, Thompson thought my item about Deanie was hilarious. Not until I went to the Graduate School of Journalism at Columbia University did I learn about the proposal to use the Fourth Amendment to limit the First Amendment. The Brandeis position became the law of the land in 1967, but has been whittled back since then.

A Polish waitress at Isaly's, the dairy where I often ate dinner, provided my first real romantic adventure. Florence Zimmer was a recent high school graduate with porcelain white skin that showed off her mascaraed eyelids, heavily painted lips, and long dark hair. I began tipping her heavily and soon started picking her up in the company Dodge after she finished work for the day. We drove out of town to a lonely spot and climbed into the back seat for some steamy smooching. Just as the torrid affair reached the point of no return she announced that she was going to visit her real boyfriend, a Polish boy, a soldier, at a camp where he was training to go overseas.

Otherwise, life in Ambridge was almost all work although I learned little about becoming a better journalist except how antagonistic police were to reporters. At first I took the hostility as personal but eventually I understood that the police, most of whom were Slavic, viewed the *Citizen* as representative of the more privileged Anglo-Saxon bosses and business class. The result: the cops refused to show me the police blotter, limiting me to oral reports of automobile accidents, minor fires, and a few burglaries.

Frustrated by the skimpy news, I started my column, P.S. by The Rambler. I wrote about anything I wanted and it was not long before I got into trouble. I had read that under new federal controls no retailer could increase prices. A small local grocer had raised the price of sugar, which was rationed. When I exposed the price increase in a column, the grocer complained that he had not violated the law. He had raised the price of sugar, but he had protected himself by charging that higher price once before the controls went into effect. Thus his higher price was legal. I ran no apology, figuring that the grocer had only technically observed the price freeze. The publisher, Vaughn R. Arnold, did not complain; the grocer did not advertise in the *Citizen.* Thompson said nothing.

I also angered the local slot-machine boss because I reported that he had cheated on paying town fees by moving the glass covers bearing the fee certificate from one slot machine to another. The religiously minded Arnold liked that column.

Neither he nor editor Thompson asked about my view on conscientious objection although it was no secret that I was a pacifist; I had told a number of people of my belief. When the draft board called me back to Erie to take the physical examination I went, postponing the ultimate decision about whether to refuse to serve. In a few weeks the board mailed me notification that I had been rejected, classified 4-F for two reasons, as "incipient manic-depressive" and because of blood in my urine.

The "manic-depressive" finding upset me. With a little spin, someone could say I was crazy. Falling back on my device of joking to deflect a personal problem, I sent a telegram home, saying the board had rejected me as "physically, mentally and morally unfit." I thought that was funny and an easy way to avoid facing the truth about myself.

Mom didn't laugh. A super patriot (she named my brother Woodrow for the World War I president), Mom was proud that two of her sons were in the service and said that if I was going to be a pacifist she was sorry I ever went to college. Deeply wounded by the person I loved the most, I tried to explain my abhorrence to war. Surely she would understand. She didn't.

A few months later, after the Japanese bombed Pearl Harbor, I received an anonymous letter at the *Citizen,* calling me a pacifist and a draft dodger. The first designation was correct, the second was wrong. I wrote a column addressing only the second point. I denounced the charge of draft dodging as a lie, citing my 4-F classification. Reluctant to stand up for my unpopular conviction, I ignored the pacifism allegation. If my mother did not understand me, who would?

No one on the paper commented on the letter or my reply. But the Ambridge librarian, an older woman with whom I confided, sized me up correctly. "So," she said, "you are a papier-mâché man." That observation by someone I respected added to my mother's wound. I began to reconsider my pacifism, but not to the extent of baring my soul in another column. Ironically, I considered my pacifism a private affair, a right I had not extended to Deanie.

Another incident demonstrated to me how weak I was. One afternoon Thompson asked me to check on a report that a woman had been raped. He gave me an address and told me to interview her. "Ask her," he said, with a rare grin, "how it felt." I was appalled, but instead of protesting or checking first with the police, I drove to the address, rapped lightly on the door and left immediately. I told Thompson no one had come to the door. "I thought as much," he said. I was relieved that my ruse had worked.

My values, however, centered on protecting myself, not on doing what was humane or journalistically right. It was not a question of worry about being fired; with the military draft, that wouldn't have happened. I feared a face-to-face meeting with the victim. I would have been ashamed to ask her any questions, let alone Thompson's crude "how it felt." At the same time my boss had given me an order and I was obliged to carry it out, even though I had little respect for him. It never occurred to me to challenge Thompson, who, being weak, undoubtedly would have backed down.

Instead, I fell back on the device I had developed as a spoiled child eager for approval. I used duplicity.

The *Citizen* was no place to learn journalism and cope with ethical problems on the job. Professor Maurer had given me the wrong advice in suggesting a small paper for my first job. It was not the size that mattered; it was the quality of the editor and publisher. Many small papers have excellent editors; a lot of metropolitan ones are led by incompetent executives.

Unfortunately, the editor and publisher at the *Citizen* let me run amuck. I used my column for personal pleasure, to tease Deanie; I used the company car to woo the Polish waitress; I neglected to check with the grocer on price gouging; I failed to stand up to Thompson on interviewing the rape victim; I made up a quotation on a traffic accident in which I was involved and attributed it to an anonymous policeman; I routinely accepted free admission to the only movie house in town; and I deceived readers about my pacifism. It would have been much better for the paper and for me if my bosses had insisted on running corrections when I strayed from the truth. Looking back it is easy to criticize my bosses, but times were different then; journalism as practiced was sloppy and corrections were few, as I discovered to my chagrin, in my next job, at United Press and even after I joined the *New York Times*.

Three years after leaving home I had not advanced my religious search or faced up to my personal weaknesses. Nor had I made much of a start on becoming a competent, let alone an ethical, journalist. Indeed, I did not learn from my mistakes. I needed discipline and guidance but even more I needed role models. A strong editor could have straightened me out.

What if I had ignored Professor Maurer's advice and gone straight to New York and offered to work on the new New York afternoon newspaper, *PM*? The one-year-old experimental tabloid appealed to my youthful idealism. Its reporters were specialists. It encouraged good writing. It accepted no advertising; instead it ran a separate consumer section written by reporters who searched New York stores for bargains. It favored no political party, although it was decidedly left wing. It proclaimed opposition to "people who push other people around." It represented the journalism I longed for and I read it avidly. Starting there would probably have been a disaster because, as I learned years later, *PM* did not impose high standards on its staff.

The year at the *Citizen* was not entirely wasted, however. It provided the stepping-stone to my next job, at United Press Associations. A Republican paper in a heavily Democratic area, the *Citizen* also put out a weekly, which ran new headlines on old *Citizen* stories and boilerplate editorials with a Democratic slant. The purpose, of course, was to draw more advertising.

In the summer of 1942, U.S. Senator Joseph F. Guffey was running for reelection. On a tour of Western Pennsylvania he stopped in Ambridge to strengthen his ties to the steelworkers union. Someone showed him a copy of our weekly, featuring a big picture of him on page one with my story about his tour. Guffey, a 100 percent New Deal Democrat of the claptrap school, was impressed. More important to my career, Jim Jennings, his press representative, was also impressed. He asked what I was doing on such a rinky-dink paper and if I would like to move up. When I said I was eager to do so, he took my name, address, and phone number.

To my astonishment I soon received a letter from Morey J. Potter, chief of the Harrisburg bureau of United Press (that was long before it merged with International News Service), expressing interest in me. I was hired without a face-to-face interview, solely on the recommendation of that PR man (perhaps also on the basis of my draft deferment). I didn't stop to think that I owed my new job to a PR man—another indication that although I demanded purity in churches I didn't insist that my ethics remain untainted.

I left Ambridge in the fall of 1942 after one year at the *Citizen*. Having reluctantly recognized that the blue-collar class could be as biased as white-collar workers, I gave up pretensions that the voice of the people was the voice of God. In my last column I spoke down to my readers:

> I want you to see that those who are against you are also against the other little people all over the world. If you are Polish, notice that those who call you "Pollock" also cuss the Jews and hate the unions. If you are a housewife remember that the same men who would slap a sales tax on the food you buy are the ones who yell loudest about the "niggers."

4. Morey J. Potter, United Press Harrisburg bureau chief and best damned janitor in central Pennsylvania, in vest, talking to John Scotzin, *Philadelphia Record* reporter, in capitol newsroom. I'm in the suspenders. Photographer unknown.

As *Citizen* readers must have felt in reading the irritating prose of a know-it-all liberal, I didn't consider myself one of the "little people." I was above them. I had a college education; most of the readers didn't.

In Harrisburg, I found the job I needed. United Press was a training ground for reporters. For-profit United Press operated on a formula that kept costs down. While retaining a few experienced old hands in key spots, it hired young reporters at low wages and worked them hard in its constant battle to compete with the Associated Press. The formula produced profits and many outstanding reporters, such as Harrison Salisbury, Neil Sheehan, Claude Sitton, John Herbers, Seymour Hersh, and Hedrick Smith, all of whom I worked with at the *New York Times*. United Press sometimes showed bad news judgment and gave me assignments that tripped me up a few times, but, all in all, it was a good place to learn.

Morey Potter ran the bureau from a sparse two-room office on the fourth floor of the *Harrisburg Patriot-News* building. Born and reared in Kansas, he retained the work ethic of a farmer. Intensely competitive, he had earned promotion to bureau chief by beating rival Associated Press on major stories. His stubby fingers flew in a V at a speed I have never seen equaled. His capacity for alcohol and friendliness at bars served him well in dealing with news sources.

He constantly ran out of money and borrowed from reporters, paying back by manipulating check accounts at two banks. He often urinated in the office sink rather than climbing the stairs to the next floor to the men's room. He would run both hot and cold faucets for a few minutes to wash away the odor. One day an unexpected visitor, a woman, caught him. She thought he was washing his hands because both spigots were running. He just turned his head and talked to her.

Because of the war, Potter had lost a number of reporters. He didn't have time to break me in slowly. I started to work August 16, 1942, and had my first byline three days later on a story about the shortage of nurses. That byline, with the designation "United Press Staff Correspondent," fooled me into thinking the work would be easy. Potter sent me to the capitol to help cover the state government, even though I had no seasoning.

A state capital is like a little Washington, with a chief executive, a legislature, lobbyists, a bureaucracy, and a supreme court. In fact, before the New Deal expanded the federal government's role, state capital reporting jobs were often considered more important than Washington because statehouse news was often more relevant to people's lives. While the New Deal made the federal government far more vital, statehouse assignments still had the advantage of being training grounds for government and political reporters. The formats were the same: press conferences, departmental actions, political meetings, legislative hearings, lobbyists' pressures, and appellate court sessions. Reporters had to know how to handle spot news swiftly, to write features, to get exclusives, to stay ahead of the opposition. I had lucked into the best training spot any young reporter could desire.

David Bramson, the lead UP reporter, and Joseph Banks, the no. 2 man, showed me around. Along with the Associated Press, International News Service, and the Philadelphia, Pittsburgh, and Harrisburg newspapers, United Press occupied a cluster of desks in a spacious newsroom in the capitol.

Bramson had the difficult job of covering the two hundred members of the House of Representatives. Banks covered the smaller and more sedate Senate. Both also covered the governor's office and all the executive departments. My job was to help on secondary legislative and departmental stories.

Bramson wrote most of the important stories, constantly adjusting his glasses while chewing a cigar and laughing at his own obscene jokes. The more deliberate Banks worked quietly. Both were in their thirties and single. Bramson had an eye for women as he looked for "pussy," a new word for me. Banks, whose family was wealthy, was neither as talented nor as driven as Bramson, who worked hard, looking for an overnight lead, which, I was soon to learn, made United Press so valuable.

In those pretelevision days most dailies were afternoon papers and their editors didn't want to run the same stories that the big-city morning papers had printed hours before. Yet afternoon paper editors needed most stories early in the morning to meet their printing schedules. United Press reporters tried, and usually succeeded, in getting new developments, so we could use "today" instead of "yesterday" in our overnight leads for what we called P.M. papers. For exclusive stories it was easy to write "today" in the lead. Under favorable circumstances the Associated Press, which served mostly morning papers, would be chasing our stories instead of developing its own.

Sometimes we could not find a new development; we had to force that "today" and came close to distorting the news. Nothing is more final than death. What do you do for a second-day lead on an obituary? The usual solution was to lead with "Funeral plans were being made today for . . . " or "Friends paid tribute today to John Jones. . . . " The story, undoubtedly apocryphal, was told of a cub reporter, unable to find a new angle, who wrote "John Jones was still dead today. . . . "

On breaking stories—a governor's press conference, legislative passage of a bill, a state supreme court decision—because of the time squeeze, UP reporters had to learn to dictate stories without sitting down at a typewriter to compose them. Otherwise the afternoon papers, which made up most of our clients, wouldn't have time to print them. These lessons, on how to get fresh information and how to dictate stories over the telephone on the fly, proved valuable for the rest of my career, especially when I sometimes shifted from editor to reporter at the *New York Times.*

I was unprepared for the UP job. Overwhelmed by deadline pressures and the need to produce exclusive stories, I violated basic norms taught in college. For example, instead of asking a colleague how to spell the name of Strawbridge and Clothier, a Philadelphia department store, or checking the ads in Philadelphia newspapers, I guessed, and guessed wrong. In interviews with legislators and officials, I often feigned knowledge instead of pleading ignorance and asking for a simple explanation. As a result I sometimes found myself unable to write a clear story without losing time and annoying sources by going back to them a second time to clear up ambiguities and fill holes. Decades later I discovered that legendary reporter Homer Bigart, who stuttered, extracted more information by, in effect, pleading ignorance, thus appealing to the sympathy of sources.

On occasion my stories remained forever exclusive; no competitor picked them up because they were wrong. The worst error I made came the first year. In reading the national press, I noted the big debate over how to give servicemen the right to vote while away from home. I interviewed the Pennsylvania secretary of state, a political hack, who was in charge of elections, and asked her if she didn't think it was a scandal that Pennsylvania's soldiers and sailors could not vote. Yes, she said, and something should be done about it.

The *Philadelphia Record*, the chief Democratic organ in the state, sky-lined my story across the top of page one. I puffed with pride until L. U. Leslie, the white-haired AP bureau chief, wandered down to the UP corner of the newsroom and smirked. "Pretty nice beat you had there. Too bad it isn't true," he said, explaining that the legislature passed a law the previous year making it easy for servicemen and women to vote. Sheepishly, I called Potter, who had edited the article. Sheepishly, he told me to wait for a chance to write a correct story. That was our way out. In those days few newspapers ran corrections. We didn't offer one. Neither did the *Record.*

Potter never lost faith in me. His swift pencil smoothed out my rough prose. I learned just by re-reading the edited stories as transmitted over the wires. He was always encouraging, the first person to praise me as a journalist. As the months went by, under his sympathetic eyes and with help from Bramson and Banks, I began to act more like a professional. The competition was stiff. The reporter who wrote most of the exclusives was Gerson (Lefty) Lush of the *Philadelphia Inquirer,* the mouthpiece of the Republican Party, which controlled the state government. At lunch and at bars, he leaned on politicians eager for publicity. They knew that the *Inquirer* could help them. It didn't take me long to realize that I, who seldom drank, and was therefore something of a social cipher, could not compete on such a basis.

While scoffing at the close relationships between Lush and other reporters with news sources I did not draw the line at accepting small perks from politicians. Every Christmas season Senator M. Harvey Taylor, boss of the Pennsylvania Republican party, would give each correspondent a bottle of gin or whiskey. Taylor would go to the newsroom with a lackey carrying a few cases of spirits. He called each reporter by name (although he did not know the likes of me), wished him a happy holiday, shook his hand, and gave him a gaily wrapped bottle. The reporter would say, "Thanks, Harvey," adding a lame joke if he was a favorite. I never summoned the courage to say no to that pitiful spectacle of a tiny payoff for a reporter's soul. Years later I was shocked to learn that *New York Times* reporters also accepted gifts and that even after they were banned some reporters had them shipped to their homes.

In Harrisburg, lacking access to key sources, I tried to learn more about issues by reading extensively and thus become more knowledgeable about some issues than others in the Capitol Hill newsroom. Every day I searched for ideas for exclusive stories. The *Wall Street Journal* provided many tips and no other reporter seemed to read it as closely as I did. I began to thrive.

My ambition at that time was to be a foreign correspondent, a natural goal with the war raging in Europe and the Japanese taking over most of Asia. I decided that I should learn Russian and bought a Linguaphone Russian language course. Although I played the records almost every day, I made little progress. I needed a personal teacher. Someone told me about a Russian woman, a widow of an American aviator. Anna Reid not only agreed to teach me Russian but also offered to rent me a room in her house. It was not total immersion, but it was a good setup to learn Russian.

Tiny and vivacious, Anna Reid was a fine teacher, but I didn't get very far in the lessons. She had two daughters. Handsome, cynical Tatiana worked for the Federal Bureau of Investigation. Plain, chubby Victoria was a bobby sox high school senior. I was turned off by the scornful Tanya but turned on by voluptuous Viki. We started going to movies and taking long walks, and before long we became serious about our relationship. Her mother encouraged the romance.

My romance did not detour me from my quest for religious faith. When I learned that the Quakers held weekly meeting at the Penn Harris Hotel, I began to attend. Their traditional opposition to war fit perfectly into my pacifist beliefs. These were the first silent prayer meetings I had ever experienced. During those quiet sessions the spirituality I sought never reached me, the Inner Light never instructed me. Not once was I inspired to break the silence and speak, as others did. Although I was disappointed in the attempt to find a religious home, the Quaker impact remained vital all my life.

Within six months of moving to Harrisburg I discovered a way to meet my desire to serve my country without violating my conscientious objection principles. I applied to the American Friends Service Committee, a Quaker organization, to work overseas as an ambulance driver. The AFSC quickly accepted me and instructed me to obtain a passport and be ready to go to India.

I went to the Pennsylvania Vital Statistics Bureau and filled out the necessary form for a birth certificate—Robert Howard Phelps, born July 19, 1919, Erie, Pennsylvania, Hamot Hospital, mother Ruth Fox Phelps, etc. I was only mildly surprised to learn that no one by the name of Robert Phelps had ever been born in Pennsylvania. Had I been Howard after all? But Vital Statistics could find no record of a Howard Phelps, either. "Try Richard," Mom suggested. That worked. Officially I had been Richard all my twenty-three years without anyone, not even my mother, knowing it.

If I wanted to be called Robert, the head of Vital Statistics advised, I should apply for a correction. All you need, he said, is a baptismal certificate. But I had never been baptized. A family Bible with my birth written in it would do, the official said. I wrote to Mom, who purchased a Bible, wrote the four children's names and birthdates in the glossy family section between the Old and New Testaments and sent it to me. The Vital Statistics man looked at the new Bible, at the entries, all written with the same blue ink and clearly recently entered, raised his eyebrows, and gave me my birth certificate. While my family and neighborhood friends continued to call me Howard for years, I was now, forever, officially, Robert Howard Phelps, "Bob," to most everyone else.

Despite its initial approval, the American Friends Service Committee rejected me on learning the draft board's reason for classifying me 4-F. Thereupon, I went to a Harrisburg psychiatrist, Dr. John H. Waterman, and said I did not believe I was mentally ill. To me the diagnosis was the draft board's way of saying that pacifists were not competent to serve. After a few sessions in which he asked routine questions about my relationship with my parents, my fears, and my sex life, Dr. Waterman said that I was not manic-depressive. Free from that shadow, I set aside my pacifist beliefs, an action proving that my convictions were not as deep as I had thought, probably because they were based more on politics than on philosophy. Guilt feelings won the long battle for my conscience. I finally concluded that freedom was more important than life. Powerful words influenced me. Long before, Emerson had put my new conviction into verse: "For what avail the plough or sail,/Or land or life, if freedom fail?"

I went to the recruiting stations, first the navy's, then the army's, and applied for a commission. My college degree qualified me for officer candidate school, but the navy and the army both rejected me because of the incipient manic-depressive diagnosis. The fact that my psychiatrist had cleared me carried no weight with the military. I wrote to the Erie Selective Service Board and volunteered for another physical examination, which I passed with the aid of a letter from Dr. Waterman. On November 5, 1943, I was inducted into the navy. Good-bye United Press, good-bye Harrisburg, good-bye Viki.

# 3. Okinawa One
## Kamikazes—An African American Hero

**I was eager** to go overseas, but first the navy wanted to whip me into shape. It sent me to a Seabee boot camp at Camp Peary, near Williamsburg, Virginia, where I slogged through the red mud in the wet, cold winter of 1943–44. By spring I was whipped but certainly not shaped for any job in a Seabee construction battalion. For eight months I languished in a general work pool where I began writing short fiction stories, goofed off, and learned to cuss like a sailor. My favorite, "Go take a flying fuck," usually drew laughs, which, naturally, encouraged me in this new vocabulary. I was becoming one of the guys.

During the hiatus I took advantage of free weekends to go to Harrisburg to see Viki. I wrote home that I wanted to get married. Alarmed, Mom replied, "Howie, are you nuts, or teasing?" Wiser than I, Viki, now at Bucknell University, said she wanted to finish college. Wiser still, in October she broke off our understanding, explaining that she wanted to enjoy the full college experience and date other men. I turned the defeat into a melodrama, continuing to write to her daily for weeks.

Without knowing what it was doing, the navy healed my broken heart by sending me to South Charleston, West Virginia, assigning me to the shore patrol guarding the naval ordnance plant there. At five feet eight and a half inches tall, I weighed 127 pounds, hardly enough heft to break up a tavern brawl.

Nor was I trained in police skills to guard the plant, where fifty or sixty sailors assembled some of the first guided bombs in a secret project. On the nights I was posted as a guard on an empty floor I wore a .45-caliber automatic on my waist. It was so heavy it pulled my jeans down over my skinny hips. I tightened the gun belt to its last notch but it remained loose; my jeans kept slipping down. At target practice I was equally inept. I not only never hit the bull's eye, but also usually missed the entire target twenty-five yards away. While practicing firefighting, I almost fell off the truck.

None of this bothered me until late one night I heard a noise as if someone were moving in the building. I had been sitting in a chair, the only guard on the floor. I pulled the .45 from its holster and was moving toward the sound when the gun went off. In seconds a dozen or so officers and sailors descended on me. I told them that I was checking out a suspicious sound. But why did I fire my gun? Did I see someone? No, it had gone off accidentally. They searched the entire building but could find no evidence of an intruder. They aimed questioning looks at me and left. The next day the guns were taken from all of us.

Charleston was an ideal post to sit out the war. We had a lot of free time and girls were plentiful. I dated a few and one invited me to her home for dinner with her parents. But, the presence of a UP bureau in Charleston attracted me more than the girls. I introduced myself to the bureau chief, offered my services, and was taken on as a part timer, without pay. United Press readily accepted slave labor.

A few weeks later the bureau chief told me that naval intelligence officers had asked about me. While the need for security was pressed on us, I did not realize that intelligence officers were monitoring my free time. It was not long before the commander in charge of the project called me in and asked how I liked being there. I said it was just fine. "What do you do on liberty?" he asked, knowing I went to the UP bureau. "Oh, I said, I go to the United Press bureau and help them out by writing a few stories. I used to work for them."

He asked if they ever inquired about the naval plant. "No," I said, realizing for the first time the real reason I had been called in, "but the bureau chief did say, 'Oh, you're out where they're making guided bombs.' The commander was startled. "What did you tell him?" "Nothing, and he didn't ask anything."

It was my turn to be startled a week or so later when he offered to recommend me for officer training school. I declined, explaining I would rather continue to write fiction and that I would have to sign up for four years if I became an officer. The navy had lost track of me once and I didn't want to run the risk again. A few days later, in late January 1945, the commander showed me a navy memo asking for volunteers to serve as combat correspondents. The navy wanted the same kind of favorable publicity that the Marines got from their combat correspondents.

"Would you like it?" he asked.

"Absolutely," I replied. Within twenty-four hours orders transferred me to the Hawaiian Sea Frontier for further transfer west. That was a neat way of getting the security risk out of Charleston. Send him to a combat area.

I took a quick trip to Erie to say good-bye to the family. Relieved that I had given up pacifism, Mom now worried that I might recklessly take risks and be killed. She worried even more when I showed her a pocket-sized edition of Mary Baker Eddy's *Science and Health With Key to the Scriptures.* In Harrisburg I had read articles about Christian Science as I searched the *Christian Science Monitor* for news tips. Mom feared that the book might persuade her idealistic son to refuse medical treatment if wounded.

I laughed at Mom's worry about the little book as I kissed her good-bye. "I'll put it in my shirt pocket," I joked. "Maybe it'll stop a bullet." When I turned to Pop I impulsively hugged and kissed him, something I could not remember having done before. I, too, wondered whether I would come back.

At Pearl Harbor I found myself in the second group of Enlisted Navy Correspondents. An ensign with no journalism experience headed the group. He assumed we were trained journalists, so instructions dealt only with our relationship to our superiors, the kinds of articles we were to write, and the procedure for filing them. As enlisted men, not even chief petty officers, we were to perform any job an officer ordered, even if that meant scrubbing decks or peeling potatoes. Hopefully, we would have time to write articles for hometown newspapers of the officers and men on the ships or stations we were assigned to. To avoid stories by a rogue correspondent, every story had to be approved by an officer, designated by the ship's captain, before sending it, by navy mail, to headquarters at Pearl Harbor, to be edited and dispatched to newspapers in the states.

Because I was from Pennsylvania, I asked for assignment to the new aircraft carrier *Benjamin Franklin,* which was about to make its first voyage into combat. Fortunately for me, someone else had already asked for the *Franklin.* On that maiden trip, two bombs from a single Japanese plane almost sank it as it maneuvered only fifty miles off Honshu. The attack killed 724, more than half its crew, and wounded 265.

Instead of the *Franklin* I was assigned in mid-March to a squadron of twelve destroyer-minesweepers training at Ulithi, an atoll in the central Pacific that had been turned into a gigantic naval base. To get there I traveled as a passenger on the *Aaron Ward,* a destroyer minelayer. We were part of a large convoy of ships headed west. With my new assignment, I received no promotion; I was a seaman first class, the highest rating below petty officer.

To give antiaircraft crews target practice, a plane from one of the aircraft carriers towed a target drone past the ships. With permission of the executive officer, Lieutenant Commander Karl F. Neupert, I climbed up to the bridge, an ideal position to see the action. As the drone approached from the rear I saw puffs of smoke from ships firing at it. Then the two batteries of five-inch guns on the forward deck of the *Aaron Ward* swung around and fired—boom-boom-boom-boom—past me. With the first boom I slumped to the deck. I could not get up. Commander Neupert came by and asked if I was all right. "Yes," I lied, "I'm just trying to stay out of the way." God, I thought, what would I do in actual combat? The next day there was more target practice. Again the guns boomed. Again I went down, but more slowly. On the third day I stayed up. From then on I could cope with the sounds of guns although they always unnerved me.

Somewhere north of Ulithi we met up with Mine Squadron 20 and I boarded the USS *Ellyson,* the lead ship, while the *Aaron Ward* joined its minelayer squadron. Gathering at the secret base, I learned later, were elements of the greatest naval fleet in history—1,300 ships, including 15 battleships, 29 aircraft carriers, 23 cruisers, 106 destroyers, and numerous support craft. From the *Ellyson's* deck all I could see were a few other destroyer minesweepers riding the gray swells.

My high-speed squadron consisted of destroyers built in the early 1940s that had seen action in the Mediterranean and at the Normandy invasion before conversion to minesweepers. Like officers on every ship I boarded, no one on the *Ellyson* knew how to treat me. Was I a civilian war correspondent, a navy officer, or a navy enlisted man? Although tempted to ask for a bunk in the comfortable chief petty officers' quarters, I played it straight from the first and told the *Ellyson* executive officer, Lieutenant W. J. Chiapella, that I was an enlisted man, so he sent me to the crowded enlisted men's quarters. There was no room there so I wound up sleeping in the chow hall and working in the yeoman's office.

More important than where I slept was how much freedom I would have to talk to the crew and to write my stories. Of course I didn't want to jeopardize secrets, but I wanted all the freedom I could get. Taking advantage of officers' unfamiliarity with how the press operated, I decided to seek the optimum. When I met Captain Richard A. Larkin, commander of Mine Squadron 20, who was stationed on the *Ellyson* at that time, I said that I didn't want to be a nuisance, asking him to read every story I wrote, and requesting his permission every time I wanted to transfer to another ship in the squadron. I asked him to sign blanket orders giving me the right to send my stories directly to Pearl Harbor and to move from ship to ship as I pleased. To my surprise, he agreed. Thus I bypassed not only the admiral but also the captains and executive officers on all ships in the squadron. Throughout the Battle of Okinawa my uncensored copy moved to Pearl Harbor by navy mail and I suffered no delay in transferring from one ship to another. No other navy correspondent, to my knowledge, enjoyed such freedom. Moreover, the lack of oversight bolstered my esteem and confidence.

I soon learned that we were headed for Okinawa, the large island southeast of Japan. Its capture would provide the jumping-off place for Operation Downfall, the assault on Kyushu, the southernmost of the main Japanese islands.

In the early morning mist of March 24, 1945, our squadron began sweeping the gray waters off the island. Nerves on edge, we found neither mines to explode nor enemy to fight. Every minute we expected an attack, but none came.

After three days of sunbathing we finally got our first taste of the Pacific war. As we swept deep waters, smaller minesweepers sailed in close to the Hagushi beaches to clear shallower areas for landing craft.

5. All 127 pounds of me as enlisted Navy correspondent
barely filled my rolled-up jeans and misbuttoned, ragged
shirt on deck of an LCI near the end of the Battle of Okinawa.
Photographer unknown. United States Navy photo.

Suddenly, in mid-morning on March 28, one of the small minesweepers,
the *Skylark* exploded. It had hit two mines and was burning fiercely. Huge
clouds of black smoke billowed from the stricken ship. Almost immediately men jumped feet-first into the water. In forty minutes the *Skylark*
sank, bow first. The USS *Tolman* pulled 105 of the crew to safety. Five sailors were killed in the explosions.

Four days later, on Easter Sunday, April 1, we watched as American soldiers and Marines landed without opposition, to some surprise.

In previous U.S. invasions, except at Iwo Jima, the Japanese had fiercely resisted our landings. As at Iwo, the Japanese avoided early casualties at Okinawa by retreating rather than facing devastating American firepower. Fighting fiercely from caves and tunnels, the Japanese army slowed the American advance on the ground. The purpose was to inflict such heavy casualties that the United States would hesitate to invade the Japanese homeland. Ironically, the ferocious Japanese resistance helped convince President Harry S. Truman to order atomic bombs dropped on Hiroshima and Nagasaki.

In an attempt to knock out American picket ships, which had surrounded the island, the Japanese launched waves of suicide planes in an operation called Ten-Go. With the seas cleared of mines, our minesweeper squadron joined other ships, most of them various types of destroyers, on the picket line. The kamikaze planes were soon diving on us. Little did we realize that we would stay on picket duty for nearly three months, the longest sea battle in history and the bloodiest of the Pacific War. Called Operation Iceberg, it involved more ships and men than the invasion of Normandy.

The kamikazes, or "divine wind," took a heavy toll. Only one of the eleven ships in our squadron (the twelfth ship hit a reef at Ulithi and did not go to Okinawa) escaped undamaged in the furious Japanese attacks. The first attacks came at sunrise on April 2 and became routine after that. The *Ellyson* drove away the first plane and destroyed a second a day later, providing me with my first good story.

It wasn't until April 6 that kamikazes succeeded in hitting our squadron. About 3:30 P.M., the USS *Rodman* sent out Mayday calls, saying its engine room was afire and water was pouring into a forward hold. The USS *Emmons* went to the rescue but it, too, was hit, first by a bomb and then by a kamikaze. We heard that Rodman's skipper had ordered abandon ship, but then it radioed that it was proceeding to Kerama Retto, our heavily guarded anchorage, under its own power.

The *Emmons* was not so fortunate. It took two more hits and its forward magazine blew up. About 6 P.M. the *Ellyson* was ordered to leave the relative safety of Kerama Retto and tow the shattered *Emmons* to safety. If that was not possible, we were told to sink it to prevent it from drifting onto the beach. All of us wore life jackets and some added flash-proof clothing, goggles, gloves, face cloth, and helmet.

About 10 o'clock, just as we reached the area—variously called Suicide Lane, Slaughterhouse Avenue, and Bogey Alley—we were amazed
when the captain secured us from battle stations. The skies were so clear
of bogies that we could sleep. Early the next morning we learned that the
*Emmons* could not be salvaged. Enemy planes had shot away its bridge and
blown off its fantail. Fires burned both fore and aft. It was drifting toward
Ie Shima, still occupied by the enemy. The *Ellyson* sank the *Emmons* with
ninety-six five-inch shells.

Attacks by two-engine Mitsubishi Betty bombers, the workhorse of
the Japanese navy, in the night compounded the threat of suicide planes
during the daylight hours. Just when we thought the danger had let up, a
Betty would hit one of our ships. These night attacks scared us even more
than the kamikazes.

One night the *Ellyson* radar picked up a Japanese plane headed, we
thought, right for us. Below deck, I watched the radarscope as A. M. Wil-
cox, the radar officer, called off the distance as the plane approached.
"Three thousand yards and closing . . . Two thousand and closing . . . one
thousand . . . 500. . . . " The plane swept over us and we heard a slight
boom. "Flares," someone shouted, meaning the Japanese had successfully
spotlighted us. "Make smoke," an officer ordered.

I ran up on deck. The ghostly orange light of a dozen Japanese
flares bathed the *Ellyson*. Knowing that Betty bombers would be on
us in moments, Captain Robert W. Mountrey ordered a hard turn. We
felt concussions from bomb explosions off our bow and stern—we had
been straddled—but the ship suffered no damage and our camouflage
smoke quickly covered us in the darkness. Enemy planes came back and
dropped more flares but not as accurately and the bombs that followed
fell far astern.

Two weeks later we were caught in flares again, but no bombs dropped.
The constant threat kept us on edge. I wrote in my journal:

> Every sound like the beeper sends my heart fluttering. When the cooks
> drop pans on the deck above the ship's office, where I work, I leap from
> my chair with the thought—we've been hit.
>
> I try to figure the safest place on ship. In case of a torpedo, it's unsafe
> below. If a suicide plane hits us, it will aim for the bridge, so it's safest

below. If we are bombed, or strafed, I had better hit the deck. Yet the ship is so small I realize it's foolish to try to find a safe spot. There just isn't any and I resign myself to the gods. I say there's no use trying to escape being hit, but to accept it when it comes. It isn't a belief in fate—that when your number's up you get it despite the precautions—it just means that it is impossible to tell where we will be hit.

The crews of our squadron said enemy fire in the invasions of North Africa, Southern France, and Normandy was nothing compared to the months-long battle at Okinawa. A tough USS *Hambleton* sailor told me that all he had to do in European battles to quiet his nerves was to light a Camel. "Now," he said, his hands shaking, "I can't even light a Camel." Another man vomited every time the loudspeaker reported a bogey in the vicinity.

Shared danger with the crew built up my morale. I was taking part in a great operation; I was contributing and, while the real sailors never accepted me as one of them—a transient with no battle station—they opened up, responding candidly to my questions. The officers talked, too, never pulling rank on me, in part because I never sought favor above my rating as an enlisted man.

Fatalism set in. Our ship designation, DMS, no longer meant just Destroyer Minesweeper; it also meant Dead Men Sure. Even victories produced a negative effect. When a landing craft reported it had intercepted two sailboats fleeing Okinawa, it shot them to pieces, adding laconically, "Survivors resist rescue. There are no survivors." We interpreted that to mean that the enemy would continue to fight to the last man, as it had, island by island, since U.S. forces turned the tide at Guadalcanal. The invasion of Japan would be a bloody battle.

All of us wondered how we would react if the *Ellyson* were badly damaged and scores of crewmen killed. I visited the *Rodman* after it took multiple hits from suicide planes. I was told that one man climbed on a life raft and began to talk like a baby. Another jumped into the water and yelled, "Swimming party." With the captain's permission some sailors abandoned ship; others were afraid to go into the water. Japanese planes strafed those who jumped into the ocean, the bullets sounding like bells when they hit the water. With the radio out and only one signalman left, the captain himself signaled by semaphore. Others searched the bodies of dead Japanese pilots for souvenirs. Everyone on the *Rodman* praised navy Hellcat fighters for brilliant flying, diving right into friendly fire to shoot down enemy planes.

While I was on the *Rodman* at Kerama anchorage, we went through an eight-hour raid, the longest I experienced. It started at 6:30 P.M. April 27 and lasted until after 2 A.M. April 28. It consisted of forty-five separate attacks, ranging from one to twenty planes. At the first indication of danger, small boats made smoke, which was choking to breathe but welcome because it was effective in hiding ships. We heard on the emergency radio—the *Rodman*'s radio room had been gutted—that a single bogey had been spotted. Then we saw an explosion. The next day we were told that a suicide plane had hit the hospital ship USS *Comfort*. The *Comfort* carried no armament. White with a big cross on each side, it was brilliantly lighted at night and kept a large distance from warships to avoid accidental attacks. Twenty-eight people on the *Comfort* were killed and forty-eight wounded.

On the *Ellyson*, Dr. William B. Walsh, the ship's physician, called us mental casualties because, without suffering any damage or deaths, we saw sailors of our squadron killed and their ships damaged.[1] We wondered how long our luck could hold out. Almost every ship we relieved was hit and almost every ship that relieved us was attacked after we left a station. Our morale plummeted. Where formerly we said "if we get hit," now we said, "when we get hit."

Never have I been so nostalgic, so wistful, so reflective, so appreciative of what others meant to me as I was at Okinawa. When I knew definitely that we were going into battle close to Japan I wanted to be sure the right people knew of the deep affection that I had been so reluctant to fully express. Yet even then I held back. I wrote Viki of my devotion but, in view of her breaking off our understanding, I could only hint of my continued love. I told my family of my love and appreciation for their sacrifices for me but my words were almost journalistic, lacking the tenderness that would have conveyed the depth of my feelings. Perhaps I felt restrained by the fact that under censorship rules all letters were read by officers whom I saw every day. Sometimes a premonition of death moved me to write. Although my letters lacked the depth of my feelings, I always felt better having written them.

Following instructions from Pearl Harbor, I made hometown stories my priority. These were usually templates saying that the ship was at Okinawa, with one or two places for names of the crew and other personal information to be inserted. I included a list of crew members and their hometowns. At Pearl Harbor yeomen typed an individual story for each crew member and sent it to local newspapers. The system worked, as shown by clips pouring in weeks later.

These routine articles hardly satisfied me and I always looked for something better. My instinct sought heroism, of course, but also mistakes, blunders, and carelessness, although fear of navy security blocked most of my ideas. I did not push against the rules because I understood their need. Looking back, I realize I could have been more creative by writing more about individual exploits. Editors and reporters did not use the term "narrative journalism" in those days; that term did not become popular until decades after the war as part of "new journalism." But even during the war I and other correspondents used narration in writing feature stories. I wrote one about a sailor operating the *Ellyson*'s Ford-built bogey tracker and another, while on a visit to the island, about an army bread baker. Generally, though, I merely wrote straight accounts. However, I did recognize the value of narration when a dramatic event happened right in front of me.

In fact, one of the best stories I wrote at Okinawa concerned a kamikaze that the *Ellyson* encountered early in the invasion. We were eating dinner on April 3 when general quarters sounded. I ran up on deck with Dr. Walsh, who was holding a dish of ice cream. In bright sunlight a small Japanese plane, an outmoded bomber Americans called Val, was skimming over the waves, heading directly at us—or so it seemed. The plane had hidden from our radar, coming in off the island, staying low, wobbling as it came. The *Hambleton,* the *Rodman,* and the *Macomb* astern were firing at it, and, as the plane neared, friendly fire ripped into the smokestack where the doctor and I were standing. Only later, when we saw the holes in the smokestack did we realize how close we had come to being hit, perhaps killed.

The kamikaze veered to the left and seemed to be headed for the *Hambleton*, which was immediately astern. "It seemed as though I could see the Japanese pilot scream "'banzai!'" I wrote in my journal. "The Hambleton rose up on a wave, like an angry bull tossing his head and snorting."

Accounts differ, but here are my conclusions of how that Japanese plane was shot down. When the 40-mm quad gun on the fantail jammed, Matthew Brooks, a second-class steward from Baltimore, jumped to a .50-caliber machine gun and started firing. That .50 caliber, welded to the rail, was to be used to destroy floating mines, not shoot at enemy planes. Brooks fired round after round and the kamikaze plunged into the water.

My journal account, based on talks with officers and the crew, credits Brooks with knocking the kamikaze down. The *Ellyson*'s official action report does not specify which of its guns hit the kamikaze—all guns were firing—noting only that the plane was splashed with an "assist," meaning that fire from one of the other ships played a role.

From my notes I wrote an article about the black sailor's feat and sent it to Pearl Harbor headquarters, exultant that I could give him the credit he deserved.

Wondering whether the navy ever recognized Brooks's feat I checked more than a dozen former Ellyson crewmen while writing this book. Reflecting the racial separation on World War II ships, none of them remembered Brooks by name although a few readily recalled the tall, thin black man at the .50 caliber machine gun. However, Lt. (jg) Germaine Davison of Hokah, Minnesota, the officer in charge of that gun, said he had recommended that Brooks receive the Bronze Star. After repeated inquiries, the National Personnel Records Center reported just before the deadline for this book that the navy did indeed award Brooks the Bronze Star, although after his discharge. The citation, dated January 20, 1948, read:

For heroic achievement as a member of the crew of the USS Ellyson in action against enemy Japanese forces in the Pacific War Area on April 3, 1945. When his ship was under attack by a hostile plane, Brooks voluntarily manned a machine gun that he had never before operated and delivered accurate and effective fire against the determined enemy aircraft, thereby aiding greatly in the destruction of the attacking Japanese plane. His courageous initiative and gallant devotion to duty reflect the highest credit upon Brooks and the United States Naval Service.

Unfortunately, I have not been able to contact Brooks himself.

In June, *Ellyson* sailors cheered as I visited the ship on returning from tours on other vessels. I thought the crew was ribbing me but the cheers seemed genuine, expressing thanks for my articles. Relatives of some of the crew had sent clips of my stories from local newspapers. The power of those simple stories reporting to their families and neighbors their role in the gigantic battle impressed me so much that from time to time after the war I, like so many metropolitan newspaper editors, flirted with the possibility of a career running a small-town daily. I never made it to that glorified life.

I learned something important from those cheers. At Ambridge I had talked down to readers as "little people." Under fire at Okinawa I realized that the military men, with their varied skills, were far more valuable than I was.

# 4. Okinawa Two
## A *Caine Mutiny* Story

**On May 27,** a suicide plane crashed into the starboard side of the USS *Forrest*, one of our minesweepers, killing five and wounding thirteen.

A few days later, I boarded the *Forrest* and reported to Lieutenant William S. Warren, the executive officer. That was regular procedure. While friendly, he went beyond the usual questions about my status, probing deeper into my relationship with higher authorities. Before the interview was over he asked me, an enlisted man, to report misbehavior of the ship's captain to the commander of the squadron. He said he feared retaliation if he reported his immediate superior. I listened and said I would talk to others on the ship.

The story that Warren, the second in command, and other officers poured out was more than a list of complaints. It was the chronicle of a martinet on the verge of exploding, with only a slight pressure needed to touch him off. Mockingly called the Red Ryder after the comic strip hero—he had red hair and a red Vandyke beard—Lieutenant Commander Sanford E. Woodard would stalk the deck, wearing two pistols, one on his hip, the other under an arm, berating the crew. Some thought he wore the pistols to defend himself in case one of the crew went after him.

"What was your rank?" I was told he asked a sailor.

"Seaman first class, sir."

"Well, it's now seaman second class."

He refused to allow church services to be held until Warren pointed out navy regulations to him. He grudgingly told the executive officer to go ahead, but then, standing outside the cabin where the worshipers gathered, he disrupted the prayers by shooting at cans he threw in the water.

Even after the kamikaze hit the *Forrest* he continued his target practice, shooting over the crew's head as it cleaned up.

He didn't mingle with the other officers in the wardroom, eating alone in his cabin. All the officers I talked with told the same story. So did the enlisted men.

After interviewing many of the crew, I sent Woodard a note informing him of my mission and asking for an interview. He called me up to his cabin one evening. As a security measure the portholes were covered; only a small lamp was burning. Leaning back in his chair, he was eager to talk.

Strangely, he didn't question my position in the navy. My rating as "correspondent" must have raised visions in his head of national fame in *Time* or the *Saturday Evening Post*. While I usually called myself "combat correspondent," because it resonated the fame of the Marine combat correspondents and thus would carry more clout than the official rating of "enlisted navy correspondent," on official business I was an "ENC."

After making sure I knew he was a 1937 graduate of the Naval Academy, Woodard proceeded to indict and convict himself. He ridiculed most of the officers and enlisted men as incompetent. I thought about asking him questions about specific incidents, but that would have disclosed that the crew had been talking about him, probably leading to more punishment. Without any prodding he opened up.

"It takes Annapolis graduates and regular navy men to run a ship like this," he said. "Reserve officers and men cause more trouble than they are worth."

"Draftees," he said, "are the worst."

"So what can you do?" I asked.

"They need strict discipline," he said, "I'm not going to baby them. Why I could run a better ship if I had a regular navy crew half this size."

There were three hundred men on board.

On and on he talked as I took notes.

It did not require much insight to know that the navy would not print a story of a martinet captain and the boiling anger of his crew during a sea battle. I was sure that if I wrote the article and sent it to Pearl Harbor the navy would have disciplined me and with good cause. Even if I wrote just the facts, objectively, without taking sides for or against the captain, reporting only what the crew said and what the captain said, I would be going beyond my authorized role. I was part of the navy, a public relations man, not a civilian correspondent. Moreover, I would be breaking the trust that Captain Larkin had extended in letting me send stories to Honolulu uncensored. I decided to report Woodard to high authorities. It was a risk but I was willing to take the chance. I did not believe that so many officers and men aboard the *Forrest* would have concocted such a tale of abuse of leadership.

After I wrote my usual hometown piece on the ship's crew, I transferred to the Coast Guard cutter *Bibb*, where I seized the opportunity to talk to the commander of the minesweepers. Conceding that I was going beyond my rank and probably violating Naval regulations, I told him what Woodard had said in the interview and what officers and crew had reported. He listened, asked no questions, and made no comment except to thank me. Weeks later I heard that Woodard had been relieved of his command. I could not write the story, but as a whistle-blower, I had done a good deed.

For sixty years I thought that report of his removal was accurate. In 2005 I checked navy records and found the rumor was false. The records show that Lieutenant Commander Woodard remained captain of the *Forrest* until it returned to Boston and was decommissioned. Naval records open to me provide no indication that he had ever been disciplined.

In fact, Lieutenant Commander Woodard received the Silver Star, the third highest naval decoration, for "conspicuous gallantry and intrepidity" commanding the *Forrest* during the attack by Japanese suicide planes and the Bronze Star for picket duty and other service at Okinawa. He was eventually promoted to captain, skippered other ships, and received a Gold Star in lieu of a second Bronze medal as commander of the destroyer USS *John R. Craig* during the Korean War.

Interviewing *Forrest* survivors by telephone in 2005 I found many, but not all, who still thought ill of Woodard. No one praised him. Most told tales of continued mistreatment, including berating some sailors in public as undeserving of the Purple Hearts they received for injuries.

On the other hand, officers and men of the USS *Craig*, who called Woodard "Red Dog," considered him an outstanding skipper. Captain

Philip G. Saylor of Front Royal, Virginia, remembered Woodard as a "helluva good officer." Commander Roy S. Nunnally of Austin, Texas, went further, calling him "a great one," a disciplinarian, but personable and likable. Richard E. Scott, who retired as a lieutenant commander, was a storekeeper second class when Woodard took over the *Craig.* He said he was "scared to death" when assigned as Woodard's sea detail talker because of complaints he had heard of him. Thus he was pleasantly surprised to find Woodard fine to work with. "He never said a cross word to me and we got along fabulously. He was a tremendous ship handler and I enjoyed trying to anticipate his orders."

Perhaps both views are correct and this is a tale of redemption. Perhaps after my report his superiors called Woodard in and privately dressed him down but wrote nothing adverse into the record about his actions on the *Forrest.* The navy certainly remembered how General George S. Patton's slapping of two soldiers in Sicily upset the public in late 1943. Perhaps the navy decided that keeping the situation quiet and warning Woodard was a better way to handle the problem. If so, it worked. Woodard learned from his mistakes and reformed, to become an ideal skipper on the *Craig.* That is what I prefer to believe.

Regardless of the truth, I regret my blindness to the potential in the story as fiction. The thought never occurred to me, even after I returned to civilian life. I still had my notes. I could have built on the facts, making it into a crew's struggle in dealing with an absolute authority on the verge of madness during the longest sea battle in history. As a civilian whistleblower, I could not be disciplined by the navy. Considering my interest in fiction while in the navy and especially for a few years after my discharge, I'm puzzled why the idea did not occur to me. I guess that by that time I was too much the journalist to see that a novel could tell the truth better than a facts-only story.

Years later I realized my failure when I read Herman Wouk's *The Caine Mutiny,* saw the play on Broadway and later the film, with Humphrey Bogart as Captain Queeg.[1] Wouk cautioned that the story was not based on a real ship captain, although he had served on two destroyer minesweepers, the USS *Zane* and the USS *Southard,* which were older ships and not part of our squadron. Queeg's ship was a destroyer minesweeper like the *Forrest*. Queeg was a lieutenant commander, as was Red Ryder. Moreover, Wouk's crew derided the captain's cowardice with a song, "The Yellowstain Blues." The *Forrest* crew didn't go that far; they thought he was crazy but not a coward. There were rough parallels between Wouk's story and reality. Woodard was never publicly disciplined. Wouk's Captain Queeg, as a witness in a court-martial of the officer who took over the *Caine*, revealed his mental instability, but instead of being disciplined he was given an easy job at a naval base.

What readers might forget, however, is that at the end of *Caine Mutiny* the navy lawyer who won acquittal of the accused officer by skillfully exposing Queeg as a mental case denounced a post-trial victory celebration. He pointed out that regardless of his faults, Queeg had enlisted in the battle against the Nazis before Pearl Harbor, while his accusers were enjoying college life. Perhaps that's what Woodard's superiors thought. They knew that as a young man he had enlisted in the navy in 1932 and showed so much promise that he was given an appointment to the Naval Academy, from which he graduated in 1937. He had volunteered to protect his country long before most of the men who served under him.

Of course the fiction writer operates on a different level; he can adjust the detail to fit his message. As a fiction writer how would I have shaped Captain Woodard? Hopefully, I would have checked his record, as I did for this book but could not while an enlisted navy man. I certainly would have written a different ending.

The Battle of Okinawa gave me more than a taste of war. I heard the calls for help from the hospital ship USS *Comfort* when it was attacked. I saw an American munitions ship blow up, filling the sky with coruscating horror as its crew died. It burned for days, a constant reminder of peril.

I had unfairly expected the navy to be more efficient than it was. Once more, I was looking for perfection. There were many examples of friendly fire inflicting casualties on our people. In the worst case, I had seen American ships shoot down American planes that were trying to protect them at Kerama Retto, mistaking them for Japanese.

The pacifism lingering in me saw how combat brings out irrational hatred. Wielding brooms, the crew of the *Forrest* beat the body bag of a suicide pilot awaiting burial. A sailor on the *Rodman* pulled an arm of a dead kamikaze pilot out of its socket in a search for souvenirs. On Kerama Shima American soldiers dug up Japanese graves and took skulls for souvenirs. Other GIs, given a few hours off, captured horses and rode one to death.

I saw compassion, too. On a trip ashore, the 77th Division showed me that the army, although fighting face-to-face with the Japanese, could be kind to the enemy. The prelanding bombardment had killed many civilians, but army doctors had treated thousands of the wounded. In a visit to hospitals, I saw cot after cot of women, their throats swathed in bandages with clamps to hold them in place. Medics said that Japanese husbands and fathers had cut the throats of wives and daughters rather than let them fall into the hands of what they feared were brutal invaders.

I met Cupcake, the name GIs gave a nineteen-year-old Japanese girl who had been shot through the left breast during the invasion of Okinawa. She wanted to die when she was picked up. Her parents, brothers, and sisters had been killed and she hated the Americans. She changed her mind after she was treated for her wounds at a mobile surgical hospital. *Our Navy*, an official navy magazine, ran my feature article about her, sending me a check for $7.50.[2]

I also saw compassion in the navy. The *Ellyson* picked up a kamikaze pilot, just fifteen, who had decided at the last minute to save his life and crashed into the sea. He was terrified. He pulled back when Dr. Walsh bent over to examine him for wounds. There were none; he was merely exhausted. Like other kamikaze youths, he said he had only five hours training before setting off on his mission. During the interrogation, a group of American planes flew over our ship. The boy, sitting on his heels, looked up and said, "Hellcats." Although only a raw recruit, he knew our planes. Our interpreter said he should be home going to school instead of fighting a war. The boy laughed.

My pacifist heart felt no hatred for kamikaze pilots. I was not alone. The officers and crew treated the boy kindly. We found it hard to believe that the Japanese military was calling on boys to kill themselves in a desperate attempt to delay the inevitable defeat. We realized, too, that the Japanese would battle even more fiercely, from street to street, in the coming invasion of Kyushu. After a day or two, the *Ellyson* transferred the boy to a ship with better facilities for handling prisoners.

While thoughts of death were constant, I didn't pray to God to spare me. Still the agnostic, I didn't believe in intervention by the deity on my behalf. I never thought of being a Johnny-come-lately convert. In response to my mother's question, I wrote home on May 26 that "little has changed in my religious thinking since I have been here." Some veterans of the European and Pacific wars told me that they turned to God when the action got hot, but most said they didn't. "I don't agree that there are no atheists in the fox holes," I said in my letter. "There are in the holds of ships, I know."

I did read my little Christian Science book. Some pages offered comfort, but usually I could not believe it. Lieutenant Warren on the *Forrest* shed some light on the faith after his left arm was ripped open by jagged steel while he was inspecting damage caused by a bomb exploding near the water line. Pulled up on deck, blood pouring from his arm, he was immediately sent to the sick bay where Dr. Robert J. Schaffer treated and heavily bandaged his wound. I asked Warren why, as a Christian Scientist, he accepted the treatment. He explained that if he had greater faith he would have relied solely on God to cure him. Because his faith was weak at that moment, he accepted medical treatment. Don't look to me for perfection, the wounded man was saying. Unlike me, he didn't require complete adherence to his belief at all times. It took me decades to accept this obvious limit on faith as normal. Oddly, my years on the *New York Times* proved crucial to this enlightenment.

On June 19, I was ordered to the LST-804, where I learned I was to return to Pearl Harbor for a new assignment. Two days later, the Japanese began another desperate air assault. The next day, June 22, the *Ellyson's* charmed life ended.[3] A kamikaze exploded as it splashed fifty feet off the bow, killing Gunner's Mate First Class H. R. Klein, captain of a five-inch gun, and wounding five. Friendly fire from a destroyer escort riddled the *Ellyson's* superstructure, injuring four enlisted men.

My charmed life continued. Of the twelve ships to which I was assigned, one never left Ulithi; ten suffered damage and casualties; only the *Gherardi* escaped untouched; and, only the *Gherardi*, the *Ellyson*, and the *Hambleton* remained operational. I had been lucky enough to escape assignment to the carrier *Benjamin Franklin*. The *Aaron Ward*, on which I had traveled to the Western Pacific, suffered heavy losses and was nearly sunk in an intense attack by suicide planes while on picket duty. And the USS *Terror,* a command ship and tender to the minecraft, was hit with heavy loss of life on May 1, shortly after I spent a day on it. Fortune somehow kept me from being one of the 5,000 sailors killed and 5,000 wounded at Okinawa, the highest casualties the U.S. Navy ever suffered in a single battle.

I left Okinawa with admiration for the navy. Despite all the griping, despite complaints about officers, despite discrimination against blacks and Hispanics, despite the inevitable personal animosities that develop from living in confined quarters week after week, despite serious errors in the cauldron of battle, officers and enlisted men put aside their divisions and pulled together as a team. At last, the pacifist could see the good side of the military and be proud to be a part of the navy.

# 5. Living It Up in Japan, Korea, and China

**Back at Pearl Harbor** I was lauded as a hero—of sorts. The officers in the enlisted correspondents section had not taken part in any battle and thus were impressed by the action I had seen. They were also impressed by my production—I had written 257 stories, most only a page long. My bosses decided that I could have any ship available for my next assignment. With a confidence I had never experienced before, I chose the first available submarine.

While waiting I read in the *United States Naval Institute Proceedings* of July 1944 that 35,000 men—or more than 1.1 percent of the U.S. Navy, Marine Corps, and Coast Guard—were either absent without leave or absent over leave at all times. Thus in the navy alone 14 million man-days of effective military service were lost each year.

My desire for justice set me to wondering how the navy record compared with a favorite target of conservatives—wartime strikes by civilian workers. By chance, I found in the *Honolulu Advertiser* an AP article reporting that strikes and lockouts resulted in the loss of one-tenth of one percent of the available working time in 1944, or 8.5 million man-days of idleness. I sent a short piece to *Harper's* magazine comparing the two reports and concluded:

> The Navy's record in this war is so magnificent that no one is inclined
> to criticize the service because a small percentage of its men go over the
> hill. But labor also has done its war job well, and should not be pilloried
> because a few workers have failed to keep the no-strike pledge.

*Harper's* printed three paragraphs as a filler in its August 1945 edition, just before the Japanese surrender.[1] It was a small start, but the item had my name on it in a quality national magazine.

I was reading the *Honolulu Advertiser* because I had taken a part-time job there as a copyeditor while waiting for my submarine assignment. Another navy correspondent tipped me off about the *Advertiser*'s need for desk help. The paper was so desperate for staff, he said, that I need not worry about my lack of editing experience. Late afternoons after navy duty, we went to the *Advertiser*'s newsroom and helped put out the bulldog (early) edition, editing wire copy, writing headlines, and reading proofs.

When the last bit of copy cleared the desk the slot man pulled out a bottle of Southern Comfort, and I had my first taste of old-fashioned newspapering. As that first sip of the sugary liquor warmed my stomach I wondered what kind of a life I was headed for. I had seldom touched alcohol in Harrisburg and felt like vomiting. To be one of the gang, I took a swig of Southern Comfort every night but the sweet taste always nauseated me.

My hope of a tour on a submarine ended when the Japanese announced their "unconditional" surrender on August 14, 1945. It was evening and I was writing a letter when Radio Tokyo flashed the news. Finally, confirmation of the rumors! I ran around, hardly knowing what to do. From the window of our Quonset hut I could see Pearl Harbor. The deep-throated roar of the thousands of sailors, soldiers, and civilians rumbled up the hill as they expressed their joy. Horns blew, sirens screamed, and whistles shrilled.

I stood in awe until Richard Cheney yanked me out of my reverie with an invitation to go for a ride. This was not the future vice president. My friend of the same name was a junior-grade lieutenant. He and another j.g. commandeered a pickup truck and off we went. At first we just tore around the navy yard, along the docks and through the huge piles of goods ready to be loaded on ships. Everyone was excited but few knew what to do except dash around madly and recklessly in cars, Jeeps, even lift trucks.

We decided to go back up the hill a few miles and get a better view. Thousands of searchlights from ships and antiaircraft batteries danced across the sky, their giant fingers pointing out planes sweeping overhead. Red, blue, green, yellow, and white flares flamed up from the ships. We drank in the glorious sight and Dick's friend decided we needed to add to our celebration. He drove to the officers' barracks and got a bottle of wine and a fifth of Milford and Taylor Reserve, a New Zealand whiskey. Like thousands of others, the three of us toured Honolulu, blowing the horn and cheering. Soldiers and sailors, with a bottle in one hand and a girl in the other, clogged the streets.

Dick's friend kept the wine for himself. He said he didn't want to get drunk. Dick took a swig of the whiskey and passed it to me. I was determined to let it just touch my lips—daily swigs of Southern Comfort warned me to take it easy—but the truck hit a bump, and the whiskey went down my throat, igniting a pleasant glow that quickly spread throughout my body. By the second drink I forgot my plan to limit myself to a taste or two and fake the rest. Dick and I pulled on the bottle the rest of the night and I had my share.

Our tongues loosened, I called the lieutenants commanders and they called me leftenant. We began to sing, first college songs like Maine's "Stein Song" and Michigan's "The Victors." When I switched to "Anchors Aweigh" Dick and his friend threatened to push me out of the truck. Reservists, they hated military life. We then settled on a popular ditty:

When the war is over, we will all enlist again
When the war is over, we will all enlist again
O when the war is over, we will all enlist again
In a pig's asshole we will.

We screamed the verses at the top of our lungs all the way to Waikiki, pausing only to pull on the bottles. At the beach a girl stood alone, screeching "Rape! Rape!" Navy and army police cruised the area but we saw no disturbances.

At a hamburger stand, where we stopped for a sandwich, we watched as a drunken teen-age sailor, who said he was the greatest lover since French movie star Charles Boyer, asked a girl if he could kiss her. She said yes; he pawed her awkwardly and slobbered a kiss on her cheek. He was having a hard time standing, so when he said he was supposed to return to his ship by 10 o'clock—it was long past that—we put him in the back of the pickup and started for the fleet landing. On the way we met a WAVE lieutenant driving alone in a Jeep. A Jeep full of soldiers was driving alongside her and she was terrified. We pulled along the other side of her and the three vehicles sped down the road. By now, fully drunk, I kept yelling at her: "Get ready for the boarding party, here we come."

We tired of the chase and eventually let the Jeeps run ahead. As we did she slowed down and pulled off the road. When we came alongside she said, "Please stay with me until we get to the navy yard." Feeling protective, we convoyed her to the yard, muttering about soldiers who would take advantage of women. At the fleet landing, we turned the drunken sailor over to a shore patrol, who promised to see him back to his ship without preferring any charges.

Early in the morning they dumped me at my barracks and somehow I found my cot. I woke up late with a violent headache, nauseated but unable to vomit. I could not get up. After a few hours I took a cold shower and returned to bed. Finally, at 1 P.M., I made it to the correspondents' hut. Everyone laughed and said I couldn't take it. When I swore off liquor forever, they laughed louder. "But I mean it," I insisted, which touched off even more laughter. That was the first time I was drunk.

They said that Lieutenant Cheney was deathly sick but the driver of our truck, who had limited himself to wine, never got beyond a bright look in his eyes. Cheney became a life-long friend. Years later we got drunk drinking a jeroboam of champagne in his backyard in Leonia, New Jersey.

As a reward for my work at Okinawa, I was ordered to accompany a public information officer to Tokyo Bay for the Japanese surrender on the battleship *Missouri*. We flew to Iwo Jima, where we caught the new destroyer USS *Perkins*, which took us to Japan.

On the morning of September 2 the *Perkins* entered Tokyo Bay, cutting through the mist ahead of a British destroyer and a British freighter. Minesweepers, including my old ship, the *Ellyson*, exploded mines, reminding us that danger was not over. On the hills American flags flew on a lighthouse and a factory. The Japanese had placed tiny white flags on the 116 guns defending the harbor. Fleets of B-29 bombers droned overhead and hundreds of carrier planes buzzed the ships, signaling signing of the surrender documents. We were a little late.

A small boat ferried the public information officer and me from the destroyer to the *Missouri*. Just as we climbed a ladder to the deck the

Japanese delegation departed on the other side. We missed the surrender and never saw General Douglas MacArthur or Admiral Chester W. Nimitz or other men of the Allied brass, let alone the Japanese. I slept on the *Missouri* that night and was listed as being aboard for the ceremony, or so a yeoman told me. The next morning I was transferred to Yokosuka, which had been the main Japanese naval base on Tokyo Bay.

Unprepared for the occupation, American officers at Yokosuka didn't know what to do with me or other navy correspondents as they arrived. There were about six of us and, lacking assignments, we moved around the country as we pleased. Without buying a ticket we would just get on a train. Conductors would argue and try to write out a pass for us. We would just wave them off, much to their anger. Japanese kids were like kids everywhere. I remember a small boy on a train, flicking an insect off his mother's arm, clearly saying "B-29." The *Enola Gay,* which dropped the first atomic bomb, on Hiroshima, was a B-29.

On one of the first days of the occupation, I met Roy S. Yamaguchi, a reporter for *Asahi Shimbun,* a leading Tokyo newspaper. He was reporting American troop landings, sending his copy to Tokyo by pigeons. He invited me to his somewhat Westernized house in a suburb for dinner on September 9. The two of us ate alone, sitting on low chairs. His tiny wife served us, crawling in on her hands and knees and putting three dishes down for each course, then backing out.

At *Asahi* I met a receptionist, an older woman, who spoke good English. She said she was the wife of Sessue Hayakawa, who had been a flamboyant Japanese star in Hollywood films in the 1920s. She had not heard from him since the war started, when he had been in Paris. Could I write to him and to try to find out if he was still living?

Using the last address she had, 19 rue Brunel, I wrote and in a few weeks received a reply from him, still in Paris at the same address. Delighted, I hurried to Tokyo to tell Mrs. Hayakawa the good news. She looked at me with a mixture of hope and dread as I approached. "It's good news," I said, and handed her the letter. Contrary to Japanese custom, Mrs. Hayakawa cried openly when she read it. He was alive and well. I was so happy for her that tears came to my eyes, too. I didn't know until decades later that she had been a Hollywood star in her own right. As

Tsuru Aoki, she played opposite her husband. After the war Hayakawa appeared again in films, including his greatest role, the Japanese camp commander Colonel Saito in the 1957 hit *The Bridge on the River Kwai,* for which he received an Academy Award nomination. After his wife died in 1961, he became a Zen master. He died in 1973.

Because of my history of pacifism, I was interested in talking to Toyohiko Kagawa, a Japanese Christian who had devoted his life to helping the poor. Kagawa had been excoriated by the Japanese military for apologizing for the 1937 invasion of China and touring the United States in 1940 on a peace mission. He and his American missionaries had broadcast calls for peace over Radio Tokyo during the war. Three other navy correspondents and I set out on what we thought would be a simple train ride to Kamikitazawa, a rural area near Tokyo, where the group lived. We quickly got lost, but a Japanese man offered to guide us. We switched to a trolley and a small boat and then walked to Kagawa's little house in the woods surrounded by farms. He wasn't there.

Disappointed, we were about to go back when the guide directed us to a Western-style bungalow nearby. Eight Kagawa disciples living there—two men and six women—thought we had come to arrest them as war criminals. We were the first of the occupation force to find them. One of the women was a Japanese American, born in Oregon, who had been visiting Japan and was interned after the attack on Pearl Harbor. The five old American ladies, who had spent most of their lives in Japan as missionaries, were ready to surrender, face trial, and go to jail. Learning that we were reporters, they deluged us with questions about their fate. They were willing to be Christian martyrs. They had declined repatriation when the war began because Japan was their real home. All thought the emperor was one of the greatest men in the world, that he had been a prisoner in his palace.

The most interesting character, I wrote in my journal, was eighty-two-year-old "Mother" Topping. Wrinkled and bent, she had difficulty walking on legs and feet swollen from beriberi. Varicose veins stood out like crooked corduroy on her scrawny frame. Her plain black silk dress—it looked like a slip—dragged on the floor and she constantly tripped over it. While others sang hymns at a piano, she took me into another room. She put a heavily veined hand on my shoulder and whispered, "I'm a war criminal."

For three years she had made radio broadcasts urging American mothers to stop the war immediately. She began broadcasting shortly after her husband died. On his deathbed he had said, "America, Japan, forgive them both." I was too polite to ask whether he had been addressing her or God. In any event, the Japanese had not asked her to make the broadcasts, she said; she had volunteered because she believed they might stop the war. I had found someone more naïve than I was. She showed me the script of a broadcast in which she had called American flyers "beasts" who machine-gunned women and children. She had asked American women to flood the United Nations founding meeting in San Francisco with telegrams to stop the war.

"What do you think they will do with me?" she asked, looking over silver-rimmed glasses with tired blue eyes. I asked if she were an American citizen. She said she was. "And did the Japanese pay you?" At first she refused, she said, but the Japanese "have a different sort of psychology and didn't understand." So she took money but "was careful not to use it for myself."

I, the former pacifist, told the little old lady she would probably be tried for treason.

"And then what?" she asked.

"They'll stand you in front of a wall and shoot you," I said, testing her reaction with a tinge of cruelty. I could sympathize with the missionaries' pacifism but not with their joining the enemy.

"No, no," she said, putting a wrinkled hand on my arm, "they'll pardon me."

She was more interested in what would happen to a half-dozen American soldiers who had been captured and made broadcasts for Radio Tokyo. On a Christmas broadcast she had portrayed their mother, they her sons. She had heard they had been arrested.

"They'll probably be lined up in front of a wall, too, and shot," I said.

"No, no, pardoned, like Pétain," she said, referring to the French marshal who had collaborated with the Nazis as head of the Vichy government. She said that she was so old that life didn't mean anything to her. But the soldiers—"they are such good boys"—should be spared.

We stayed for dinner but I could not eat the simple meal of seaweed soup, heavy synthetic bread with bean paste, and tea.

We met Kagawa the next morning. He had suffered from consumption and looked older than his fifty-seven years. Although he must have weighed less than a hundred pounds, he grabbed my hand and shook it vigorously in a wide arc. He was concerned whether American Christians, who had given him much financial support before the war, had turned against him. He said his broadcasts had not been anti-American but were appeals to end the fighting, which, in effect, would have been to recognize Japanese conquests, a conclusion less important to him than stopping the war. I filed a story by airmail to the newspaper *PM*, but don't think it was used.

Civilian correspondents found Kagawa and the missionaries much later. Neither Kagawa nor his missionaries were prosecuted. Nor were American prisoners of war who broadcast on Radio Tokyo. After the war Kagawa continued his preaching in Japan and overseas, was nominated for a Nobel Prize, and died in 1960. His followers erected the Kagawa Archives and Resource Center next to a church in Kamikitazawa.

I admired the little man. While I had renounced pacifism, Kagawa had stood fast. The pressure on him from the government and most of the Japanese people must have exceeded by far the family pressure on me. The military jailed him as a traitor; I had been free to sit out the war. Yet his heroic example didn't convince me that I had made a mistake. Three months under fire made me proud of what I had done.

What I didn't yet realize was that the navy experience was further eroding the high standards I had set for myself. At boot camp, the clues were small. I didn't hesitate to sneak out of work details. My "flying fuck" expostulations made me one of the gang. On ship I sometimes sarcastically berated married sailors who boasted of conquests, some probably true, ashore. Certainly I felt morally superior. But when the opportunity came to make some money illegally, I didn't hesitate.

In exploring the Yokosuka Naval Base another navy correspondent, Thomas Mackin of Kearny, New Jersey, and I found a cave on a promontory overlooking Tokyo Bay. It was dry, but lacking a flashlight, we didn't go deeply into it. We knew, from silhouettes of American planes on the walls, that aircraft spotters had used the cave. One silhouette showed a B-73, a plane that had never been built.

Looking for souvenirs, we found a few cases of Japanese naval officer epaulets in small boxes. Mackin suggested we sell them to American sailors who were swarming ashore on a few hours of liberty. "They'd pay a lot for these," he said. We set up a stand in town. Soon we had our pitch down. Standing on a wall, I babbled variations of this:

There are no kimonos, there is no sake
But you've got to have a souvenir before you go backy.

Mackin handled the money. In a few hours we were sold out and each had $157.

Not for a moment did I think I had done anything wrong. After all, we were told, an American commander at the naval base regularly browbeat Japanese officers to give him swords of the defeated admirals.

I lucked out on a boondoggle trip. The army had outfitted a ship named *Spindle Eye* as a communications center for civilian correspondents during the planned invasion of Kyushu. With the surrender the invasion was called off and correspondents moved into excellent facilities at American headquarters in Tokyo. Eager to use the new ship, the army public relations staff invited correspondents to take a voyage on the *Spindle Eye* to Nagasaki, the target of the second atomic bomb, Korea and Shanghai. In a drawing of straws, Frank Harris of Boston and I won the two slots open to navy correspondents. Hal Boyle, the much-admired AP reporter who had won a Pulitzer Prize for coverage of the European theater in 1944, was among the civilian correspondents on the trip. Harris and I enjoyed eating at the same mess and playing Ping-Pong with Boyle and the other big boys but we didn't learn anything about war reporting from them because we never saw the stories they filed.

Pacifism tugged at me only mildly at our first stop, Nagasaki. A lot had been written about the devastation, but we were unprepared for the miles of rubble that marked the center of the once-prosperous city. What amazed me was that at ground zero and at small pockets here and there a building remained standing. Even though the bomb had killed hundreds of thousands, I didn't question the morality of using it. We didn't visit a hospital, nor did we get even a glimpse of the sick and the wounded, thus we missed the human suffering.

6. Aboard the Army communications ship *Spindle Eye* on way to Shanghai. Photographer unknown.

After a side trip to Korea, we sailed to Shanghai. Docking at the Bund, we forced our way through the ragged kids pushing obscene pictures—"Dollar, Joe?"—and walked the few blocks to the Palace Hotel, the head-quarters of a contingent of navy correspondents. They had gone to China without any combat experience and, true to their journalistic backgrounds, exploited their "correspondents" roles shamefully, as Frank and I soon did. The correspondents had a suite of rooms in the second-class hotel, and from the moment we arrived, succeeded in impressing us.

Frank and I were wearing standard blue work shirts and jeans. The Palace Hotel correspondents had switched to khaki Eisenhower jackets and slacks that Chinese tailors made to their specifications, with "US Navy Correspondent" in English and Chinese above the left pocket and "War Correspondent" shoulder patches. Three correspondents invited us to sit on cushions on the floor of the living room. At the ring of a bell a Chinese servant rushed in, fell to his knees and exclaimed: "Yes, master, yes master."

"Chop chop—beer," an American ordered.

"Yes, master, yes master."

The Chinese servant backed out and raced off, returning, in a remarkably short time, with another Chinese man carrying a silver tray with bottles of cold beer. Tipped with the equivalent of three cents, they prostrated themselves.

"Sank you, master, sank you," and they scooted away.

We navy correspondents theoretically represented Allied forces that helped liberate the Chinese, but in truth we treated them as an inferior people. In turn, the Chinese, dominated for centuries by foreigners, submitted—"yes, master." What else could they do at that time? Our language in addressing the hotel employees—"chop chop"—denigrated them. Our willingness to accept prostrations and backing out of rooms showed a lack of respect. Perhaps the navy segregation policy, which reflected American social life at that time, contributed to our behavior. While I opposed segregation even then, I never thought of challenging it in the navy.

Our hosts offered us the city of Shanghai. We could stay with them in the Palace; there was plenty of room. Bursting with pride and arrogance, they told us everything was available in this newly liberated city.

"Want to get laid? A blow job?"

The bell rang, a servant rushed in, "Yes, master, yes master."

"Chop chop—woman, nice young woman."

"Yes master, yes master" and he ran out, darting back in a few minutes with a sad and messy woman. "Clean girl, master, young, clean girl."

Harris and I said we sure liked their Eisenhower jackets. They would get them made to measure in a day. "And how about a woman?" The Chinese woman had cuddled up to one of the men. Far from young, she looked old and ill. "No, no," we said. We were not going to take a chance of catching venereal disease. Ready for whiskey? How about Scotch? Bourbon? Gin? We would have Scotch. "Yes master, yes master." A bottle of Johnny Walker—at least a bottle with a Johnny Walker label—magically appeared. Whether it was the real thing or not, it tasted like Scotch.

For the next few days, caught up in the hectic pace of the city, we dashed from place to place through the crowded streets in rickshaws. We went to nightclubs with neon signs glittering with their new names—Atomic, Brown Derby, the Jungle, Mike's Place. While a band jangled "My

Blue Heaven," beautiful white Russian women, refugees from the Soviet Union, tantalized the newly arrived Americans, as, we suspected, they had tantalized Japanese officers during the occupation. They had quickly learned to say "I love you" in English, in response to the servicemen's line of "we'll get married and I'll take you to America."

Beggars stretched out trembling, filthy hands. Lepers, part of their faces fallen off, clawed at us, fireworks crackled under foot, shopkeepers beseeched, rickshaw drivers implored. Fierce-looking Sikh traffic officers somehow controlled the chaos. In a scene that still haunts me, a tattered girl—she could not have been five—sat on a curb, sobbing and holding a dead baby in her lap. I stood for a moment paralyzed. Was she faking? Was she begging? No, she didn't even look up at me. What could I do? Nothing. Poverty and despair overwhelmed me. I hurried off.

To silk row, where store after store was stacked to the ceiling with pajamas, house coats, shirts, blouses scarves, stockings. All silk, 180 percent silk. Handmade. A thousand years old. Beautiful. Lavish. Wonderful. Then to the leather shops, the jewelry district, the art dealers. Silver. Jade. Lacquerware. Rubies. The treasures of the Orient, real and fake, available for a price. How did the Chinese hide all these riches from the Japanese?

Caught up in the excitement of liberated Shanghai, free of the ordinary constraints that govern conscience, I did something for which I remain, more than sixty years later, profoundly ashamed. It happened the night before the *Spindle Eye* sailed back to Japan.

Six of us had a big dinner at a crowded restaurant. As we ordered, we got to talking about the hopelessness of the Chinese poor. There didn't seem to be any way they could pull themselves out of poverty in China as they could if they lived in the United States. One of us, I suspect it was I, noted that it would be easy to smuggle a Chinese person to the United States aboard a navy vessel.

We turned to the waiter, a smiling young man in his late teens or early twenties, who spoke a little English, and asked if he would like to go to America. He said yes, bowing again and again, his black eyes glowing. As he kept leaving our table to serve others, we worked out a plan. He could stay below deck out of the sight of the officers. Any officer who did see him would think he was a Filipino mess boy. Once we landed in the United States we could get him out of the naval base with little trouble.

Halfway through the meal we told the young man we could take him to America. When we saw his excitement we began to wonder whether we had gone too far. We tried to back off, telling him he would have to leave the next morning. Sadly he said it would take him two days by bicycle to go to a village in the country to tell his mother good-bye. Sorry, we said, relieved; the ship would sail tomorrow. We thought we had escaped the hole we had dug for ourselves.

But the waiter wouldn't give up. All right, he said, he would leave without saying good-bye to his mother. Where would he meet us? We told him on the Bund. And would I—by this time I was doing most of the talking—write my name for him? He gave me a piece of paper and, in a desperate attempt to tell him this had all been a bad joke, I wrote "Mickey Mouse." He read it, pronouncing the words slowly, "Mick-ee Mouse." Then, nodding vigorously, he bowed and, doing his best with the different "th," said "Sank you Mr. Mouse, sank you." Too ashamed to tell him the truth, we tipped him liberally and left the restaurant. The next day before dawn, before the Chinese youth was to meet us, the *Spindle Eye* sailed back to Japan.

For a day or two I was bothered by what I had done, but didn't dwell on the cruelty of our joke or my leading part in it. Not until months later, after my return to civilian life, did my conscience catch up with me and remorse set in. Rejoining the Harrisburg Quaker meeting—pacifism had not entirely left me—I recounted incidents in which the military corrupted people. I told of the sailors gleefully stabbing the body bag of a kamikaze pilot and of GIs digging into graves for skulls to take home as souvenirs.

Pointedly, I didn't mention our denigration of the Shanghai hotel staff and the joke on the Chinese waiter. Had the war corrupted me? Or had the real me just been lying there, waiting for the opportunity to spring out? At times I wondered whether I was thinking too deeply about the incident. Perhaps the Chinese waiter did realize it was a joke. He must have told his friends and certainly one of them would have been familiar with Mickey Mouse. But my conscience never let go. My guilt has grown over the decades.

On returning to Yokosuka, I realized that I had tired of Japan, with its endless grays, its rainy cold, its blocks of devastated buildings, its bombed-out warships rusting in Yokosuka docks, and the confused, unfriendly people. I was ready to go home. I was serving no useful purpose as a navy correspondent. Only twice did my nominal bosses give me assignments. Once they told me to put on my white dress uniform and play enlisted man with some officers at a dinner with geishas. This was a navy public relations event to show how well we were getting along with the Japanese. *Liberty* magazine ran a story with a picture of a geisha feeding me.

The second assignment was to escort an AP photographer looking for a Navy Day picture. With Japan one day ahead of the United States, the picture would arrive just in time for Navy Day. I showed him a long line of enlisted men waiting to enter a brothel. A shore patrol objected. When I protested that the war was over, the SP threatened to break the camera. Nevertheless, the photographer took—or pretended to take—the picture. I do not think the Associated Press ever transmitted that picture if one existed.

Obviously my mind had already left the navy. I asked for reassignment in the States. Instead, I was ordered to fly back to Pearl Harbor by way of Guam and Johnson Island. In Honolulu I calmed down. At least I was out of Japan. There would be no dysentery. With John Dewey's *Human Nature and Conduct: An Introduction to Social Psychology* to keep my mind from wandering stateside, I resigned myself to four more months before discharge. The navy again offered to make me an officer and I again declined.

Although I wouldn't be eligible for discharge until spring, the navy, responding to a little prodding, transferred me to the hospital ship USS *Benevolence* for the voyage home. On February 7, 1946, I leaned on the rail of the big white ship, my eyes misting. As a Marine band played "California Here I Come," a loudspeaker cut through the music. I could only make out "specialist X second class, report to the ship's office immediately." I went below and was told my orders had been canceled. The month that had been added to my life had been taken away without explanation. "He who gives can take away," I wrote home, "and the Navy is God."

It was not until late March that I sailed for home on a destroyer, landing at Long Beach, California. That night, on liberty, I went to a drug store and ordered a wonderful snack, a chocolate milk shake and a grilled cheese sandwich. Within minutes my stomach bloated and I vomited. When I returned to the base I found that someone had stolen the Japanese rifle that I had stolen at Yokosuka.

A few days later I boarded a train headed east. At Braintree, Maryland, I was discharged on April 7, a month earlier than I should have been. Brushing aside the question of justice, I had called Morey Potter at United Press, who wrote a letter saying I was needed. I still used my media status to get a personal favor. Would I ever learn?

# 6. Two Loves
## Betty and Editing

**Back in Harrisburg** I called on Viki, who was home from Bucknell University. She opened the door and stepped back—not toward me—and then sat down in a chair. Feeling I should do something dramatic, I dropped to my knees at her feet. Unbelievably, at twenty-six years old I was still an unreconstructed romantic. In the next few seconds I grew up.

I saw a stranger. Viki was no longer the fresh young girl I left behind; she was a woman who had not discovered how to use cosmetics with restraint. Those blue-gray eyes exuded not love, not even warmth, not icy indifference, either, but a curious puzzlement, as if to ask what we were doing there. We went out to dinner although we both felt uncomfortable. I never saw Viki again.

Before I went into the navy I had met another young lady, Elizabeth King, a secretary at the Pennsylvania Federation of Labor. She was an Irish beauty with long hair so brown it was almost black and green-flecked brown eyes that could turn mournful. One of the first telephone calls I made when I returned to United Press was to the labor federation.

"Miss King, please," I told the operator. When she answered I asked, without identifying myself, "Is it still Miss King?"

"Yes it is, Robert Phelps," she replied. She had remembered my voice.

We began to date and before long we were dining together almost every night. Neither of us owned a car so we were confined to movies and walks in parks for entertainment. Within months we were engaged and on January 10, 1947, we were married in the rectory of St. Francis of Assisi Church in a ten-minute ceremony. Diocesan rules barred Catholics from marrying non-Catholics in the church itself. Raised as an unquestioning

Catholic, Betty made sure I understood that she would remain faithful to her religion, although she wouldn't ask me to convert. I said I belonged to no church and wouldn't object to raising our children Catholic.

Because of our lack of sexual experience, we had serious problems. I was "a quickie and Betty a lightning bug" who needed plenty of warming, I wrote in our combined diary. Practicing the rhythm method of birth control countenanced by the Catholic Church compounded the problem by restricting the days for sexual relations. I often wished that Deanie, the Ambridge telephone operator who jumped naked into my bed, had given me the sexual lessons I needed. If virginity demonstrated purity, it also ruined many nights of love. Purity, a hallmark of my idealism, didn't seem so important any more.

We didn't panic; the depth of our love gave us patience. We went to sleep in each other's arms and woke up in each other's arms. At the end of our first month Betty thought she was pregnant. It was the first of years of false alarms. We never had children although we sought help from doctors. Nor would adoption agencies approve us because of our difference in religion. In those days there were fewer babies available than couples seeking to adopt them. That was fortunate, my mother jested, because Betty would have had the poor kid on his knees praying for hours and I would have him studying the rest of the day. He would never have had any fun.

Betty and I started out on the basis of equality. Neither would make a major decision, we agreed, without the approval of the other. In discussing this ideal, I made a major mistake. Emphasizing that we could never fuse into one being nor totally understand each other, I quoted Thomas Wolfe.[1]

> Which of us has known his brother? Which of us has looked into his father's heart? Which of us has not remained forever prison-pent? Which of us is not forever a stranger and alone?

When I first read those well-known lines as a college freshman, I thought they applied to me. I could not understand why my father and my brother Woodrow had remained so distant from the rest of us and why my brother John had become an alcoholic. The answer, Wolfe seemed to be saying, is that isolation is part of the human condition and is difficult, if not impossible, to overcome. I wanted Betty to realize that truth and accept differences between us as normal. To me, the passage must be true because the words were so beautiful. "Beauty is truth, truth beauty—that is all ye know on earth and all ye need to know," Keats wrote. But he was writing about a Grecian urn, not a personal love. It never occurred to me that I was doing something a journalist should never do—taking words out of context.

The idea of separateness disturbed Betty; she had thought of marriage in the Biblical sense of "one body, one flesh." A marriage devoid not only of union but also of understanding frightened her. Did that mean inevitable conflict and failure of the marriage? I assured her that as long as we practiced equality and talked our problems through we would build a sound and happy marriage. She certainly felt no competition from another church because I stopped attending the Quaker meetings. She believed in me then and believed in me on her deathbed fifty-six years later even though I regularly ignored the equality I had pledged. This was decades before the feminist rights movement.

Betty helped me overcome much of my awkwardness in dealing with people. She also brought me new respect in the newsroom at the state capitol. How could I get a wife as good looking and personable as she was?

Joe Banks had quit United Press, so Potter gave me the no. 2 reporting job, covering the state Senate. Keeping track of the fifty state senators was much easier than covering the two-hundred-member House of Representatives, where Dave Bramson still labored. My beat also included much of the state bureaucracy. My reporting skills were improving but, as before my navy tour, I rarely received tips. I continued to pick up ideas from the trade press and close reading of the national press, especially the *New York Times,* the *Wall Street Journal,* and the left-wing New York tabloid *PM,* still my favorite newspaper.

A good example was my exclusive story on community property. I had read in the *Wall Street Journal* that people in community property states, formed from Hispanic areas, like California, New Mexico, and Arizona, paid less in federal income taxes than people in states basing their estate laws on the English system. A few of the English-tradition states had decided to give their citizens a tax break by adopting Hispanic community property laws, which presume joint ownership by husbands and wives. Most states had not.

I talked to a number of Pennsylvania legislators, none of whom knew about the situation. But one senator liked the idea and said he was going to look into it. This was the peg on which to hang the story. The rest of the press jumped on it and the Republican governor, James H. Duff, seeing an easy way to give Pennsylvanians a tax cut without any cost to the state, asked the legislature to adopt community property, even though it might complicate some estate plans. The plan was easily approved. Eventually federal tax laws gave equality to all states.

From the *Wall Street Journal* I was slowly learning how to personalize my writing. I blatantly copied *Journal* leads, adapting them to state house subject matter. Remembering a *Journal* story reporting that "nickel beer" was going the way of the five-cent cigar, I wrote that the five-cent call from pay telephones was going the way of the nickel beer because the state Public Utility Commission was about to raise the toll. That story was played in papers throughout the state. No one, not my United Press colleagues, not even my competitors, mentioned my copycat theft, probably because they never read the *Journal.* Yet years later friends remembered I had written that article.

Journalists' reluctance to read publications other than their immediate daily newspaper competitors puzzled me then and puzzled me later in Providence, New York, and Boston. Reporters and even editors seldom read trade magazines and newsletters, which were often ahead on a story because they followed their special interests closely. To me it was better than talking to lobbyists. I got on the mailing lists for many of those publications.

Another story I took the lead on was the unionization of major league baseball players. Short items had come out of Pittsburgh in 1946 that Pirate players were joining the newly established American Baseball Guild, led by a Boston lawyer, Robert Murphy. His demands for big leaguers included a guaranteed minimum salary of $7,500 a year, pensions, and removal of the reserve clause, which barred players from signing with other teams when their contracts ran out. Club owners said such outrageous demands would bankrupt financially weak teams. Some Pittsburgh Pirates joined the guild, which petitioned the Pennsylvania Labor Relations Board for recognition as bargaining agent. General opinion was that the board would reject the petition. Coming from a union family I was not so sure. I tried to cultivate the labor board examiner who investigated whether, under Pennsylvania law, the players had such a right.

The day before the labor board handed down its decision I called on the examiner. He wouldn't give me a clue to his recommendations, no matter how I phrased the questions. When he stepped out of his office to take a call, I peeked, in timeless journalistic fashion, at the draft of the order on his desk. It called for union recognition. Because there was no alternate draft on the desk, I wrote the overnight story as a hard decision, but Potter wisely toned it down so that it said the union was on "the verge of victory." The next day the board ruled for the players. While my original article would have been right, I never forgot Potter's lesson—don't go beyond what you know.

The union's victory was short-lived. On June 7, the Pirates voted 20–15 to stay off the field in a game against the New York Giants but the vote lacked the two-thirds margin the guild required for a full walkout. Because so many players were opposed, the guild decided against a partial strike. The guild, which soon collapsed, did lay the groundwork for the founding in 1954 of the Major League Baseball Players Association, now one of the strongest unions in the country.

Besides scanning publications and peeking at documents, I used other tricks to turn routine stories into beats. One of the issues Pennsylvania newspapers were interested in was milk prices, a consumer as well as an agriculture story. The state Milk Control Commission had the right to set milk prices, but, being controlled by farmers, set only minimum prices that dairies had to pay, not maximum prices they could charge consumers. The orders were complicated and varied by geographical areas.

I convinced H. N. Cobb, the gruff, no-nonsense chairman of the commission, that errors in news articles could be reduced if I could look at the complex orders a day ahead of time. Thus the night before their release he gave me the orders and I had plenty of time to write a story on each district. To make them look like hot news I wrote each story with the first paragraph as a bulletin and the remainder as an addition to the bulletin and sent the copy to Potter on a hold-for-release basis. He had our Teletype operator punch the stories on a tape. When the commission made its announcement the next morning I called Potter, who would flick a switch and send the bulletins out, quickly following up with the rest of the stories. As a result we were far ahead of Associated Press and International News Service, which had to spend valuable time trying to understand the technical language of the orders. Moreover, we were accurate.

I had tremendous energy and became a stringer for the *Wall Street Journal* and *PM*. The *Journal* didn't ask much and paid well. *PM* editors asked for ideas before filing. Getting no response from my wires, I began sending complete stories. With great pride I wrote home when I received a $7.50 check from *PM*, for an item about a Superior Court case about a mouse found in a Coca-Cola bottle. I was chagrined when the headline erroneously said it was the state Supreme Court.

Older reporters viewed me as immature, idealistic, and stupid—and I was all three to a degree. I really believed that the press should represent the people and the people had a right to know what was going on in government. That's why I liked *PM*'s aggressive reporting. Statehouse reporters for newspapers were often personal friends of sources. Experienced in years of shaping news to fit their publishers' convictions, they often scoffed at the public watchdog role.

My idealism overcame in part my basic shyness. With my blue-collar background and my lack of old-school ties, I didn't feel socially equal to governors or cabinet officers or legislative leaders. I didn't dream of inviting any of them to lunch or dinner nor apparently did any of them dream of inviting me. In those days the more experienced reporters would go out drinking with officials and especially with the legislators, most of whom would be available because they would be without their wives in Harrisburg for the two- and three-day a week legislative sessions. When I did go to cocktail parties and social events to which the press was invited, I stood aside, nursing a single drink. The delicate balance between source and story I sought in the navy worked only in part in political situations.

At Okinawa, with the threat of death always imminent, we talked easily with each other. In Harrisburg, I was ill at ease at small talk but confident when discussing substantive issues. To me, the freedom of the press clauses in the federal and state constitutions gave the media (and me as one of its representatives) license to ask tough questions. I became especially adept at news conferences. Others would ask the governor questions, dutifully write down his reply, and go on to the next subject. Only a few of us bore in with follow-up questions. Other reporters called me brash and lacking respect. They said I acted like a prosecuting attorney. My style was to phrase first questions sympathetically, trying to understand the politician's position, before probing for weaknesses. I was always (I hope) careful to keep my personal beliefs private and not argue with politicians.

Over the years, watching reporters work all over the country, I noticed, with personal satisfaction, that many of the best, including a number at the *New York Times*—Meyer Berger, Harrison Salisbury, John Herbers, and Homer Bigart, for example—were shy, too. Was it an act, as some observers thought? Bigart was noted for stuttering while asking questions. Sympathizing with him, sources would go to great lengths to talk, reaching out to fill in the gaps, often revealing more than they desired. I believe Bigart's stuttering was no act; it was a basic shyness, which he used to advantage. He died in 1991.

The biggest byline I ever received came on the story of a crash of a United Air Lines DC-6 in the anthracite mining region southwest of Wilkes-Barre on June 17, 1948. All forty-three persons aboard, including Earl Carroll, the Broadway theatrical producer whose *Vanities* featured racy comedians and undressed girls, died in the crash. I was in charge of the bureau because Potter, who was angry with Bramson, had designated me to fill in for him while he was on vacation. Following UP's skinflint ways, Potter cautioned me to spend no money without authorization from the regional headquarters in Philadelphia.

A few days after he left, the editor of the *Shamokin News Item*, a United Press client in the area, tipped us that an airliner had gone down near Mt. Carmel. After checking the state police, we immediately knocked out a bulletin, but not before the Associated Press carried a few paragraphs that a TWA plane had crashed, killing all passengers. In a message on the open wire, the Philadelphia bureau asked who was heading for the scene. I replied that Mt. Carmel was in its territory, not ours. Besides, we were not allowed to leave Harrisburg without permission.

DAILY NEWS, FRIDAY, JUNE 18, 1948

# 43 Die as DC-6 Hits Mountain

J. O. Fleet of Civil Aeronautics Board looks over twisted remains of an engine torn asunder by force of impact.  CAB Inspector H. G. Meyers (left) and John Olinger of Civil Aeronautics Administration begin on-the-spot study of crash with examination of mass of wreckage including parts of an engine.

(NEWS foto by Pacter)

## DC-6's Passenger List

Chicago, June 17 (P).—The passengers aboard the United Air Lines DC-6 which crashed in Pennsylvania today were:

Earl Carroll, Hollywood theatrical producer.
Mrs. Jack Oakie, Hollywood, divorced wife of the motion picture actor.
Beryl Wallace, star of Carroll's theatre restaurant show.
E. George Von Beho, New York, head of the warehousing and ....

feature of business English at the University of Illinois, Urbana.
Hugh McCloskey, the Texas Co., New York, 15 Rugby Road, Manhasset, L. I.
Lieut. Comdr. C. S. Avery, San Francisco.
Nathan Berks, Berks Bakeries, New York

### By ROBERT H. PHELPS

Mount Carmel, Pa., June 17 (UP).—A United Air Lines DC-6 struck a transformer station on a mountainside in the northeastern Pennsylvania coal fields today, disintegrated in flames and killed all 43 persons aboard.

Among the 39 passengers were theatrical producer Earl Carroll and his longtime friend, actress Beryl Wallace.

None of the passengers and crew of four had a chance to escape. The holocaust of flames started a raging brush fire which drove would-be res-

on the Chicago-New York leg of liner larger than a few square feet a flight from San Diego—appar- found in the wreckage.
enty had trouble a few minutes be-   Charred fragments of bodies and fore it rammed the transformer luggage were scattered over the station of a high tension line at hillside for 600 feet on each side of the crash and an area of three city (2) P.M. (New York daylight blocks was burned in the brush.

7. My biggest byline, in the *New York Daily News,* for an article I did not write. Following custom, United Press rewritemen in Philadelphia bureau put together the story from various sources, but the byline went to the reporter at the scene, although I contributed only a few paragraphs about the wreckage of the airliner. © New York Daily News, L.P. used with permission. Photo of article taken by Maureen Costello.

"Permission granted," Philadelphia shot back on the Teletype.

"We still can't go," I replied. "No one here owns a car," thus telling editors everywhere how low-paid we reporters were. The New York office busted in with its own message: "Rent one and get going."

Another staffer and I raced to the crash site in a battered rental Plymouth (saving money over renting at Hertz). Despite our late start we were there ahead of the Associated Press and metropolitan papers. By the time I phoned details to Philadelphia, the UP story already ran more than 1,000 words. A rewrite man said all they wanted was a description of the scene. The story, with my byline, led the *Daily News* of New York and many other papers because we were first with the correct information and had more details. The *New York Times* used the AP version, which had to correct its earlier erroneous bulletin that a TWA airliner had crashed.

United Press reporters chafed under such biased preference because we knew that our stories often—not always, but often—were better written, had more facts, and were delivered earlier. Its member newspapers owned the Associated Press, a cooperative, but I thought that discriminating editors at the *New York Times* would be less susceptible to that influence. (International News Service, the Hearst service, chafed, too, but with less reason because it was chronically understaffed. The INS slogan was "Get It First, but First Get It Right," which editors who had been burned by bad stories turned around to "Get It First and Get It Right Later.") I could never shake that feeling of inferiority generated by the discrimination for Associated Press. However, it did much to sharpen my natural competitive instincts.

The principal lesson I learned from the airline crash, however, was to spend whatever is needed when faced with a big story. Brush aside all questions of saving money. While we were first with the correct facts about the plane crash we lost at least a half hour by my delay in getting to the scene because I was following instructions on keeping expenses down. My mentor, Potter, was wrong, but he had long been in trouble because of overspending.

After nearly five years at United Press, I took stock. I was good at interviewing sources, but with few tips from government officials, I had to think through every exclusive story on my own. I still lacked flair for writing. For the most part I was a straight declarative writer: subject, verb, object. I had improved a little, but most of what I wrote lacked a human quality.

I did learn to dictate straight news stories without typing them out first, thus saving valuable time. Sitting in the press areas in the legislature or in a courtroom, I would scratch out paragraphs in long hand as the proceedings went on. When the session ended, I would scrawl a quick lead on the story and phone it in. Years later this skill served me well on those occasions when I switched to reporting at the *New York Times*. Few reporters developed on the *Times* learned to dictate complete stories. They either phoned notes to a rewrite desk or went to the office and typed out their stories, often missing an edition.

I wondered about my future. Would United Press send me to Washington because of my state capital experience and interest in politics? Should I move to a metropolitan newspaper? Before I went into the navy I had turned down a reporting job at the *Philadelphia Bulletin* but only because I didn't want to leave Viki. After the war I had rejected a *Wall Street Journal* overture to move to Cleveland because I feared I would be typed as a business news specialist even though I admired the paper's writing. More important were my continuing doubts about myself personally.

Trivial incidents shook my confidence. On a weekend trip to central Pennsylvania, our borrowed Plymouth got a flat tire. "Don't worry," I told Betty, "I'll put on the spare." Despite strenuous efforts I couldn't take the flat off. The lugs wouldn't move. A local gasoline station attendant came and quickly spun the lugs off. Embarrassed, I asked what I had done wrong. He explained that I had turned the lugs the wrong way. The threads on the wheels of Chrysler-built cars were designed so that the motion of the car wouldn't throw the lugs off. On some wheels that meant turning the lugs to the right to loosen them. Seeing my humiliation, this small-town guy, who probably never finished high school, said something that has helped me through decades of dealing with others who make mistakes. "Don't feel bad," he said, "I'm sure you can do things that I can't."

Severe indigestion also made we wonder about myself. Only the blandest foods stayed down. Tests by Dr. Stuart Harkness, an osteopathic physician, showed no apparent cause. While examining me, he said that some people were "constitutionally inadequate," living only because advances in medicine permitted them to continue, albeit functionally crippled. He insisted he was not talking about me, but I thought he really meant me and for years that remark troubled me.

Approaching thirty, I still doubted my abilities and faced a career crisis. What should I do? Despite my failed attempts while in the navy, I continued to write fiction, short-short stories, 500–1,000 words, which fit on one magazine page and were popular at that time. I received rejection after rejection from weekly magazines like *Collier's* and newspaper Sunday supplements. I was following the same path to writing oblivion as my mother. It took a few more years before I gave up on fiction.

I did enjoy journalism, but, after being rejected for a Nieman Fellowship at Harvard, I settled on the idea that perhaps my career should not be as a reporter, but as an inside man, where social graces were not important—or so I thought. Perhaps editing was my calling. Whatever you accomplish, Betty said, it won't be handed to you. "It will be by the sweat of your brow."

I decided to apply to the Columbia Graduate School of Journalism because *New York Times* editors taught there. Other reporters at the statehouse thought I had too much experience to return to school, but I applied under the GI Bill and was accepted.

Contrary to my promise before we were married, I didn't consult Betty about applying to Columbia. Having operated on my own for so many years, I didn't think about talking to her. It didn't occur to me that she would have to give up her fine job as executive secretary, a position she had worked for years to achieve. It didn't occur to me that she would be leaving her sisters and brothers and the support of her close-knit family. Proving Thomas Wolfe right about lack of understanding those close to us, I had thought only of my career. As a loyal wife she accepted my decision without complaining and, contrary to her instincts, which told her she would live and die in central Pennsylvania, quit her job. She was making $110 a week; I was making $102.50.

We moved to New York in the fall of 1949, never to return to Harrisburg except for short visits. Within weeks after we left, my chronic indigestion also vanished—confirmation that I was doing the right thing.

I quickly discovered, as I had been warned, that the Columbia School of Journalism was primarily for reporters with far less experience. *New York Times* editors, headed by assistant managing editor Theodore M. Bernstein, were good teachers, but their courses were a small part of the curriculum and limited to copyediting.

Only luck saved me from wasting those nine months. Montgomery Curtis, director of the American Press Institute, let me attend four week-long seminars held in the journalism building. Well over six feet and broad shouldered, Curtis taught old-fashioned tough editing. A former city editor at the *Buffalo News*, he emphasized basics, from covering police news to obituaries to politics, with the need to spell names correctly, to use middle initials, to get the facts right and the quotations precise. In his gravelly voice he preached the value of simple, straight leads. He dismissed "new journalism" trends toward light features with fancy leads. The newspapers' role, he said, was to cover the news. Entertainment was subordinate.

I learned a great deal about dealing with reporters, photographers, and editors from those seminar discussions that Curtis led with city editors and managing editors from around the country. He taught that personal relationships were vital but the more important policy was to be clear and firm so as not to be misunderstood.

I stayed in touch with Curtis and for years found him a valuable person to discuss career options.

Another valuable help was the Columbia course on libel. Taught by a New York lawyer, Harold Cross, it provided a solid basis on what could and could not be safely printed. My test paper was graded as "A—Excellent paper. As close to perfection as such an exam can be. It is seldom, indeed, that a student bats 1.000."

The course made me wish that I had studied law, which I had considered as a teenager. (All my adult life people, noting my aggressive questioning, have told me I should have been a lawyer.)

Eventually I used my notes to write, with E. Douglas Hamilton, a New York lawyer, who succeeded Cross at Columbia, a handbook aptly named (by Betty) *Libel: Rights, Risks, Responsibilities,* widely used in newsrooms.[2]

Through Columbia's employment office, Betty got a job at the luxurious Hotel Pierre, helping Nola Luxford, a New Zealand actress who had appeared in Harold Lloyd films, put on weekly fashion shows. While she did not make a good deal of money, Betty enjoyed the job more than her secretarial work in Harrisburg. With Betty's salary supplementing my veteran's allotment under the GI Bill, we attended many plays, usually sitting in the cheapest seats high in the second balcony. Cheap in those days meant $1.20 or $1.80. Living in a converted army barracks in Shanks Village, in Orangeburg, New York, we commuted in our Chinese red 1948 Studebaker, our first car.

Early in the new year we learned that Dick Cheney, whom I had not heard from since our Pearl Harbor celebration of the Japanese surrender,

8. In 1950, Betty and I celebrated in the Cotillion Room of the Pierre Hotel in New York, courtesy of Irwin Dribben, the New York fashion photographer, who gave us this picture. Photo by Irwin Dribben.

had settled in New York with his pregnant wife. After a few months in Paris, where they had gone to write fiction, they decided to seek their careers in Manhattan. We visited them often in their tiny upper West Side apartment. Their enthusiasm for France rubbed off on us and before long we decided that the next job could wait; we would tour Europe. With a $1,500 traveling scholarship and $1,250 from the sale of our Studebaker we spent nine months in Western Europe.

The trip to Europe proved to be more of a vacation than a reporting assignment, although the *Harrisburg Patriot* liked my proposal for some articles on how low-level government workers lived. I wrote those articles and took some pictures to go with them but did not see the clippings until we returned. In a way they were mirror images of my navy hometown stories. Ever on the lookout for bigger game, I lucked into a classified

American report on how to revive the West German railroads, which had been badly damaged by Allied bombing during the war. Based on those suggestions I wrote an article for *Tracks,* a railroad magazine. Caught up in a near-revolution in Belgium, I sent a review of the press's handling of the uprising to the Columbia School of Journalism, which never succeeded in finding a buyer.

On our return, I wrote an article that the *New York Times* ran in its Sunday travel section on March 16, 1951, under the heading "Doing the Continent on Only $5 a Day." We had kept strict accounting during our trip, and the expenses, not counting steamship passage, for hotels, meals, transportation, entrance fees, tips, and entertainment, had been $3.69 a day. Playing safe, the *Times* editor had raised the figure to $5. That was my first byline in the *Times* and my first encounter with conservative *Times* editing. I was puzzled; to me the story was as inaccurate as if I had written $2 a day. If the editor didn't believe my figures why didn't he just spike the story?

On returning from Europe we rented a third-floor apartment in a house in Jackson Heights, Queens. The landlady almost refused to rent to us because she had heard that newspapermen held wild boozy parties. She didn't realize that I had not reached that exalted status. Betty's demure appearance overcame the landlady's fears.

My immediate problem was finding a job as an editor. The hunt took longer than expected. One of my first stops was at the *New York Times.* I tried to see Ted Bernstein, because I had taken his copyediting course at Columbia. He sent me to the personnel director, who advised me to get a job as a copyeditor in another city and, after a few years, work on the desk of another New York daily. Then, he said, I might be ready for the *Times.* I would be nearly forty years old before becoming eligible for the *Times.* On that schedule I might never work there.

Revising my plans, I sought a reporting job. *Time* magazine, looking for vibrant, confident young reporters, was not impressed. No wonder, considering how I felt about myself. The *Philadelphia Inquirer* told me, as it probably told others, that I was a close second for a business reporting slot. The *Charlotte Observer* was looking for a combination editor-reporter, writing some editorials but also serving as an investigative reporter, and expressed strong interest in me. I replied that I wondered whether I would fit in at the *Observer* because I disagreed with the predominant Southern view on racial segregation. The *Observer* answered that they were prepared to accept me as I was but it seemed that I was not ready to accept them. That showed me who was prejudiced.

We had bought a 1950 Pontiac and our money was running low. Acting on Dick Cheney's advice, I broadened my search to public relations jobs. J. C. Penney, the department store chain, was interested but the company struck me as too settled in its ways. In June I took a job as a writer at Carl Byoir and Associates, then the largest public relations firm in the world. Our offices were high in an old skyscraper on East 41 Street, right off Fifth Avenue.

I was hired at $150 a week for the American Can Company account. That was $47.50 more than I had been making at United Press, but this was New York and living costs were much higher than Harrisburg. Executives of American Can, the largest maker of cans and cardboard milk cartons in the country, had long been irritated by the fact that the public in general was more familiar with the no. 2 manufacturer, Continental, which was headed by General Lucius Clay of World War II fame, whose accomplishments included running the airlift during the Soviet blockade of Berlin. Using an opinion poll to confirm Continental's preeminence with the public, Carl Byoir talked American Can officials into spending millions on a campaign to sell itself as no. 1.

The campaign was a straightforward public relations program. Byoir set up a team consisting of an account executive, an editor, four writers, and an economist, a former professor at the University of Pennsylvania. The economist researched food production on a county-by-county basis. We writers worked that material into articles that were sent to newspapers and radio stations. In other words, the stories would provide a constant reminder of how important American Can was to local economies.

My first assignment was to write a story based on the Maryland dairy industry. I wrote four paragraphs, with a heading saying that "Bossy" was setting record milk production in the state. Everyone was pleased, especially when the clips came in. To my astonishment, even the highly touted *Baltimore Sun* ran the piece unedited on a section front, retaining a key phrase noting that much of the milk was bottled in cartons made by the American Can Company. These stories were cousins to my hometown articles for the navy.

As the months went by I wrote the same little story for counties in California and other states, changing only the figures on milk production. The clips kept coming in. I was shaken about the quality of editing, or lack of it, in the newspaper industry. Newspapers needed good editors. Why couldn't I get an editing job? I kept looking, writing to papers and studying help-wanted ads in *Editor and Publisher*, the weekly magazine of the newspaper industry.

The Byoir people, except for the no. 2 man, George Hammond, seemed to like me. In a few months I was sent to Chicago to get some ideas from American Can officials at its headquarters. That trip might have been a test to determine if I could get along with the client. In any event, I was asked to transfer to the Chicago office. Convinced that I wanted out of PR, I didn't want to cement my commitment to Byoir by taking the Chicago position. It was not wise to say that so I gave another legitimate reason. Betty and I were trying to have a baby and we didn't want to change doctors. That angered Hammond, but I didn't budge.

I was surprised that he wanted me in the organization; I didn't think like a PR man. One clue was the expense account I turned in on the Chicago trip. I ate breakfast at a cafeteria, had lunch at American Can, and had dinner with an aunt. The only meal listed was the breakfast, at $1.90, which seemed expensive to me but outrageously low to Byoir people. In a job in which padding the expense account was considered normal, I refused to add a cent and felt superior in doing so.

From the first week at Byoir I knew that public relations was not a career for me. At a series of meetings, heads of departments introduced the American Can group to the Carl Byoir way. The head of the magazine department was typical. Her job was to place material on Byoir clients in magazines. She said she wanted to give us the "benefit of her thinking." That was as specific as she got. We visited officials at American Can. We had lunch with the economist. I came out of each meeting ignorant of what had been said. Everything was mushy. I must not have been creative enough to come up with any big ideas. Neither did anyone else.

In 1952, a year after I joined Carl Byoir, the personnel man of the *Providence Journal* called, asking if I was interested in a copyediting job on the afternoon *Bulletin*. The Columbia journalism school had given him my name. I was more than ready.

I had just taken part in one of those false anniversary projects for which public relations is noted. The idea was to hit the media, especially television, in Utah with a ceremony on the production of the five billionth can produced by American Can at its Provo, Utah plant. The president of American Can, W. C. Stolk, would present the can, mounted on a plaque, to Utah Gov. J. Bracken Lee at the annual convention of the Utah Canners Association. The can would then go to a state library for permanent display.

Several dozen cans were sent from Provo to New York, where Byoir sent them to a shop to be enshrined in Lucite. All the cans collapsed when put into Lucite. Byoir sent for another batch of cans, with the same result. For weeks, as the failures continued, Byoir called the Provo plant for more cans, eventually turning to the Tampa, Florida, plant and finally the Long Island plant to save time. With the presentation only four days away, one of us thought of calling the chief of research at the Provo plant. With his technical expertise, he ought to know what to do. He said to fill the can with tops and it wouldn't collapse. That worked. We had a shiny chromium plated can inside Lucite. It wasn't a Provo can; it wasn't a Tampa can. It was from the Long Island plant.

What number was it? That task was turned over to our economist, Dr. H. E. Michl with the hope, clearly explained, that he would come up with a round number. He triumphantly announced that when president Stolk arrived in Utah he would be carrying the 4 million, 6 hundred thousandth can. "There's a nice round figure for you," he said.

"Can't you find an extra 400 million cans somewhere?" I asked.

"No," the usually cooperative Dr. Michl said. "I have scraped around in all the records and know that the figure is right. It just couldn't be off more than a few thousand cans, even if we discover some hand-made ones I didn't know about."

I consulted my bosses. "Mike never cooperates," steamed Bill Seely, the affable head of the account. Seely was known as the Sponge, because he absorbed complaints both from clients and top Byoir executives.

"He just doesn't see our problems," complained Frank Westbrook, the lead writer.

"Well, he will," vowed vice president Hammond. He called Dr. Michl and, I was told, the conversation went something like this:

Hammond—"I understand you've had some problem with the figure."

Dr. Michl—"No trouble at all. I just gave the total to Bob."

Hammond—"Yes. There must be a mistake somewhere. One of those girls of yours must have misplaced a couple of zeros somewhere along the line. That figure isn't right."

Dr. Michl—"I'm afraid it is. I checked it myself a couple of times."

Hammond—"One of those girls must be playing tricks on you. I know it isn't right because I was talking to Bill Stolk just a couple of days ago—you know this project is really his idea—and he told me there were five billion cans made in Utah."

Dr. Michl—(after pause) "Where'd he get his figure?"

Hammond—"I don't know, but he must know what he is talking about because this is a pet project of his. He'd be very disappointed if something interfered with it."

Hammond—"Well, I could have made a mistake. Give me a half hour and let me check my figures."

Twenty minutes later Dr. Michl called with good news. The total was five billion. He had overlooked a factory of the old Sanitary Can Company, which American had purchased. He didn't say so, but he knew there was no way that Sanitary had produced 400 million cans in its short existence as part of American Can.

No matter. As Hammond said, it was all symbolic and didn't detract from the message that American Can had contributed mightily to the Utah economy.

As we admired the finished plaque, I noticed in horror that the engraving had misspelled Governor Lee's name. We had to pay night overtime rates at the engraver's to fix that error in time to make the plane to Utah. Then Hammond read the news releases I had prepared and discovered that Mr. Stolk had been mentioned more times than Governor Lee. I had learned something at Byoir—please the client, above all.

However, Hammond had higher standards. "We can't have that," he said, "the papers will think we're just publicity crazy."

The event went off smoothly and Stolk proudly presented the five billionth can to Governor Lee at a luncheon, followed by a television appearance in which the reporter asked the questions we had prepared and Stolk replied as he had been briefed.

Months after Betty and I moved to Providence, American Can dropped Byoir. The hard-boiled Stolk had asked for proof that the first year of the campaign had worked. Byoir tried a number of tricks in a vain attempt to hold the account. I had heard of such tricks. One was to have a bunch of men dressed like post office employees rush into a meeting of top executives with huge mail bags filled with clippings, dumping the contents on the floor. Only one of the thousands of clips didn't mention the client. Find that clip and win a prize. The executives then dived into the pile.

Whatever trick Byoir tried American Can was not fooled. It insisted that Byoir run the same public opinion survey that it had before the project. That second survey showed fewer people recognizing American Can than in the first. Of course Stolk fired Byoir.

Byoir people could not believe I was leaving. Go to a run-down old mill town in New England from vibrant New York? That didn't make sense. Nor did it make sense to move from public relations to journalism when movement was overwhelmingly the other direction. Why would anyone want to be a copyeditor? Sitting on the rim of a horseshoe desk trying to make sense of garbled prose was a refuge for old reporters. And take a cut in pay, from $150 a week at Byoir to $110 in Providence? For me, the answer was simple. At last I could really start on my career as an editor. Ethics was a powerful motivating force in my decision. I still believed that journalism, when practiced with high principles, was a pillar of American democracy. Public relations skidded too often too close to misleading the public.

In Providence first-hand evidence showed that prayer works to solve even small problems. We had stored our furniture in a warehouse in Nyack, near New York City, when we went to Europe. When the furniture was delivered to our Rhode Island apartment a chest-on-chest was missing. For weeks I called the warehouse in a vain attempt to get the chest delivered. Finally, the manager conceded he could not find it.

One Saturday I drove to Nyack. The manager gave me the key to the room on the third floor where our furniture had been. I found the room jammed tight with mattresses, tables, lamps, chairs—all kinds of furniture. I gave up without trying to move the huge mass of someone else's furniture out of the room. As I walked down the stairs I remembered what Betty had told me before I left Providence. "If you want to find it," she said, "you'll have to pray to St. Anthony."

Just then my eyes focused on a huge jumble of furniture in the middle of the floor. Peeking out from that big pile was the fluted corner of a piece of furniture that looked familiar. Two brawny workers pulled the pile apart piece by piece. A yank on a mattress revealed more of that fluted edge and a metal plate with the name "Goldsmith's Harrisburg."

When I told Betty I had found the chest she laughed and asked, "What more evidence do you want?" I stuttered something about a coincidence. Then I made a joke of it, "You didn't tell me which St. Anthony." In those days I rarely went to Mass with her and Betty didn't press the case for Catholicism. She never did, although she was still a true believer.

It was the work, not the pay, that counted in Providence. I settled down on the rim of the afternoon paper's copydesk and proceeded to learn. My immediate boss was the copydesk chief, Kenneth Roberts, who became another important guide in my career. Ken, small and wiry, had a sharp tongue, which he used to keep the seven copyeditors in line. I liked him because he patiently helped me learn such skills as weaving three or four wire accounts into one story, using the best from each. As acerbic as he was, he nevertheless taught me a valuable lesson on dealing with people.

When a friendly printer came out of the composing room and confronted me with an error he had caught, I cut him off curtly because I had already spotted the mistake. Afterward, Ken admonished me to listen politely and thank people who called attention to problems in stories. Otherwise, he pointed out, they will not bother to tell you of errors that you might miss. That little lesson served me well in my relations with printers at the *Times*.

Ken brought me along swiftly and in a matter of months I was editing all the copy from Washington, selecting the stories from the *Journal's*

Washington bureau and the wire services, editing them and writing the headlines.

Even though working with older men, I didn't wonder whether I had made another mistake, whether I was, in a sense, retiring early. Editing challenged me. Constrained by rules of grammar and syntax, I had trouble writing lively headlines, but as the months went by I began to loosen up. My best headline was either on a story of a clock that ran backward—"Tock Tick, Tock Tick"—or on the cesarean birth of the thirteenth child, all boys, to a Catholic mother—"O boy, O boy, O boy, O boy, O boy, O boy, O boy, O boy, O boy, O boy, O boy, O boy, O boy."

I had kept in touch with the *New York Times,* writing an article on summer boating in Rhode Island, advising Richard D. Burritt, the newsroom's personnel man, of my advancement, and stopping to see him on one trip to New York. In the fall of 1954 Burritt called and asked me to go to New York for a physical examination, although there was no job opening. That seemed strange to me and I didn't believe it. I passed the exam and within a few weeks was offered and accepted a job as a copyeditor on the International Edition of the *Times.* Finally, at age thirty-five I had made the big time.

PART TWO • **The *New York Times***

# 7. Early Success
## A Substitute for Religion

**When I walked** into the block-long newsroom of the *New York Times* on 43d Street just before 8 P.M. on Monday, November 1, 1954, I was challenged by a midget of a man demanding to know what I was doing there. He was Sam Solovitz, assistant head copy boy. Only four feet nine inches, Sammy took no nonsense from the college graduates under his command. One of his jobs was to keep strangers away from reporters and editors who didn't want to be tied up talking to fanatics. Sammy told me to sit down and wait for Herman H. Dinsmore, the editor of the International Edition, to arrive.

The *Times* hired Sammy during World War II from Western Union, where he had been a messenger. Over the years Sammy's antics enlivened the newsroom. When he died, in 1999, the *Times* ran a long obituary with a picture of him, indefensible when contrasted with the short shrift given the deaths of far more important or interesting people. To me, the overplay showed how even *Times* editors would set aside standards for personal reasons. In effect the paper became a house organ. I saw this at the *Boston Globe,* too, where every columnist seemed to mourn in print elderly colleagues who died. A single obituary was not enough; the pages dripped with their tears. Unlike the *Times,* however, the *Globe* published obituaries of ordinary people regularly.

Three of us edited the International Edition. Dinsmore was a disgruntled former foreign desk copyeditor convinced that communists were influencing the selection and editing of the paper. Ted Sweedy, a former reporter who had succumbed to alcohol, was assistant editor. I was the copyeditor. Two of us worked every night, one in charge, the other copyediting, which meant primarily trimming stories to fit into the smaller news hole of the eight- to fourteen-page International Edition, and writing new headlines for the minimal changes in makeup.

As I looked around the newsroom those first few weeks the ages of copyeditors on the regular paper struck me. If the *Providence Journal* copyeditors were old, the *Times* desks were ancient. Gray haired, many had held top jobs on other New York newspapers. I told Betty that I wouldn't be surprised if I would retire as a rim man on the *Times* because there was so much talent and experience for the more important jobs. That wouldn't be a bad career, I said. I would be doing work I enjoyed on the most important paper in the world. In fact, it would be quite an accomplishment for the violinist who had failed despite years of practice and for the student who had struggled through the University of Michigan and never distinguished himself as a reporter.

In my new job I seldom dealt with reporters. About the only ones I talked to were night rewritemen. (Night rewrite was a giant step up from the dead end of day rewrite, which handled one-paragraph fillers.) Each night a rewriteman would put together a roundup of New York stories for the International Edition and every Saturday night one would do a roundup of college sports for us. Thus editing was simple and only occasionally did I question an article.

I did ask for a change one night when Gay Talese brought me the Saturday college football roundup. I looked it over and asked what Notre Dame had done. He said he didn't think it was important. I told him that when it came to football Notre Dame was always important. (If I had been candid I would have said important to me because my older brother, John, had gone to Notre Dame for one year and played on the practice squad until an All-America lineman damaged his ankle.) Gay shrugged and wrote an insert. A few years later, Gay, his writing constrained by *Times* editors, quit to write magazine articles and books, with great success.

Within six months I was transferred to the staff of the regular edition. I was assigned to the national news desk, which was my first choice even though the foreign desk was considered the élite editing desk and I had been warned that the national desk slot man, the man in direct charge of the copyeditors, was a despot with an explosive temper. To my relief, Samuel M. Sharkey Jr. was considerate in the short time I worked under him.

A few weeks later he took a much higher-paying job with the National Broadcasting Company.

The first story I edited on the national desk was a one-paragraph filler. When I finished it, I tossed the copy (those were the days when stories were typewritten on paper and pencil-edited) back to John Stephenson, who was filling in the slot and would soon become permanent head of the desk. Without a glance at what I had done, he put it in the basket to go to the composing room. I was surprised by his confidence in me, a beginner, and decided that I had better be very careful and work hard to justify his faith. It was up to me and me alone. No one was going to carry me. I made up my mind that I would never let Stephenson down. He became my first mentor at the *Times* and I quickly grew quite fond of him. Years later, I was grateful when he made it easy for me to give him orders when I moved to more important positions.

A bulldog of a man, with shaggy black brows and heavy jowls, he sat hunched over the desk, the sleeves of his white shirt rolled up his hairy arms, a cigarette in his mouth. His background in classical Greek and Latin belied his deft touch with a pencil. (At the *New York World-Telegram*, where he had been slot man, he wrote this headline on a short article reporting that the condition of Mustafa Kemal Atatürk, the ailing founder of modern Turkey, was improving: "Ataturk!")

When I learned that Steve had been the first copy desk chief at *PM*, I told him it was the favorite newspaper of my youth. In a few minutes he destroyed my illusions about that radical experimental sheet. The "General" who wrote World War II analyses of military strategy for *PM* was any reporter who happened to be free, not a retired military officer. A *PM* editor sent a reporter to the affluent suburb of Ho-Ho-Kus, New Jersey, to dig up a scandal so he could headline it "Hocus Pocus in Ho-Ho-Kus." Editors sought stories where "store teeth" could be used for dentures to annoy dentists who had complained about the phrase.

Like so many others at the *Times*, Steve drank too much. (In those days the saying was that liquor was the curse of the *Herald Tribune* and sex the bane of the *Times*. I found both failings common at the *Times*—and, from what I heard, at the *Tribune*, too. In Boston, the *Globe*, with a much younger staff, personal weakness tilted more toward sex.)

9. John Stephenson, national desk copy chief, whose guidance provided a smooth beginning for a new copyeditor at the *New York Times*. John Orris/The New York Times.

The first problem for me in my new assignment was where to eat lunch. At 8:45 P.M., when we finished editing copy for the first edition, middle-age copyeditors, like Tom Daffron and John Randolph, crossed West 43d street to Gough's, a smoky saloon, where they had a drink or two and a sandwich. The older men (there were no women copyeditors on the major *Times* desks at that time) went upstairs to the *Times* cafeteria. Where did I belong? Not being a drinker, I avoided Gough's. Not wanting to classify myself as an old man, I didn't go to the cafeteria. Most of the time I ate alone, often walking up to 55th Street for a corned beef sandwich at the Carnegie Deli.

One night Socrates Konstantin (Chick) Butsikares, a copyeditor who had risen from copyboy to the desk, invited me to join him for a drink at the Times Square Hotel. As we stood at the bar sipping our drinks and munching peanuts, a man a dozen feet away called to Chick. "Hey baldy," he yelled, "how about sharing those peanuts?" Chick, although still in his twenties, had lost most of his hair. Turning his head slowly and puffing out his massive chest, he challenged the man. "Come and get them yourself." As they glared at each other I thought that maybe I would have to join in a fight, Chick against his tormentor and I against the guy's companion. The bartender deflated the tension by giving the man a heaping container of peanuts.

One of the reasons why I enjoyed early success on the national desk was that in Providence I had prepared for the *Times* by studying *Headlines and Deadlines,* the book on copyediting written by two assistant managing editors, Theodore M. Bernstein and Robert E. Garst. Bernstein had developed strict standards for copyediting at the *Times* and he used the book in teaching at the Columbia School of Journalism. Much of the material was valuable in Providence. But the standards for headlines were much looser there.

At the *Times* each line had to be a separate thought; it could not end in a preposition, an adjective, an adverb, or an article. Each line had to be approximately the same length as others in the heading. I spent hours in Providence learning to count headlines to determine whether the words would fit in *Times* columns. Like other newspapers, the *Times* set the width of each letter on a scale in which most lowercase letters were worth one unit; spaces, i's and sometimes l's and t's were worth a half unit, and w's and m's were worth one and a half units. Capital letters had correspondingly larger values. This method usually worked well, but sometimes, in especially tight situations, the headlines didn't fit even though the count indicated they would.

Refining the *Times* count, I set the numerical value of letters on a more precise basis, like 8, 10, 11, 13, 19 for each of the most common typefaces. This method called for a lot of memorizing, but it helped in tight situations. Few of my headlines at the *Times* bounced back from the composing room as too long. Older copyeditors soon turned to me to check their headlines when unsure whether they would fit. Today computers instantly show whether a headline fits.

I soon learned that Ted Bernstein was the most powerful editor in the newsroom. Aided by four news editors, he decided how many columns of news to give each department, which articles and pictures would go on page one, and how prominently other stories were played on inside pages. Supremely confident, he sat in his small office in the southeast corner of the newsroom, smoke from his ever-present cigarette circling his Manhattan pale face, and drew the dummy for page one with his tobacco-stained fingers. Attesting to his power, Bernstein was the only editor in the newsroom with a private office other than managing editor Turner Catledge. Significantly, Bernstein's territory was known as the bullpen.

Although he had never been a reporter, going from Columbia University directly to the *Times* copydesk, Bernstein governed writing as well as editing. His strict tenets frustrated reporters eager to break away from the turgid style that marked much of the paper. Full names of agencies had to be used in first references, such as Federal Bureau of Investigation instead of FBI, even though most readers recognized the agency more readily from its initials. Initials were permitted in second references but only with periods—F.B.I. With the exception of the president of the United States, the Roman Catholic archbishop of New York, and a few others, people had to be introduced in a story with their first names and middle initials.

Nicknames were forbidden except in sports stories and an occasional feature. Second references had to carry courtesy titles, such as Mr., Miss, and Mrs., except on the sports pages. And courtesy titles for a foreigner had to be in the language of the individual, for example, Mlle. for an unmarried French woman and Herr for a German man.

These niceties led to comical dilemmas. What if a sports story started on page one? Should the star Yankee centerfielder be referred to as "Joseph P. DiMaggio Jr." and then "Mr. DiMaggio" on the front page and just "Joe" and "DiMaggio" when the story jumped to the sports pages? Bernstein knew such a ruling would make the *Times* look ridiculous; he let informality rule on sports stories wherever they appeared.

In Bernstein's desire to block permissiveness, pay increases had to be "rises," not "raises," unless in a direct quotation from a source. Motorists could not buy "gas," they bought "gasoline" because "gas" referred only to vapor, not to liquid fuel. Bosses didn't "fire" employees; they "dismissed" them. Not long before I joined the national desk a slot man with an itchy pencil changed "fired" to "dismiss" on a proof only to read the headline in the paper that a cannon had been dismissed, or so I was told.

Near the end of the twentieth century, with Bernstein retired, editors threw out many Bernstein rules and gave wider freedom to talented writers, with a marked improvement in readability and reporter morale.

The first big story I worked on dealt with President Eisenhower's heart attack early in the morning of Saturday, September 24, 1955. The first public announcement from Denver, where Eisenhower was vacationing, came at 11 A.M. eastern time and said that the president had had a "digestive upset." That was worth only a short story for the inside of the paper.

But at 4:30 P.M., just before the first edition deadline of the Sunday paper, the illness was upgraded to a "mild heart attack." That was page one. John Randolph edited the story in swift takes.

(Randolph had been demoted to copyeditor on the national desk because, as picture editor, he had run a photograph of Marilyn Monroe, her mouth open, about to kiss Joe DiMaggio. Even though the two were engaged and about to be married, the bullpen decided the picture was in bad taste. After serving a few years in copydesk limbo, Randolph was appointed hunting and fishing columnist, where he breathed new life into the sports pages.)

Randolph was fast with a pencil; as he edited the Eisenhower copy the rest of us worked on the headline and sidebars. There was only sufficient time for a one-column headline on page one. The *Times* prohibited use of the president's nickname, Ike, except on an occasional feature. "President" wouldn't do in this case because lots of organizations had presidents. We had to use "Eisenhower." The trick was to write Eisenhower with a short verb but Eisenhower took so much space there was little room for a strong verb. The best we could come up with was "Eisenhower Has/A Heart Attack," violating the Bernstein ban on using weak verbs like "has" instead of "suffers." For the second edition the page was remade and the headline covered three columns: "Eisenhower Is In Hospital/With 'Mild' Heart Attack/His Condition Called Good." Why that second-edition headline used the weak construction "Is in Hospital" instead of "Hospitalized," which would have fit, was beyond me. Perhaps it was not considered acceptable English. In any event, the headline showed me that *Times* editors, like those elsewhere, could violate their own rules.

Two serious blunders stand out in my copyediting days. One blunder was mine. Anthony Lewis, then the Supreme Court reporter, referred to

Senator Edward M. Kennedy as "Ted" in a story. Knowing that Bernstein banned nicknames, I changed "Ted" to "Theodore." The next day an irate Tony, who was a personal friend of the Kennedys, screamed at this changing of the Senator's given name, Edward. All I could do was apologize.

The other blunder was not really mine. I was given a profile of Senator John O. Pastore of Rhode Island to edit. Because I studied Bernstein's *Winners and Sinners,* a newsroom publication of advice to the staff, I knew that every profile should have negative as well as positive elements on the basis that no one is perfect. Joseph Loftus, the Washington bureau's labor specialist, had written a 100 percent laudatory piece. From my Rhode Island days I knew that Pastore had his critics, which I mentioned to national editor Raymond B. O'Neill. He told me to write it into the piece. I did, but it was O'Neill's duty to inform Loftus. This he forgot to do. Loftus was justifiably angry when the story appeared.

Neither Lewis nor Loftus held the errors against me. In fact, both became friends. To them, the errors just showed how "New York" damaged the informed and careful reporting of the Washington bureau. I was learning about the antagonisms in the large *Times* bureaucracy and I resolved to never take sides, but to give my honest opinion in any dispute—a decision that some superiors found impossible to accept, with resulting damage to my career.

Those errors didn't stop me from changing the copy of one of the icons of the *Times,* Arthur Krock, the long-time head of the Washington bureau, who had retired but still wrote a column. One of the perks of copyediting on the late shift in those days was an extra $15 for reading Mr. Krock's Sunday column. (He was Mr. Krock to everyone except his successor, James B. Reston, who called him Arthur. Reston was Scotty to everyone.)

Sometimes the Krock column fell to me. I was instructed to just make the paragraph marks. Mr. Krock not only wrote the heading, he would also copyedit the column after our editing, and, within an hour, send any corrections back to the national desk. For weeks I followed instructions, but eventually Mr. Krock's awkward syntax got to me and I began to make small changes. When there was no eruption from Washington I told the other editors what I had been doing. They warned that Mr. Krock didn't countenance meddling. While I never came close to recasting his columns, I did make changes that some editors thought drastic for Krock. If he noticed, he never said a word. (Some of my awe of this *New York Times* legend disappeared when I learned that he had won a Pulitzer Prize in 1938 for the mere fact that he had interviewed President Roosevelt. That was considered a journalistic breakthrough.)

During this early period I formed my philosophic defense of daily journalism. I realized, of course, that the *Times,* like other newspapers, made many errors, and seldom ran corrections. That refusal to publicly fix the record bothered me. I found Krock's reply amusing, but arrogant, when he was informed that he had misquoted John Keats as writing in his sonnet "On First Looking Into Chapman's Homer" that "stout Balboa" discovered the Pacific Ocean. Refusing to run a correction noting that Keats had written "stout Cortez," instead of Balboa, Krock said he wouldn't "perpetuate the poet's historical error."

I concluded that what saved newspaper credibility from the multiplicity of errors was the fact that they came out daily and thus could correct the record in subsequent stories even if they didn't admit their misstatements in a corrections box. Including correct information in follow-up articles, I reasoned, served the same purpose as constant corrections of a ship's course. A ship does not go in a straight line toward its destination. It veers a little to the left and then to the right because of the motion of the water. That Jesuitical explanation does not mitigate the need for corrections boxes, anchored in the same place day after day. After decades of resistance to critics, the *Times* now prints corrections generously.

The national desk copyeditors indulged in a lot of camaraderie in contrast to the more serious foreign desk. One week, to pass the time during a lull in the news, each of us wrote *Times*-style headlines for our fake obituaries. I wrote two: "R. H. Phelps, 67, Overhand Bowler" and "R. H. Phelps, 59, Owned '50 Pontiac."(I sure underestimated how long I would live.)

We also had fun writing headlines on biblical and historical events, at which Irvin Horowitz shone. One of them: "Jehovah Rests on Seventh Day." And one by me on Jesus's crucifixion: "Sect Leader Executed in Palestine." My headline indicated how I thought modern journalism would handle the death of a man billions of people have worshiped as the son of God.

As I settled in on the National Desk, I gradually realized I had found the guide to my life I had been searching for. It certainly wasn't religion in the classical sense; it was a secular substitute for religion. It was journalism as practiced at the *New York Times.*

Here was a noble purpose—giving people information they needed to participate in a democratic society. Here was a canon of behavior—strict rules on coverage, editing, and writing imposed over decades by thoughtful, dedicated editors. Here was tradition—stemming from Adolph Ochs's promise, when he acquired the *Times* in 1896, to give the news "impartially, without fear or favor, regardless of party, sect, or interest involved." Here was authority—news was not news until it appeared in the *Times.* Every night the Associated Press carried a list of stories the *Times* was running on page one, and editors around the country used the advisory as a guide to how they played the news.

Here also were fine companions, fellow editors to discuss the news and our profession, to rib each other and, on occasion, to party together. Four of us formed a car pool and, at the instigation of Tom Daffron, put in $100 each and bought an old Cadillac to drive into town. Because the others lived farther from New York I was the last pickup and, as a result, never drove it. In fact, I rode in it only a few times before my working hours were changed.

Wrapped up in my job, I found little interest in pursuing my religious quest, although two colleagues talked openly about accepting Jesus as their savior. John McCandlish Phillips, a metropolitan reporter, kept a Bible on his desk and sometimes in slack news periods, conducted Bible studies in the back of the newsroom for any who would listen. Phillips, one of the best writers on the staff, was well liked and quiet. Perhaps that is why the editors allowed such proselytizing. Rooted to the desk, I never attended his sessions.

Phillips wrote his most memorable story in 1965, an exposé reporting that Daniel Burros, the leader of the state Ku Klux Klan and official of the American Nazis, was a Jew. When the article was printed, Burros shot and killed himself. Phillips, who had sought to convert Burros, displayed no remorse, seeing the event as the will of God with him as God's instrument. Years later he resigned from the *Times* and became a street missionary.

Bob Slosser, like Phillips an evangelical, was a national desk copyeditor. He sometimes rode to work with me from northern New Jersey. While we occasionally talked religion, we more often discussed poetry. After wild years at the University of Maine, he converted to evangelical Christianity, living a quiet suburban life with his wife and small children. Bob's noteworthy editing decision came on a page one article by Harrison Salisbury on April 12, 1960. Slosser warned senior editors that the article on Southern racial segregation, headlined "Fear and Hatred Grip Birmingham," should be reviewed for libel. The editors decided to publish it as well as a second Salisbury article the next day. Alabama officials sued, asking $3.15 million in damages. The United States Supreme Court threw out the cases. Years later I appointed Slosser as an assistant editor in Washington. He did a fine job, but religion called. He quit to join the Rev. Pat Robertson's right-wing evangelical movement as a writer and authored a half-dozen books, including a biography of Ronald Reagan.[1] Bob died in 2002.

Phillips and Slosser stood out as unusual on the news staff for their outward profession of faith, but only once, in nearly two decades on the *Times,* did I hear anyone utter a disparaging remark about any religion. That was at a party when a copyeditor who had too much liquor denounced the Catholic Church. Betty said that as a Catholic she had to leave, and we did.

On Wednesday night, July 25, 1956, I was editing stories on the national desk for the Sunday paper when the Italian liner *Andrea Doria* and the Swedish liner *Stockholm* collided off Nantucket. Max Frankel, a young reporter on night rewrite, wrote the story. When it became clear that this was not just a bumping, but a major disaster and that the *Andrea Doria* was sinking, the bullpen directed me to move to the metropolitan desk, which was in charge of the story. Chick Butsikares, the slot man that night, gave me the lead story to edit. We constantly updated the story until just before 8 A.M. the next day, when, under a New York publishers' agreement, the *Times,* as a morning paper, could no longer put out another edition. For the next twelve hours the afternoon papers had a clear field.

Like so many reporters, Frankel tended to get ahead of a breaking story. Using ship messages monitored by the *Times* radio room, he began to write it as a second-day story, without first providing the essentials: two ships had collided, one was sinking. When I took the story back to him he immediately understood, not arguing as many reporters would. With a confidence that marked his entire career, he did a masterful job of pulling together all the material fed to him by other reporters. As a result the bullpen put his byline on the story, and he won one of the monthly publisher's awards.

The day the awards were posted Frankel put a brown paper bag on the desk in front of me.

"What's that?" I asked. "It's a tradition on rewrite," he said with a grin, "to give the editor a gift if you win an award."

It was a bottle of gin. The national desk copyeditors said they had never heard of such a tradition. When I told Frankel what they had said, he arched his thick eyebrows as if in disbelief, and said, "Well, there ought to be such a tradition."

The *Andrea Doria* sinking laid the basis of a fine professional and personal relationship between Max and me.

I cried when the *Andrea Doria* took her final plunge; the ship had become almost human to me. That was the only time I cried over a news event. I was shocked, but didn't weep, over President Kennedy's assassination, although Tom Wicker wept while writing the lead story.

Frankel won more than a publisher's award and a $25 a week raise for his writing of seven leads on the *Andrea Doria* disaster. A few months later he was sent on a team reporting the Russian invasion of Hungary, the start of a magnificent career as Moscow bureau chief, diplomatic correspondent in Washington, Washington bureau chief, Sunday editor, editor of the Editorial Page, and the top job, executive editor.

During a break in the editing of the *Andrea Doria* story I walked over to the bullpen where news editor Ernest Von Hartz had taken command, coming into the office as soon as he heard the news. I suggested a story on why, in the days of radar, ships collided, since they were able to know each other's positions at all times. No one else had thought of the idea, although it was an obvious question, and he had it assigned right away. It was a page one sidebar. Von Hartz remembered that story and put in a strong word with Bernstein on my behalf.

10. A. O. (Punch) Sulzberger, the publisher, and Turner Catledge, the executive
editor, visiting the special press room in September 1964 to check on publication
of the text of the Warren Commission report on the assassination of President
John F. Kennedy. Sulzberger is leaning over to read the documents Catledge is
holding while I, on the right, and the printers wait their reaction. Reproduced
with permission by The New York Times Company.

Bernstein, who had years before been cable editor, a title dropped
after World War II, considered the foreign desk the best, followed by the
national desk and the city (later called metropolitan) desk, and specialty
desks, such as business and sports, located in other parts of the building.
Bernstein showed his preference by choosing most of his news editors
from the foreign news desk—Lewis Jordan, Larry Hauck, Robert Cran-
dall, and Von Hartz. (Von Hartz enjoyed the additional advantage of having worked with Turner Catledge at the *Baltimore Sun* in the 1920s). Those
selections were understandable because the *Times* placed heavy emphasis on foreign news. Now, as well as then, news from abroad, in addition
to occupying a prominent position on page one, leads the inside of the

paper. On top of the hierarchy, foreign desk copyeditors felt superior. Tom Daffron, a national desk colleague, broke the pattern when he was named a news editor.

When the Soviet Union launched its first satellite on October 4, 1957, the story logically belonged to the foreign desk because it was more than a scientific accomplishment; it was an international political coup. Blind to the politics, the foreign editor decided that the event was somewhat of a stunt, not important, and shoved it off to the national desk, which handled science stories. In subsequent days, as the importance of the launching sank in, some national desk copyeditors donned sputnik T-shirts to bug the foreign desk. From that point on, the national desk held on to exploration of space, one of the biggest stories of the century.

Soon I was filling in during vacations as assistant on the dayside national desk. In those days it was essentially a clerk's work, going through wire service copy and typing the early schedule of stories, but the job did give me an opportunity to see how the day national editor set up coverage and to talk to reporters in bureaus around the country. I would also attend Catledge's 4 o'clock meeting, where the top editors discussed the major stories of the day. Gradually I became a full-fledged utility man, subbing for day national editor Harold Faber and also filling in as national editor Ray O'Neill's assistant on the night side, taking a first look at stories before sending them to Stephenson's desk for copyediting. About the same time I became one of the substitute slotmen, running the copydesk when Stephenson was not working.

My old problem, a lack of candor, showed one day when I was in the slot. I gave Alden Whitman, one of the copyeditors, a short item on a figure caught in the communist witch-hunt of the 1950s. I realized instantly that I had made a mistake. Alden, admittedly at one time a communist, had been cleared of contempt of Congress for refusing to testify against others in the newspaper industry. But the *Times* didn't want anyone to edit a story in which he or she had an interest, which Alden obviously did. I asked for the story back and Alden asked why.

"I'm as capable of editing this as anyone," he said.

Instead of answering him candidly, I said I wanted him to handle a longer story.

Alden was a fast, but not a particularly skillful, copyeditor. He suffered from glaucoma but always had a book to read in down time on the desk. After leaving the desk he became famous writing advance obituaries of important people. He traveled the world interviewing presidents, prime ministers, Nobel Prize winners, and other distinguished people for their obituaries. Although known as "Mr. Bad News," he found no difficulty in setting up the interviews. Important people wanted the *Times* to get their obituaries right. His reputation was so good and his manner so charming that he persuaded Colonel Charles A. Lindbergh, who despised the press because it had exploited the kidnapping of his first child in 1932, to let him join an expedition to study a primitive tribe in the Philippines. Of course Whitman wrote Lindbergh's obituary.

The biggest advance in my fortunes came when I began to be rotated into the bullpen during vacation periods and holidays. I enjoyed being in charge of the paper when Bernstein and his crew went home at 10 P.M. even though I had to work until 3:30 or 4 A.M. Soon my goal became clear. I was not aiming for managing editor Turner Catledge's job; I had no pretensions there. I wanted assistant managing editor Bernstein's job when he retired. In short, I wanted to be in overall charge of putting out the paper.

I liked Ted. He was soft-spoken and easy-going, and, for a time, I thought decisive. He looked on himself as the real managing editor of the *Times,* barred by the Jewish Sulzberger family that controlled the paper from the title because of a long-standing policy against Jews in the top editor's job. I liked his chief assistant, news editor Von Hartz, a huge man with a thick, broad mustache and a gentle manner, even more. (He had not been gentle years earlier when Herman Dinsmore, then working on the foreign desk, charged into the bullpen on one of his anticommunist missions. Von Hartz picked up the slight Dinsmore and set him down outside the bullpen with a warning never to violate the territory again. After Dinsmore retired he wrote a book about what he interpreted as communist influence within the *Times*.[2])

Bernstein scarcely hid his contempt for managing editor Catledge, viewing him as a nuisance. A silver-haired, back-slapping Mississippi-born former Washington bureau chief, Catledge willingly abdicated newsroom duties to Bernstein. Despite his title, Catledge had little interest in the chores of putting out the paper. He thought like a chairman of the board and envisioned consolidation of the independent Sunday department and the semi-autonomous Washington bureau under one editor—himself.

At the regular 4 P.M. conference, Catledge would ask questions and make some general remarks about articles planned for the next day, often urging that lead paragraphs be short. He would smile and say, yes, the leads he wrote while Washington bureau chief were far too long, but he wanted them shorter now.

Then Catledge went to dinner. With him out of the way, Bernstein took over, feeling free not only to lay out the paper as he pleased, deciding on what appeared on page one and the first page of the second section, but also to dictate the writing and length of stories. He could, and did, order changes in every section of the paper. Extending his reach to assignments, he directed department heads like national editor O'Neill to move reporters from one city to another to cover stories for subsequent days. When the publisher sent word that he wanted a column of one-paragraph items on page one, Bernstein complied for a short time, then took advantage of a news development to stop the practice. No one in Bernstein's crew thought of today's solution—one paragraph items, some with tiny pictures, at the bottom of page one as indexes of stories on the inside pages, plus an extensive summary of the news on pages two and three. Of course the Internet did not exist then.

Thriving in my expanded role and enjoying Bernstein's blessing, I embraced my mentor's rules. For years he was the most important influence on my development as a journalist.

Nevertheless, two incidents raised doubts in my mind about the Bernstein operation. One came on a night when two stories vied for the lead on page one. After the usual discussion, Bernstein made his decision. There was no dissent from the other news editors. Then, about 6 P.M., they all went out to dinner. As a substitute late man in the bullpen, I read proofs of big stories and checked wire service copy, watching for new developments. Bernstein and the others returned just as the first edition of the *New York Herald Tribune* arrived. It led with the other story.

To my astonishment, Ted decided that the *Tribune* was right. He drew a new dummy, leading with the story the *Tribune* had chosen.

"I guess they're right," he said.

A similar scenario played out at the *Tribune*. When editors there saw the first edition of the *Times*, they reversed their play. I was not surprised by the *Tribune*'s switch, but I was shaken by what I viewed as Bernstein's lack of confidence in his judgment because neither story had changed. To Bernstein, he was demonstrating only his willingness to change his mind.

The second incident occurred in November 1958, when assistant news editor Lewis Jordan laid out the edition reporting the off-year congressional elections. He asked me to get the edition covering the 1954 election. In those precomputer days old editions were bound in big albums. Jordan looked at the 1954 album and carefully drew a page one dummy almost exactly like the one four years before. To me that was taking tradition down a dangerous path. It didn't allow for changes in circumstances or in the value of other stories. Again, the bullpen showed a lack of confidence in its judgment.

When I first worked in the bullpen I felt somewhat intimidated. These were the editors who made the final decisions. Jordan, a big man who wore metal plates in his heels that clicked when he jackdawed across the newsroom's tile floor, personified that intimidation. The longer I worked there the less anointed the bullpen editors seemed.

Something happened to me as I moved from one job to another. If my bosses were confident in me, why could I not be confident in myself? They showed their confidence in my judgment by assigning me to sensitive positions. Why could I not believe in my judgment? This change came gradually and I did not become a new man overnight. Most of the questions I raised dealt with tradition.

For example, Bernstein and company seemed beholden to the foreign policy establishment. When critics pointed out that there wasn't much difference between *Pravda*'s routine page one pictures of Soviet leaders and the *Times*'s habitual page one photographs of Secretary of State John Foster Dulles, I had to agree.

On Saturday, July 18, 1964, when a Harlem protest against a white police officer's killing of a black youth turned into an all-night riot, I decided, as the editor in charge, to violate the prohibition against double bylines. Gerry Gold, the late man on the city desk, pleaded that both Paul

Montgomery, the reporter on the scene phoning in information, and Francis X. Clines, the night rewriteman putting the story together, deserved bylines. I agreed and both names were used on the story, which appeared at the top of page one.

On Monday, Turner Catledge asked if I knew the rule. I acknowledged I did but explained that because of the unusual circumstances, thought both men should get credit.

"Well," he said with a twinkle in his eye, "watch it."

That rule persisted until a few years ago. Double bylines now appear almost daily in the *Times,* partly to bring more reporting to a story, partly to prevent single reporters from making errors and partly to prevent young, untried reporters from indulging in outright fakery.

On occasion, I also found my sense of ethics tested. I did not understand how the *Times* could permit reporters to become overly friendly with sources, as Tony Lewis was with the Kennedys and Felix Belair was with President Eisenhower. I wondered, too, about William L. Lawrence, the only reporter the government allowed to follow the secret development of the atomic bomb on condition that he could not write about it until the explosions over Hiroshima and Nagasaki. His first stories were press releases for the project. After that he wrote for the *Times.* The relationship certainly confirmed the *Times* as part of the establishment, not as a neutral observer. That was wartime, however, and the nation was in peril. Having survived the Pacific War and seen the ruins of Nagasaki, I accepted that secret relationship as reasonable. If any publication could be counted on to offer a disinterested view of the atomic bomb project, it would be the *Times.* After living through the Pentagon Papers and seeing instance after instance of official lying, I now believe that a Lawrence-like relationship would be unethical.

But who was I in the 1950s to question the common practice of a close reporter-source relationship? In my small way I took advantage of my position to get a discount on buying a new Mercedes. True, it wasn't much of a discount, 10 percent, which I probably could have negotiated on my own, but in fact, at my request, Joseph C. Ingraham, the *Times* auto writer, asked Mercedes to give me the price break, which it did. (Justice was served, however, because that little black Mercedes turned out to be a lemon. Betty and I called it Hitler's Revenge. Perhaps the god of newspaper ethics was trying to teach me a lesson. My friends on the paper never raised a question about the transaction.)

Slowly I was learning that, while on a day-to-day basis editors and reporters did a fine job, lapses did occur even at high levels, as happened later when A. M. Rosenthal and Arthur Gelb, in charge of metropolitan coverage, became chummy with New York Mayor John Lindsay.

As a utility man I worked for years on an ever-changing schedule, sitting on the national desk rim copyediting stories on Mondays, Thursdays, and Fridays, moving to the day national desk setting up coverage on Saturdays and Sundays. I was off Tuesdays and Wednesdays. Mondays I started at 4 P.M., Thursdays at 6:30 and Friday at 7, Saturday at 10 A.M. and Sunday at 11 A.M. The situation was compounded when, sometimes with little more than a day's notice, I would be rotated into the bullpen to work the last shift, starting at 8 P.M. and running the newsroom until the paper closed at 3:30 or 4 A.M.

That schizophrenic schedule was harder on Betty than on me. She could never take a full-time job because she was never sure when to prepare dinner, but she adjusted admirably. As a fast-food operator she was years ahead of McDonald's, and of course the food was far better. Many a day, when we were working in our garden in Saddle River, New Jersey, where we had built a house, the *Times* would call me in early. While I showered and dressed she somehow put together an entree, vegetables, and a salad. In an hour I was driving down Route 17 to the Lincoln Tunnel.

My work schedule gave Betty the opportunity to develop her skills as a birder. Stiles Thomas, who sold us the insurance policy on our house, stimulated her interest in birds. At Betty's urging he put up a birdhouse in our backyard. Exactly as he predicted, a bluebird was perched on that box as Stiles walked away. Stiles took Betty on her first bird walk, in the celery field in Allendale, adjacent to Saddle River. On that walk Stiles spotted a glossy ibis, the first reported sighting of the decurved beak marsh wader in northern New Jersey. I wrote a box for the first metropolitan page.

From then on I was the *Times*'s ornithology expert, which, if I had thought about it, should have cast doubt on my faith in the *Times*. Sometimes I wrote short items on other unusual sightings, which added to my undeserved reputation. Editors often checked with me to determine the news values of bird stories from other parts of the country. I always checked with Betty, who had developed into a real expert but I received the credit. Her skill at identification was as good as or better than many more experienced birders.

For years we took most of our vacations looking for new species. We went up and down the East Coast from Nova Scotia to Florida, along the Gulf of Mexico and the Rio Grande in Texas, from the desert to the mountains in Arizona, from San Diego to Puget Sound along the West Coast. We met people eager to guide us to the best spots and to locally popular restaurants. As the years glided by we become ardent conservationists. Those were pleasant, rewarding trips.

Bernstein continued to encourage me. In January 1959, he asked me to edit in book form an annual compilation of profiles, based on the *Times* daily feature "Man in the News"; Lippincott published the first volume in June. I set up a system for editing the profiles as they were published in the paper. On the basis of the first volume I wrote a memo on how to write a profile, which Bernstein circulated to the staff. It was another signal to the staff that I was one of Bernstein's favorites.

My advancement amazed me. Other copyeditors possessed attributes I envied. Irvin Horowitz was faster. Bill Robbins, with a surer grasp of grammar and syntax, edited copy flawlessly. Cleve Mathews understood science, was widely read in history and politics, and possessed a sensitivity for writing styles. All wrote better headlines, with Betsy Wade, the first woman copyeditor on a major news desk, especially adept at composing catchy headings on feature stories. She was praised regularly in *Winners and Sinners*, Bernstein's words of advice to the staff. Robbins eventually became a national news correspondent in the Midwest. Mathews spent a few years with me in Washington, then quit to join National Public Radio and helped create *All Things Considered*, the long-running radio news show.

Clever headlines seemed to pop out of John L. Hess, who edited copy on the business-financial news desk. He waited in vain to discover an error in the daily item on grain prices so he could put this heading on a correction: "Apocryphal Rye." John went on to become a foreign correspondent in Paris, returned to New York as a restaurant critic and eventually an investigative reporter who exposed nursing home scandals nationwide, and succeeded Alden Whitman as an obituary writer. In every job his muckraking approach ran afoul of editors who spiked many of his articles. After leaving the *Times* he turned his harsh typewriter on the paper in his bitter report of his career.[3] He died in 2004.

In the summer of 1960 the *Times* decided to upgrade the International Edition, which was still edited in New York and printed from plates made from mats flown to Amsterdam. The edition had always been a day late. It never gave the *New York Herald Tribune*'s Paris edition any serious competition. To repair that problem the *Times* dispatched Bernstein to Paris to put out a paper that would be edited and printed there from articles wired from New York.

Ted asked me to go along as one of his assistants. It was a great opportunity to work shoulder to shoulder with Ted, but I wanted to know how he envisioned the Paris edition and what my role would be. He said he wanted the paper to be as close to the New York edition as possible within space limitations. We would use the same stories and play them in the same positions. Our major editing role would be to cut the stories to fit the smaller space. Only a few stories would be written in Paris. Thus we would rarely develop new articles or work with reporters. To me this was similar to the first job I had at the *Times,* working on the old International Edition. There would be no opportunity for creativity.

Paris tempted Betty because of the many opportunities it opened. We could tour Europe. She could explore the art galleries, learn French cooking, and visit friends we had made during our tour as students. She would learn to speak French fluently. But when I said I did not want the job she quickly said we should not go. My career was more important. I accepted her view without discussing it further. I turned down the offer, to Bernstein's and everyone else's surprise. It marked a critical point in my career. I was abandoning Ted Bernstein, the precise journalistic technician, as my mentor and substituting the brilliant, mercurial Harrison Salisbury, with unimaginable consequences for the rest of my life. It was also a turning point in Betty's life. I passed up an opportunity to think of how, if we moved to Europe, her life could expand in a direction best for her. Sadly, I did not seize it.

# 8. Harrison Salisbury
## A Flawed Role Model

**In February 1962,** soon after becoming managing editor, Clifton Daniel appointed his friend Harrison Salisbury editor of national news, with instructions to shake up the department. Under the benign hand of Ray O'Neill, a former printer, the national desk had drifted into a comfortable routine of turning out solid but predictable and unexciting stories.

The move disturbed reporters and editors alike. Some doubted that he fit in at the *Times* even though he had won a Pulitzer Prize in 1955 for his reporting from the Soviet Union.

He was hard to like. Stone-faced behind steel-rimmed glasses, with a bristly gray mustache and thin gray hair, he seldom indulged in small talk. Yet, on his return from Moscow he accepted the rank of general assignment reporter for the metropolitan desk. He swiftly turned out blockbuster stories from routine assignments, such as why New York streets were so dirty, a favorite request of Iphigene Sulzberger, the publisher's wife. His series on juvenile delinquents became a book.[1] Taking over the national desk, he quickly set about to change the national news report and in the process changed my career goal. Planning coverage, Salisbury thought, was the most important job an editor could do. He shoved aside Harold Faber, the day national editor, and let O'Neill continue to work the night shift, processing copy, with no power to make major changes.

Salisbury reshaped the national report. The ideas flowed out of him and he set young reporters afire with his suggestions. They appreciated his eagerness to fight for their stories against the bullpen's demands for cutting and the copydesk's nitpicking.

110

Some correspondents preferred their old way of acting independently, of deciding what was news in their territory and telling the national editor what they planned to do. Salisbury would listen, of course, but he had strong ideas of his own. If the reporter resisted, Salisbury didn't hesitate to send someone else into his territory to do what Salisbury wanted. Because he had toured the country lecturing on the Soviet Union, he met a lot of people in business, the professions and academia. He would come up with not just ideas but also sources for reporters. When blacks marched in Southern cities he went beyond the obvious and asked for stories on what the black establishment—the professionals, the doctors, the dentists, the funeral directors, the businessmen, who thrived on segregation—were doing. Often he would provide phone numbers as well as names.

In May, Salisbury asked me to be one of his assistant national editors. Despite his aloof nature, I accepted with alacrity. I wasn't so sure after my first few hours on the job. He asked me to check proofs of four articles written by Nan Robertson about a struggle between conservative and liberal organizations on college campuses. As I read through the proofs I saw that Nan had accepted as true what campus liberals of the National Student Union had told her had happened and had not given the conservative students' side, represented by the Young Americans for Freedom. She had not been at the campuses for the events she described so she was not a witness.

Reading along, I began muttering to myself. Salisbury, who sat at the next desk, turned and looked at me, but said nothing. After I had muttered for some time he said, "What's wrong?" I pointed out that Nan had accepted the liberal version without getting the conservative view. Irritated because he had already read and approved the stories, he said, "If I didn't trust her I wouldn't have sent her out on the story."

Having learned to keep my anger to myself, I said nothing. If Salisbury wanted only approval, I thought, to hell with him; I didn't want the job. I finished reading the proofs, marking occasional typographical errors, and turned to other matters. A half hour later Salisbury asked where the proofs were. I handed them to him and he marched—that's the way he walked—through the newsroom to Nan Robertson. An hour later he returned, said that Nan was redoing the series along the lines I had proposed and to let him know if I had any other suggestions.

From that point on Salisbury and I got along fine. I learned that he was not as cold as he seemed. One morning when I arrived at work he turned, and leaning on his typewriter, which sat back to back with mine, asked: "Did you have a couple of good days off?" Taken aback at such small talk, and wondering what it meant, I stuttered, "Yeah, yeah."

"What did you do?" he said, smiling.

"Well," I replied, "I chopped a lot of wood."

"I always enjoyed splitting wood," he said.

Yet, many times the man from Minnesota marched past me in the newsroom without a nod. Eventually I learned that his eyesight was so bad that he often did not recognize people.

As the months went by and I saw Salisbury's impact on the national news report, I no longer wanted to be the next Ted Bernstein. I still enjoyed working in the bullpen despite misjudgments it continued to make. In the 1960 presidential election, Bernstein had jumped the gun and written this headline for the second Late City Edition, which had the largest circulation: "Kennedy Elected President." As Kennedy's lead kept shrinking, the bullpen was forced to pull back for its last edition, at 7 A.M., to "Kennedy Is Apparent Victor."

Certainly I enjoyed my power when late at night in the bullpen I threw out advertising to make room for a late-breaking story. But, to me, the pleasure in being one of the architects of what the *Times* front page would proclaim to the world the next day dimmed when compared with forming the national news report. Setting up the coverage called for creativity and sensitivity. Thinking through events and deciding the stories that would best tell and explain what happened required creativity. Assigning reporters to those stories, dialoguing with them about their ideas, and guiding their copy into shape called for sensitivity. An editor experiences no greater sense of accomplishment than successfully producing a well-rounded, well-written report of a major event. Eventually, as I worked with Salisbury, I wanted to be the national editor when Salisbury moved on, an ambition never fulfilled.

I had a chance to leave the *Times* for more money in the spring of 1963 at the end of the printers strike that had closed New York newspapers for four months. I had written newscasts for NBC radio throughout the walkout and it offered to keep me on permanently. I was grateful not to miss a paycheck but loved the *Times* too much to leave.

Salisbury and I had developed a fine working relationship. He gave me important stories to edit, such as M. S. (Mike) Handler's report on the black power movement. At that time the *Times* had only a few black reporters and none covering the civil rights struggle. Salisbury borrowed Mike from the metropolitan staff, where he had been assigned on returning to the United States after thirty years in Europe. Black leaders, who distrusted most white reporters, liked Mike, a gentle man, and they were candid with him.

Unfortunately, Mike, who had spent nearly all his career covering diplomatic events, never developed a sense of narrative, so his stories tended to be wooden. I found that if I debriefed him he would add anecdotes and color that helped the stories. But the debriefing took hours. I became desperate to make the stories more readable. In one case, with Mike's permission, I wrote into his story an anecdote based on an experience that Betty and I had. We had gone to dinner with Theodore M. Jones, a young black reporter, and afterward offered to drive him home. As he got out of the car he thanked us for the ride. "It was mighty black of you," he said. That was the only time I wrote something I experienced in a reporter's story.

The article was the first extensive treatment in the *Times* of the black power movement and quoted Malcolm X as well as more conservative black leaders. It didn't get the play it deserved, running on page twenty on April 23, 1963. (The metropolitan desk didn't tap into Handler's close relationship with black power leaders until fifteen months later when Harlem rioted after the police killed a black youth.)

The news editors in the bullpen often found reason to delay publication or to downplay not just the Handler article but also many other Salisbury stories because they were not based on spot events. Salisbury looked beyond events to see news in trends and social analyses. He didn't neglect breaking news; in fact, his fecund mind found ways to expand a story beyond the bare facts. For example, when I informed him that quadruplets had been born in the Midwest and a reporter was on the way to cover the event, he directed me to assign another reporter to develop the economic side: which companies were vying for the rights to supply baby food, clothing, and other items to the family?

Supported by Clifton Daniel, Salisbury never let up. When out of the office, either on his days off or on a lecture trip, he would call to check on news developments and to determine whether the bullpen gave our stories good play. Often it would hold out stories for days. Sometimes, using my relationship with bullpen editors, I talked them into running stories that had been held out. On one occasion, I reported to Salisbury, in a poor choice of words, that "I got rid" of a long story that been held out for days. Ever supportive of his stories, he admonished me never to use that phrase again. "Say," he said, "you succeeded in getting it into the paper."

Shortly after noon on Friday, November 22, 1963, as I was working in the garden, Betty rushed out to tell me that President Kennedy had been shot in Dallas. "I've got to go to work," I said and hurried to the house to shower. In less than a half hour, after a lunch that Betty had on the desk in minutes, I was on my way. Other editors were already there when I arrived. Irvin Horowitz handled the lead story of the assassination; I handled the off-lead, the swearing-in of Lyndon B. Johnson as president.

For days we worked long hours, through the Kennedy funeral and the assassination of Lee Harvey Oswald. No one worked longer than Salisbury. With his Moscow experience and his instinct for conspiracies, he had reporters tracing the possibilities of Soviet and Cuban involvement. Johnson was not overlooked, either. (Again the bullpen tripped up, writing a headline that flatly called Oswald the assassin, although he had been only arrested.)

Ten months later, when Chief Justice Earl Warren's Commission finished its massive report concluding that Oswald had acted alone in the assassination, Salisbury sent me to Washington to pick up two advance copies and skim them on the return flight. Handing them to Salisbury I said, "We ought to print the whole thing." It ran to 888 pages. Salisbury grinned and said, "Oh you do, do you?" I didn't realize that for months the *Times* had been talking to the commission about publishing the full text of the report.[2]

The job was monumental, because in those days of hot lead each letter, space, and punctuation mark of every word was typed individually into a typesetting machine. Neither the *Times* nor any other newspaper had enough machines or operators to set that much type so quickly. But, as the paper of record the *Times* wanted to publish the entire report and do it fast because of its historical importance and the rumors about conspiracies involving President Johnson, Fidel Castro, and the Soviet Union.

The production department solved the problem by creative use of photoengraving. One of the reports was torn apart and each page stripped into a newspaper-sized form, which was photographed and engraved. Thus only headlines had to be set in type.

I was in charge of getting the pages in shape and had the assistance of Nat Brandt, a copyeditor, and John Radosta and Mort Stone of the picture desk. We started slowly, partly because the production department boss held back and partly because, realizing this, I didn't move faster to give him orders. Once we started, the pages flowed at a steady pace. Nourished by sandwiches and stimulated by coffee, we worked nonstop from 1 P.M. Friday until 2 P.M. Saturday, when the last page was pasted up. Salisbury was alarmed right after midnight when I told him of the troubles, but when he saw the pages the next morning he was pleased.

The *Times* published the report in a forty-eight-page special section on Monday, September 28, 1964. It included all the 186,000 words of the report, but not all the 110,000 words of appendices and not all the 150 illustrations. It was the longest official text the *Times* had ever published. Today computers make such jobs routine. They also produce far more attractive, easier-to-read pages because of advanced graphics and color.

Salisbury took a big risk on me early that year when he gave me a plum assignment. Calling me at home, he came right to the point.

"How would you like to cover Rockefeller's campaign for president?" he asked.

"You must have meant to call someone else," I said. "This is Bob Phelps."

"I know," he said.

"But I haven't been a reporter for nearly twenty years and I don't know anything about Rockefeller."

"Don't you want to do it?"

"Oh yes."

11. Like any dogged politician, Gov. Nelson A. Rockefeller, in his unsuccessful campaign for the Republican presidential nomination in 1964, took advantage of a picture opportunity like this one, shaking hands with man's best friend. He later sent a print to me, seen behind him in the hat and glasses. Photographer unknown.

On Monday, January 14, with New York tied up in a howling snowstorm, Betty drove me to the George Washington Bridge. Carrying the necessities of a national reporter in those days, a portable typewriter, a credit card and a telephone credit card, plus a briefcase loaded with clippings of news stories, I boarded a bus to New York where I caught a train to Albany. Thus began a two-month assignment covering the campaign of Governor Nelson A. Rockefeller to win the Republican presidential nomination.

To this day I'm not sure why Salisbury selected me. Perhaps A. M. Rosenthal, the new metropolitan editor, didn't feel he could release any political reporters in New York or Albany as he reorganized local coverage. Or perhaps Salisbury wouldn't accept anyone that Rosenthal proposed. Fiefdoms were strong. In any event it proved to be a stepping stone to Washington.

The first few days in New Hampshire were scary. The Rockefeller bus was constantly on the move, stopping briefly in town after town, halting about 5 or 6 P.M. to give reporters a chance to file their stories. I thanked Potter and Bramson of my United Press days in Harrisburg for teaching me how to dictate stories without writing them first on a typewriter. Nevertheless I was astonished to watch my chief competitor, James F. Clarity of the *New York Herald Tribune*, pick up a phone and dictate a 1,000-word story flawlessly, seemingly without looking at any notes. What, I thought, have I gotten myself into? Am I over my head in big-time reporting? After a few days I realized I had more time than the *Herald Tribune* reporter because of a later deadline at the *Times*. Rusty, I needed that extra time.

I liked Rockefeller, but was wary of becoming too close. Just as in Harrisburg, national political reporters had a reputation of becoming so friendly with sources that they could not be objective. *Times* reporters in Washington were not immune, either. As I eventually learned, Arthur Krock and Scotty Reston dined regularly with high officials and advised them on policy matters, just as the much-revered Walter Lippmann did before them. William H. Lawrence, the *Times* chief political reporter in the Kennedy administration, took pride in calling the president "Jack." Anthony Lewis often was a guest at Attorney General Robert Kennedy's home.

Although I didn't want to be viewed as antagonistic, I was determined not to get overly friendly. With Rocky that was sometimes difficult. In a mid-February tour of New Hampshire, he went into a drugstore to shake hands with clerks and customers. I asked him if he was going to buy a valentine for his new wife, Margaretta Fitler Murphy. He did a double take and chose a heart-shaped box of chocolates for her. Grateful for the reminder, he asked me if he could buy one for my wife. I declined.

A few weeks after I started on the assignment I interviewed Rockefeller on his private plane while traveling to Washington. As always, he was friendly, but nonconfiding. It was a routine interview and the answers didn't differ from his public statements, with one exception. I asked him how long he, a multimillionaire's son, had wanted to be president. "Ever since I was a kid," he said. "After all, when you think of what I had, what else was there to aspire to?"

That interview ran on an inside page in the *Times*. *Newsweek* and a number of subsequent *Times* stories picked up the quotation and it is at the beginning of a Rockefeller biography and attributed to me.[3] Privately, but never publicly, Rockefeller's staff denied the quotation because of implications that he viewed the presidency as a natural honor for someone so wellborn.

Rockefeller's divorce of his first wife, Mary Todhunter Clark, in 1962 and marriage the following year to Murphy, the wife of a dentist and a mother, was a heavy liability in New Hampshire. Because it was the first state to hold a presidential primary, he counted on carrying it to defeat his chief rival, Senator Barry Goldwater of Arizona, for the Republican nomination. The far-right *Manchester News-Leader* called Rockefeller a "wife-swapper" and said his campaign was based on "deceit, deception and divorce."

I wrote about the issue, which was real, and how Rockefeller was handling it, but didn't stress it in questioning him until one of his aides asked me if I would appear with some other reporters on a panel discussing the campaign. Assured that the Rockefeller people were not sponsoring the event, I agreed, without thinking too much about it. Once we were on stage, however, I realized the crowd strongly favored the governor. I had to show that I was not a patsy for him. So I asked Rockefeller a tough question about the divorce. The enmity that rose from the murmurs of that crowd struck like a physical blow; I had never experienced anything like it. The wave of hostility subsided only after the governor made a soothing reply.

Traveling with a candidate who made a campaign swing every week provided little opportunity to develop in-depth stories. I was confined, for the most part, I thought, to the daily story of the candidate's activities, where he went, what he said, and the crowd reaction. Yet I had to avoid repeating his standard speech, which often ended with "the brotherhood of man and the fatherhood of God"—bomfog, in reporters' shorthand.

For the most part the best I could do was to put a little extra into a story, such as my lead on his visit to Dartmouth, where I pointed out that he was seeking votes for president at the college where as a student he had come in third in an election. On February 23, I wrote that it was so cold that the valves on the horns of the New Skokie Chiefs Drum and Bugle Corps froze.

My best story appeared March 12, two days after the New Hampshire primary, which Henry Cabot Lodge, ambassador to South Vietnam, won, "swamping," as the *Times* headline proclaimed, both Goldwater, who placed second, and Rockefeller, who ran third.

During the campaign I had met Paul D. Grindle, a Boston public relations man, who, with a Boston lawyer, David Goldberg, had been the on-the-scene strategists of the Lodge write-in drive. From Grindle I learned that Ambassador Lodge, in violation of a federal law against diplomats' participation in politics, was guiding his campaign by telephone from South Vietnam. My story was played prominently on page one. Tom Wicker, who had succeeded Scotty Reston as Washington bureau chief, wrote me a note praising my coverage, citing the Lodge story in particular and expressing the hope that I would continue on the campaign trail.[4]

However, at Bernstein's insistence, I was sent to the bullpen, again as a temporary assistant news editor. I had good reason to hope the move was permanent. It was Bernstein who had asked me to write the book on libel. So he must have still thought well of me. Although news editing was no longer my ultimate goal, I wanted the promotion, talking myself into believing that in the bullpen I could help Salisbury by clearing the way for his type of stories. I was, I thought, more diplomatic than my blunt boss. I never got the job although key bosses from circulation and advertising and even tough "bowwows" in the composing room urged Bernstein to appoint me. Bernstein's refusal was fortunate; the job would have bored me after working with Salisbury.

A year later my career took another unexpected lurch. One evening A. M. (Abe) Rosenthal asked me to go to the cafeteria for a cup of coffee. When I replied that I didn't drink coffee, he didn't take it as a small-talk joke (as I in my deadpan manner meant it to be) and, irritated, said I could have tea. Even in that relaxed atmosphere he seemed ready to spring out like a tightly wound toy spring coil. His pockmarked face grim, he explained over the next hour his problems in his first year as metropolitan editor in getting the stories organized. He wanted me to put the stories in shape before they went to the copydesk.

Like Salisbury with national news, Abe had replaced routine local coverage with deeply reported, lively articles. I was impressed. However, his intensity—the locks of his thick black hair falling over his forehead annoyed him and he kept brushing them away—indicated to me that working with him would involve constant stress. After thinking about the offer for a day and talking to Joseph Durso, the head of the metropolitan copy desk, who was moving on to a career covering the Yankees, I told Abe I didn't want the job. No single editor could whip all the copy into shape in the short time available, I said. Besides, I preferred national news.

My rejection upset Rosenthal. Who could refuse to join the ride on his exciting express train? The next day he went to Bernstein who called me in and insisted that I take the job. He said that Abe would give me an assistant when the workload got too heavy. Accepting the inevitable, I asked for a pay increase. I got a paltry $10-a-week raise and took the job.

As I suspected, the job proved almost impossible for one editor, at least me, to do successfully. (After I left, two editors shared the work.) I never had any real run-in with Abe while working for him, and we didn't talk very much. He devoted most of his time to the larger questions of building up the staff and expanding coverage. I think he looked on me as a somewhat glorified copyeditor. Arthur Gelb, his personal friend and chief assistant, was easy to work with and I learned some things about writing from him.

I worked unhappily at this job for about a year. Naturally, then, I was excited when Clifton Daniel called me into his office in the early summer of 1965 and asked if I was interested in becoming the news editor of the Washington bureau. Tom Wicker was looking for a new editor, Daniel explained.

Daniel had not been liked when Catledge brought him home from overseas to groom him for the managing editor's job. Daniel's Savile Row suits and his formal manner ran counter to the rolled-up shirtsleeve informality of the newsroom. He astonished the staff one day by taking off his jacket when the air conditioning failed. Daniel moved in high society, meeting lords and ladies in Europe, and marrying Margaret Truman, the only child of former President Harry Truman, after returning to the United States. Moreover, he had a sarcastic tongue, which he used to put subordinate editors in their place, and a quick temper to match.

Urged, I am sure, by Salisbury, Daniel had tested me a few months earlier when he took me off the metropolitan desk for a few weeks to suggest improvements to the daily News Summary and Index. My report proposed making the index more attractive with pictures and better typography and changing the name from "News Summary and Index" to "Around the World in Five Minutes." The most convenient place for the new index for readers, I proposed, was on the back of the first news section. Daniel made some ambiguous comments about my report and never changed the index. When Max Frankel became executive editor he reduced the size of the index and moved it back to page two. In early spring of 2008, the index was expanded to two pages, with photographs. At the same time page four was devoted to an index of the *Times* Web site and the daily set of corrections. Teasers for many stories run at the bottom of page one.

In another test, Salisbury borrowed me from the metropolitan desk in early September to pinch-hit for Felix Belair, the *Times* expert on Dwight D. Eisenhower. The *Times* and the *Washington Post* were offered interviews with the former president because both were going to publish excerpts from the second volume of his memoirs.[5] Belair, who sometimes golfed with Eisenhower, didn't want to return from his vacation for what he saw as mere publicity for the book.

Betty and I drove to Gettysburg, where Eisenhower in retirement worked in an office on the Gettysburg College campus, near his farm. The ground rules prohibited use of quotations from the book, but I decided to go beyond the book and ask questions not directly covered, as if I were an editor seeking to fill holes in the manuscript. Kicking off his army clod-hoppers, Ike settled back and, for an hour and a half, readily answered questions. Occasionally he flashed the famous Ike smile, but quickly returned to a thoughtful mien.

My two stories, one on foreign affairs and one on domestic matters, ran at the bottom of page one on consecutive days. The editors of the *Washington Post* were furious when they saw the *Times* articles. Their one story, which ran the same day as my first, was also based on an interview. It dealt only with how Ike had worked as an author. The *Post* insisted we had violated the rules. Nobody at the *Times* thought so. I had merely taken advantage of ambiguity in the conditions for the interview to get more information.

My aggressiveness in handling the interview may have convinced Daniel that he should choose me as news editor of the Washington bureau. I told Betty the possibility of moving to Washington as we sat under a clump of birch trees in the backyard of our house in Saddle River.

Although she feared the destruction of her way of life, which had finally come together after so many years of stops and starts, I didn't think much about the effect on her. She loved our little house. She had become friends with dozens of members of her bird club. Moreover, she did not like politics. She did not like the uncertainty of a move to Washington. But she saw how much the job meant to me and without a whimper agreed to the move. We did not explore the impact on her, just as we had not sufficiently discussed the offer to go to Paris.

Daniel's approach, however, was not a solid offer. Would Tom Wicker accept me?

Wicker's editor, Fendall Yerxa, a former managing editor of the *New York Herald Tribune,* had resigned after two frustrating years mediating with New York editors. The bureau, under Krock and Reston, had been fiercely independent. They were so powerful that they hired their staffs with little or no input from New York editors. Their prestige was greater than the national editor and the foreign editor and their clout within the Sulzberger family was so strong that they ran the Washington bureau in their own way, presenting their stories with barely a discussion with New York editors.

Wicker didn't enjoy a sufficiently close relationship to the Sulzberger family to inherit Reston's power. Catledge, who had moved up to the newly created job of executive editor, had long wanted to get control of the bureau. Enlisting Daniel as the front man, he saw in Wicker his opportunity. Day after day Catledge, Daniel, the foreign editor, or the national editor would call Wicker with complaints about getting beat by the *Herald Tribune* or the *Washington Post.* Wicker, a gifted writer who didn't want to be tied up by day-to-day operations, would turn to Yerxa for help. Yerxa had little stomach for dissension and wanted out. He resigned, went to the state of Washington, taught journalism, and sailed on the lovely waters of Puget Sound.

I didn't know this background when Daniel asked me to go to Washington to talk to Wicker. Daniel said that Tom had proposed a number of men to replace Yerxa, but none was acceptable to him or Catledge. At no time did he express the overall goal: to break the Krock-Reston system and get control of the bureau.

Because of the secrecy surrounding the choice, Tom had me meet him at his house, instead of the bureau. Although Tom and I scarcely knew each other, he had written me in praise of my Rockefeller stories. A liberal North Carolinian, he, like so many Southerners, could turn out graceful prose quickly. I liked Tom immediately. A big man with short curly blond hair and a laborer's rough hands, he looked more like a Marine than a man who made his living at a typewriter. Blunt and outspoken, he told me of his frustrations in dealing with New York on a daily basis and Daniel's rejection of every editor he had proposed. It was clear I had not been on Tom's list. While emphasizing that he had not definitely made up his mind, he seemed quite positive about choosing me. He wanted the situation resolved. I said Betty and I were going to Wisconsin on vacation to finish my libel book. He said to call him from there for a definite answer.

At Dollar Lake in Wisconsin Betty and I finished editing the book and I called Wicker from a pay telephone at an Esso gasoline station. Tom seemed surprised by the call and evasive, certainly not ready to say yes. When we returned to New York Daniel told me that someone else's name had come up and Tom wanted to pursue him.

A month or so later Daniel told me the "someone else" had been Wallace Turner, the Pulitzer Prize–winning reporter based in San Francisco, who was agreeable to Catledge and Daniel. Tom offered him the job but Turner, who disliked bureaucracy as much as Wicker and who loved his San Francisco assignment and its extensions—one month every summer in Alaska, one month every winter in Hawaii—turned it down.

At our second meeting Tom apologized for the yanking around, explaining that he knew Wally better than he knew me. I told Tom that I had worked with Wally on a number of stories, including a series on the impact of gambling money on American life, and admired him. He turned the series into a book.[6] So I didn't feel hurt by being a second choice. After I became the Washington editor Wally and I worked harmoniously together on a number of political stories. In the early 1970s, I seized the opportunity to do a favor for Wally. I alerted him to a plan to transfer him from San Francisco, giving him time to invoke a pledge made years before that he could stay there as long as he desired. Wally remained there until his retirement.

# 9. On to Washington
## Gradual Acceptance

**The New York newsroom** gave me a fine send-off with an oversize mock page one carrying an eight-column headline:

BOB PHELPS HEADING SOUTH;

CAPITAL FLOCK IS ADVISED

TO ADJUST PECKING ORDER

A huge picture under the heading showed me with binoculars, the national Capitol, and the sky filled with geese in the background. The caption quoted me reeling off the Latin names of birds (which I didn't know) and ending "but where's Lady Bird?"—President Johnson's wife. Under the caption scores of reporters and editors had written their names.

I made sure that no one in Washington ever saw that poster. Years of contention had generated worry that New York was imposing an iron fist on the bureau. I didn't want to intensify that fear.

Despite my mild appearance, the thirty-five correspondents received me coolly when I arrived in November 1965. They favored Alvin Shuster, the assistant editor, who had started as a youth carrying supplies for the bureau photographer, George Tames. Wicker would have been happy with Al, but New York editors would have none of an old Washington hand. Before I arrived Wicker told the staff that I was a good man and to treat me fairly. The correspondents were guarded. The most suspicious was Marjorie Hunter, who told friends that I was making an example of her when, early on, I rejected one of her stories from Congress.

Although understandably disappointed at not getting the job, Al was always friendly and helpful in breaking me into the bureau routine.

124

BOB PHELPS FLYING SOUTH:
CAPITAL FLOCK IS ADVISED
TO ADJUST PECKING ORDER

12. The *New York Times* newsroom made this mock page one when I went to Washington. No one in Washington ever saw it. Photo by Maureen Costello.

Scotty Reston assuaged that disappointment by getting him a Nieman Fellowship the following year. After his year at Harvard, Al never looked back. He became a reporter in Europe and eventually chief of the London Bureau, the most coveted foreign post. He was able to parlay that experience into the position of foreign editor of the *Los Angeles Times*, a job he held with distinction as he built a formidable staff, until his retirement.

While I was struggling to earn the confidence of Wicker and the staff, Betty was suffering the trauma of moving from the house we had built, the life she had constructed in northern New Jersey, and the friendships that had blossomed and deepened. She was a respected member of birding circles, a nurse's aide at a hospital, universally liked and admired. "An era has ended," a member of her bird club commented at a farewell party for her.

Like everyone who moves to Washington we found housing prices astoundingly high. We were poor by Washington middle-class standards. Real estate agents took Betty from one dilapidated house to another. She became depressed. I suggested that we look in the suburbs but she held firmly to living in the city because she said I should be near my job. After months of discouragement we bought a small brick townhouse on Harrison Street, NW, right off Connecticut Avenue. All I had to do to get to work was to walk a few feet to Connecticut Avenue and catch one of the frequent buses, which took only a few minutes to reach the bureau.

Betty was never happy in that house. Alone in the big city, disliking politics, caught in the shadows of huge elms spreading their limbs across our roof, her husband gone from morning until 7 or 8 P.M., she soon sank into a deep depression. It was not until years later, when we moved to a beautiful house in McLean, Virginia, that she brightened and became her true self again.

As the no. 2 man in the bureau I had access to the pay scales of all the reporters and editors. Not surprisingly I found that I was near the bottom, along with the three women reporters, Eileen Shanahan, who covered economic news; Nan Robertson, who had been transferred from New York and wrote features, and Marjorie Hunter, who covered the House of Representatives. The Sunday Department's two representatives, Nona Brown and Barbara Dubivsky, also were in the lower pay tier. They were not reporters.[1]

On my first visit to New York I complained to Clifton Daniel about my low pay. He told me to be patient. "What if you don't work out?" he asked. "Then we would be stuck with you at a high salary," hastening to add that he fully expected me to be a success.

The New York Newspaper Guild also delayed recognizing my new status, insisting that I continue to pay dues even though my position was exempt from union jurisdiction. Fortunately, I had never signed up for automatic deduction of dues from my pay. Having modified my strong pro-union views, I just stopped the payments and after nearly a year the Guild sent me an honorable discharge card.

I found that Guild rules on hours and working conditions clashed with the interests of reporters in the bureau as well as those of the newspaper and sought ways around them. I often asked reporters to cover stories in their specialties on their days off without extra pay for overtime. They were quite willing because they liked their freedom to begin their workday at any hour and take long lunches instead of following Guild rules religiously. All were paid above the union scale. When one reporter questioned the no-overtime practice, I noted that I could always ask another reporter to cover the story. In effect, that would mean that the story might be taken away from the reporter permanently, which no one wanted.

It took a number of years for me to move up to near the top of the pay scale. I learned then, however, that just because they are in charge, editors should not expect to be paid more than all the reporters. Like professional football coaches, editors must recognize that stars deserve more money. It is wise to pay some reporters high salaries so they remain satisfied doing the job they do best, reporting.

New York editors watched me closely and the Washington reporters and the bureau reporters watched me even more closely. Would I bring the bureau to heel? Would I protect the reporters from unreasonable requests for stories? Would I fight for their stories? As a clue that I didn't consider myself a big shot I signed my memos "bp" in lower case, a practice I followed the rest of my career. To reduce tension I tried to bring a little levity into the newsroom. At one point I asked every reporter to take a bird name. R. W. (Johnny) Apple Jr. was Puffin, an apt description. When Clifton Daniel came to Washington I named him Phoenix, on the basis that he had risen from his "death" as managing editor to bureau chief. I was confident enough to call myself Eagle.

It didn't take long for me to see why the bureau distrusted New York editors. About the time of my arrival in Washington, Wicker had scored a coup by luring David Broder, widely regarded as one of the best political reporters in the country, from the troubled *Washington Star* to the *Times*. The hiring immediately increased *Times* credibility among political experts. He was especially knowledgeable about Republicans, an area of *Times* weakness, although he was not ideological. He didn't stay long. Shortly after laying his plans for covering the 1966 congressional elections he quit and went to the *Washington Post*.

A demand by the national desk that Broder set aside his plan for a tour of the country so he could cover a news conference by former President Eisenhower—a routine event that any trained reporter could handle—triggered the action. In a long memo Broder explained that he realized that he wouldn't be able to carry out his careful plan for national political coverage. He would be micro-managed. This was the Washington bureau's major fear of New York editors. Seven years after his short stint at the *Times* Broder won a Pulitzer Prize for commentary. Forty years later he continues to win awards and appears regularly on television talk shows. His son John is a *Times* reporter.

Like editors everywhere, *Times* editors monitored the Washington bureau's performance by comparing our reports with competitors' stories, especially those in the *New York Herald Tribune.* Fair enough, but the New York editors pushed us to match almost every story in the *Herald Tribune,* not just major exclusives. In one case I was asked about a Douglas Kiker story in the *Herald Tribune* reporting that President Johnson, a favorite target, was so upset by prying reporters that he had ordered a wall built between the White House and the Executive Office building. John Pomfret, the White House correspondent at the time, wrote a memo explaining that the "wall" was a foot-high brick backdrop for one of Lady Bird's flower beds. On another occasion a bullpen editor asked that we have our new national security correspondent, William Beecher, write an obituary of a low-level admiral because the *Daily News* in New York was carrying a short AP dispatch on his death.

After a series of these requests, I told Daniel my frustration.

"The easiest way to edit a paper," I said in a visit to New York, "is to tear out a story in the *Wall Street Journal* or the *Washington Post* and scribble a note to me asking 'why we no have?'"

Of course we will check on any important news beat, I said, but release us from these harassments and we will outreport the opposition so they will be following us. He was furious but never brought up the question again.

In truth, the Washington bureau was a clubby place with more social interaction among reporters than among the New York staff. The reporters in the bureau considered themselves special; they viewed the *Times* mystique as emanating more from the Washington report than from any other aspect of the paper. It was difficult not to consider yourself special when officials readily opened their doors to you; the fact that the officials

were recognizing the power of the *Times,* not the reporter, was but grudgingly acknowledged. They viewed all things Washington as superior.

So certain were reporters about the fine food at Washington restaurants that Nan Robertson persuaded Craig Claiborne, the *Times*'s celebrated food critic, to try them. When a waiter brought the first dishes
at Chez François, a favorite luncheon spot, Claiborne sniffed and said
"margarine." In a gentle judgment, the often acerbic Claiborne declined
to compare Washington restaurants with those in New York or San Francisco. New York editors, concerned with more important things, judged
the bureau on harsher standards.

While the bureau might grumble about a particular colleague, they
defended him or her if a New York reporter infringed on a Washington
staffer's territory. On the other hand they welcomed a New York reporter
wanting to do a story considered light or unimportant, especially those
involving social affairs at the White House.

Gradually the bureau accepted me. Joe Loftus, the labor reporter, and
his wife, Mary, invited Betty and me to their house for dinner. Bill Blair,
the agriculture specialist, took us to the National Press Club, where he had
just been elected president, and introduced us to many correspondents.

My status in the bureau jumped on March 22, 1966, when I wrote a
profile of Ralph Nader, who had just published the book that made him
famous, *Unsafe at Any Speed,* about the dangers in the design of the Chev-
rolet Corvair. I worked hard on the Nader piece, calling his mother, his
sister, and various other people to get such facts as his frugal living (he
lived in a rooming house and to get him I had to call a pay phone in the
hall outside his room), and his prodigious eating habits.

My lead read: "Talk with Ralph Nader about food and sooner or
later he will laughingly tell of the time he won a $20 bet by eating two
twelve-inch strawberry shortcakes at Boston's Durgin-Park restaurant."
When Wicker read the piece, which carried no byline, he popped out
of his office and asked who had written it. The profile, which said that
Nader had "scared the auto industry to its front-wheel bearings," gave
him national exposure and helped establish him as a legitimate source
on car safety. It also helped establish me as a competent reporter in the
eyes of the bureau staff.

In my first year at the bureau, Salisbury showed me how to use the system to get around obstacles. I didn't realize his aim when he called March 25 and asked that a *Times* reporter—any of them—ask Secretary of State Dean Rusk at his news conference if the United States was studying the possibility of extending diplomatic recognition to Outer Mongolia, a Soviet-protected country historically close to China. Benjamin Welles, who covered Latin American affairs, startled Rusk when he asked the question. Rusk replied that while it was useful for academics to consider such possibilities the time was not ripe to make such a move.

His response was worth only a few paragraphs, but that was all Salisbury needed. By this time an assistant managing editor, he convinced Mongolian authorities that the *Times* was interested in their country and obtained a visa to travel there. He wrote stories about Mongolia and then went on to other lands along China's perimeter. On his return he wrote a long story on what experts in those countries thought about the Cultural Revolution that was tearing China apart.

Salisbury was not through. He piggybacked on the China story to get a visa from North Vietnam, which was at war with the United States. The State Department, eager to get a reporter's view about the enemy's situation, granted him permission to go. Salisbury arrived in Hanoi in late December and immediately began writing a series of dispatches. The first article, printed on Christmas Day, attributed widespread destruction to bombings by the U.S. Air Force, and gave casualty figures without saying that the information had come from the Vietcong government.

I was dismayed that Salisbury had violated a basic rule of journalism—not making a clear distinction between what he saw and what he was told. Here was the same man who years before, on my first day working with him, had approved a story slanted toward liberal students. Now he had made the same error on a much more crucial story. But I was equally angry that no one on the foreign desk or in the bullpen had asked him to write a qualifier into the story, or if unable to reach him, had not done so in the editor's note that preceded the article. Top editors did not work on Saturday and Sunday, but they were always available by phone, even on Christmas Day. Lacking evidence, I could only wonder whether Salisbury's enemies had decided to let him suffer. In any event, it was not until Wednesday that Salisbury qualified his reporting, and then, not prominently. Deep into his story for Thursday's paper he wrote: "It should be noted, incidentally, that all casualty estimates and statistics in these dispatches are those of North Vietnamese officials. However, descriptions of damage are based solely on visual inspection."

The damage, however, had been done. He was widely criticized for giving aid and comfort to the enemy. For that mistake an advisory board denied Salisbury the Pulitzer Prize for international reporting in 1967.

Convinced that I would be a better Washington editor if I knew some of the principal players, I began to take trips with some of them when reporters were tied up on other assignments. One of the first trips, in November 1966, was with Richard Nixon, who was thinking about running for president again. I called Patrick Buchanan, his press aide (who later ran for president on third party tickets) and asked to fly with Nixon on a small private plane to Manchester, New Hampshire. Buchanan, who had been a student of mine at the Columbia School of Journalism, was friendly, and I assumed he had told Nixon that I was not antagonistic.

In New Hampshire I watched the former vice president close up as he campaigned for Republican candidates for Congress in the off-year election. Having recently questioned President Johnson's conduct of the Vietnam War, Nixon seemed delighted that the president had responded with an attack on him. With a typical ploy, he raised himself to a higher plane, feigning shock at the president's display of temper: "I regret that the president has chosen to reduce this debate to personal levels, and I will not travel that road with him."

When I asked whether the "old Nixon" would have snapped back, he grinned and said that "obviously" Johnson thought there would be an "old Nixon" answer but "I'm the only expert on the old and new Nixon." While not chummy with me, he was quite affable, winking while asking, in an aside, whether he had been too harsh on the president. Certainly he demonstrated none of the antipress and anti–New York Times attitude he had displayed in earlier campaigns.

For that single trip "Dick Nixon" made me, as he did other reporters who covered him on other trips in the campaign, a member of the "Bird-watchers of 1966." The paperweight he gave us was a Winston Churchill commemorative crown coin, encased in Lucite. He quoted Churchill's statement regarding the 1939 Munich settlement with Hitler: "The belief that security can be obtained by throwing a small state to the wolves is a fatal delusion." This was the principle, he said, that he discussed "ad infinitum as it applied to Vietnam."

The uneasy relationship between New York and Washington continued; there was little I did that eased matters. Roy Reed's coverage of Vice President Hubert Humphrey's trip to Southeast Asia in the fall of 1967 illustrated the problem. When Roy, a sound reporter who took exceptional care in writing, returned to Washington he checked on how the foreign news desk had edited his stories. They were so mangled that Roy fell ill and had to go to bed for a few days. Roy was unusually sensitive about his prose, but he was not the only correspondent who cared about how New York editors edited their articles. I fielded protests almost daily.

Although out from under Abe Rosenthal, it was not long before I clashed with him again. He had been promoted to assistant managing editor without portfolio, a step toward managing editor. With little to do, he could only make suggestions. One day he called and wanted a light feature done. I don't remember the details, but I had learned to be cautious about promising stories until I talked with a reporter. "I will see what I can do," I said. The logical writer was Nan Robertson, but she was not working that day. The only two available reporters were Harold Schmeck, a science writer, who was tied up on another story, and Jack Morris, the bureau expert on federal taxes, who was suffering from depression. I decided not to do the story on the basis that the idea was no better than the one Schmeck was working on and that Morris would view an assignment to a nonsubstantive story as another indication that his career had ended.

Early the next morning Rosenthal telephoned, screaming. "You promised that story." I reminded him that I had said only that I would see what could be done and explained why I didn't assign the story. His answer: "You should have ordered the story done and then thrown it away if it wasn't acceptable." That, I said, would be damaging to the reporter.

I did garner a few brownie points with New York editors June 23, 1967, when, with just a few hours notice, I set up a mini bureau in Glassboro,

13. The *Times* set up a minibureau in Glassboro, New Jersey, to cover the three-day meeting of President Lyndon B. Johnson and Premier Alexei Kosygin of the Soviet Union in June 1967 by taking over the only inn. Blackstone Drummond Ayres is editing copy and a local girl is answering the phone. I'm at typewriter. Photographer unknown. Reproduced with permission by The New York Times Company.

New Jersey, to cover a hastily arranged meeting of President Johnson and Premier Alexei Kosygin of the Soviet Union.

Under the *Times*'s bureaucratic guidelines, the metropolitan desk should have been in charge because geographically the meeting was held in New Jersey, its territory. I was asked to organize the coverage because so many foreign affairs reporters were based in Washington. Bill Blair, our key Washington man on logistics, called the Glassboro Inn and reserved all the rooms. He knew, from years of setting up bureaus at presidential nominating conventions, what I had learned at United Press in covering an airline crash; it's better to overspend then to pinch pennies. I took Betty along to help; we flew to Philadelphia and drove to Glassboro.

The *Times* ordered a platoon of reporters into the little college town— far too many and some had no stories to write. Seymour Topping, then the foreign news editor, sent a courier with $2,000 in cash to cover expenses. We turned the inn's dining room into our newsroom and kept a telephone line, hanging from the ceiling, open so we were in constant touch with the foreign desk. Except for Max Frankel, who called the lead story directly into New York, reporters dropped their stories off with me and Betty dictated the edited versions into the New York recording room. The two-day event produced no real news; it was primarily a public relations event for Johnson. When we returned to Washington, Tom Wicker, still bureau chief, told me that Johnson had bamboozled the *Times* into overplaying the story on page one. Topping praised me highly.

My second-hand knowledge of birds came in handy. In late August 1967, Bill Blair handed me a news release from the Interior Department, which he covered along with agriculture and the environment. The release said that John V. Dennis, a specialist on woodpeckers, had sighted an ivory-billed woodpecker, which ornithologists feared extinct, in the Big Thicket in Texas on December 10, 1966. Bill said I should write the story because he was not an expert on birds and I was. Of course Betty was the expert; my undeserved reputation had followed me to Washington. But I wrote the story, which a friendly bullpen placed, with a big Audubon drawing of three ivory-bills, on the bottom of page one on August 27.

In my enthusiasm I made a major mistake. Despite all my experience, I accepted the report as true and wrote the sighting without qualification because the Interior Department said it was true. I should have attributed the report to the department and to the ornithologist, an expert on woodpeckers, who spotted the bird. Moreover, I should have called other ornithologists for their comments. Many ornithologists soon dismissed the Texas report.

Thirty-seven years later a recording of the calls of the 1966 sighting was found and Cornell University ornithologists, using advanced technology, confirmed the identification as an ivory-bill, although they have never said so publicly. In 2005 a group of Cornell experts joined an expedition that reported spotting and photographing an ivory-bill in an Arkansas swamp. That sighting also made the front page of the *Times* and has also been questioned by leading experts. The hunt continues, using high-tech equipment.

Eager as I was to write, I made sure I was not neglecting my primary job as the bureau editor. I was equally careful not to displace any reporter on a major story. Some reporters welcomed the opportunity I offered to substitute for them, knowing they would go right back on the beat.

In mid-March 1968, both White House reporters, Max Frankel and Bob Semple, wanted the weekend off, so, along with other correspondents, I flew with President Johnson to Texas. After a few days at his ranch, Johnson decided to go to Minneapolis to speak to the Farmers Union. We correspondents were crowded into Air Force One, while wives (including Betty) and children followed in the chartered press plane.

The president's speech on March 18, calling for "austerity" and a "total national effort" to win the Vietnam War, led the paper the next day. On the way to Washington in Air Force One, Johnson called the correspondents to his cabin. I squeezed my way to a spot on the floor near his feet and when the opportunity came asked a question about Senator Robert F. Kennedy, who, two days before, had announced his candidacy for president in a direct challenge to Johnson. Johnson slowly turned his massive head toward me, a look of contempt on his face. He didn't respond. His dislike of Kennedy was too great to dignify with an answer.

Two weeks later a half dozen of us sat in Wicker's office watching Johnson's March 31 speech on television. In his prepared remarks, distributed to the press, he said he was halting most air and naval actions against North Vietnam. Then, breaking off from the text, he solemnly announced, "I shall not seek—and will not accept—the nomination of my party for another term as your president."

Wicker leaped up and took command. He would do the story on Johnson's decision not to run, Frankel would write the Vietnam story, I would assign the reaction and the rest of the stories. To me, this was the way that Wicker could have led the bureau if he had been given the same freedom as Reston and Krock. Instead, he was harassed to the point of paralysis.

In a sense it was also Wicker's farewell as bureau chief. Months before, in a tense internecine battle, Reston had fought off an attempt to replace Wicker with an outsider, but at a heavy cost in damage in relations between New York and Washington. The civil war merely delayed Wicker's removal to the end of the year.

# 10. The *Times* Civil War
## My First Setback

**Pressures on the bureau** mounted in 1967 with the hiring in New York of a Rosenthal long-time friend, James L. Greenfield, as an editor without portfolio. Greenfield, who had been deputy assistant secretary of state for public affairs under President Kennedy before promotion to assistant secretary by President Johnson, told editors in New York of confidential information he had heard. Many of these tips, relayed to me, were based on his conversations with George Ball, the undersecretary of state, who opposed continuation of the Vietnam War. I would pass the tips on to Wicker, Frankel, and Hedrick Smith at the State Department and to Bill Beecher and Neil Sheehan at the Pentagon.

But tips are just that, tips; sources often offer them in the hope that reporters will write stories supporting a particular point of view. Facts necessary to support a story are harder to gather. Ball didn't supply the facts and didn't want to go public; he preferred to work against the war inside the administration. He wanted the press to carry his message anonymously, which, while tempting to antiwar editors, was rejected even by antiwar reporters concerned about journalistic values.

The New York editors, despite their experience, could not understand why these tips didn't automatically turn into stories. To them the bureau was sitting on its hands and Wicker was to blame. It didn't help matters when, on occasion, we sarcastically suggested that Greenfield write the stories. He never did.

One day, when Wicker was away, executive editor Turner Catledge paid an unexpected visit to the bureau. He strode into Tom's office, set his bags down, and called me in. Without any preliminaries, he asked what could be done about Wicker. He was not doing his job, Catledge said, he was not running the bureau; the bureau was not doing a good job. I replied that the best thing to do was to get off Wicker's back. Give him a chance, I said. Catledge just shook his head. I never told Wicker about the conversation.

The situation didn't improve and a few months later, in January 1968, Wicker and even Reston were taken aback when managing editor Daniel (Catledge let him do the dirty work), with only a brief call to Wicker, announced in New York that Greenfield had been named Washington bureau chief with the blessing of the publisher, Punch Sulzberger.

Young reporters, such as Frankel, Smith, Sheehan, and Beecher, burned by constant requests for stories based on Greenfield tips, reacted bitterly. They consulted with Reston and talked of quitting. At heated meetings in New York, Daniel, Reston, Rosenthal, Greenfield, and Wicker fought the battle. During those meetings I called Scotty and suggested a possible solution: Wicker would stay as bureau chief but Greenfield would replace me as editor. Scotty didn't think that was a good idea and he was right; Greenfield would have been a Trojan horse in the bureau.

In the midst of the Wicker-Greenfield affair, Tom told me that the happiest moment of his life was when Scotty informed him he would be the bureau chief. Now, he said, he realized it was the worst thing that had ever happened to him professionally. Hounded by New York, he never had a real chance to put a distinctive stamp on the bureau. Thomas Grey Wicker did achieve one small breakthrough. He insisted on "Tom Wicker" as his byline. Up to that time the *Times* prohibited writers from using their nicknames.

Catledge had moved wisely, getting the publisher's approval before Daniel announced the change. Only one man could persuade Punch to reverse his approval. That was Reston, who was closer to the Sulzbergers than anyone else on the news side—except Catledge. For years Turner had fostered Punch, encouraging him at a time when the Sulzbergers ruled out the young man for a major role on the paper. He was considered a lightweight compared with his brother-in-law, Orvil Dryfoos, who was named publisher. But Dryfoos had died in 1963 and the Sulzbergers chose Punch to replace him.

Scotty thus faced formidable odds in asking Punch to overrule his mentor. Scotty told Punch that this was a battle between young men and old men and he was on the side of youth. This analysis was somewhat skewed. True, Catledge and Daniel were old compared with Wicker, but Rosenthal and Greenfield were young. Regardless, Punch feared the possible loss of Scotty, who had once flirted with an offer to be editor of the *Washington Post*. Mortified by the airing of *Times* linen publicly, Punch reversed himself on February 7 and announced the day before Greenfield was scheduled to take over that Wicker was staying as bureau chief.

Greenfield resigned immediately, leaving the *Times* building without cleaning out his desk. Rosenthal came close to quitting. Furious, Daniel refused to talk with Punch and sulked in his managing editor's office, powerless. Wicker didn't survive the year as bureau chief; as part of the peace deal, he took over Krock's column on the editorial page, a job he held until he retired many years later. Frankel, then diplomatic correspondent, was appointed to replace Wicker.

Merely an observer, I didn't think I had been injured by these developments. However, Wicker cautioned me to keep my guard up; Rosenthal had ripped me to pieces during the New York discussions. While Rosenthal, with his hair-trigger temper, often said things that on reflection he didn't mean, I felt that he and I would never work well together. Our differences were basic and our relationship awkward. But the thought of quitting the *Times* didn't occur to me then. There was too much news.

Ten months before the 1968 election, the presidential race had heated up. In March Senator Eugene McCarthy stunned the country with his "children's crusade" against the Vietnam War by coming within 230 votes of defeating President Johnson in the New Hampshire Democratic primary. Within days Senator Robert F. Kennedy entered the contest for the party's presidential nomination. Right after Johnson pulled, out Vice President Hubert Humphrey jumped in to oppose McCarthy and Kennedy.

On the Republican side, Nixon had long made it clear that he was running again and formally announced his candidacy February 2. Having lost Broder, the reporter best connected to Republicans, and concerned about fairness, Wicker wanted to make sure that the *Times* could not be attacked as anti-Nixon in its news coverage (the editorial page was another matter). He asked me which reporter in the bureau could do a balanced job of covering him. Wicker said he was thinking of Robert Semple Jr., the youngest staff member, who had been covering Johnson's program to revitalize cities. Bob, I thought, was a fine choice because he had never developed any antipathy toward Nixon.

In later years, I kidded Semple as the man responsible for Nixon's election. The *Times*'s even-handed coverage of Nixon, I reasoned, led other papers to follow suit. Nixon won by only 500,000 votes of the more than 73 million cast. If Semple had been unfair, the rest of the media, which often took its cue from the *Times*, might have been tougher on Nixon and enough of the vote might have shifted to elect Humphrey. Of course that was a highly speculative conclusion.

While the media and the country were trying to digest the 1967–68 winter developments, James Earl Ray shot the Rev. Martin Luther King Jr. with a 30.06 rifle in Memphis. The assassination on April 4 set off riots in major cities across the country, including Washington. Our political reporters were not experienced in covering riots but the staff was eager to go out. Wicker, still the bureau chief, told reporters to be careful. Gangs of young African Americans were roaming the streets, setting fires and looting stores. We had not heard of any attacks on white people, but with reports of violence from other cities and as the Washington uprising widened, our reporters, all white, pulled back. Thus we didn't know what black leaders on the street were telling the mobs.

We did, however, employ an African American news clerk, Carleton Spriggs, who lived in the city. In his thirties, quiet and serious, he said he would feel safe on the street. Within an hour he came back with a report that Stokely Carmichael of the Student Nonviolent Coordinating Committee was telling young blacks to "go home and get your guns." Wicker questioned Carleton closely and decided that the quotation, although provocative, was accurate. Ben Franklin, who covered District of Columbia news for the *Times*, used the quotation in the body of the lead story. The next day Carmichael confirmed the quotation at a news conference.

Wicker was so pleased with Carleton's performance that he offered him, on behalf of the *Times*, a scholarship to a journalism school and an eventual job as a reporter. Carleton thanked him but said he was too old. He stayed on the *Times* staff as a library clerk.

Listening to the news alone at home, Betty was nervous. She knew there were casualties (8 people died and 987 were injured) and she worried about mobs moving up Connecticut Avenue toward our house. Russell Baker, the columnist, who lived two blocks away, thought of Betty. He picked her up in his car and took her to his house, where she stayed, drinking Earl Grey tea with him and his wife, Mimi, until I arrived after midnight. The Bakers' concern cemented Betty's attachment to the bureau family.

Daniel's fallout with the publisher and Rosenthal's defeat in pushing Greenfield left the New York newsroom practically leaderless. At an early-morning chat, I told Reston I hoped he was going to do something about the vacuum. (Reston was usually in early. Knowing high-level officials were at their desks at 6 A.M. or even earlier, he called sources before most reporters were out of bed. As a result he learned developments before others.) Scotty said he guessed he would have to go to New York to straighten things out. In one of the plays on words that he loved to use, he said that Daniel, the managing editor, was not managing or editing the paper.

Reston moved to New York in May 1968 as executive editor, replacing Catledge, who was elevated to vice president. Daniel was allowed to stay on for months as managing editor but eventually was moved out of the chain of command to head the Times News Service. The Washington staff cheered but Scotty failed in the new job, partly because he continued writing his column and partly because he never had been a hands-on editor.

Confined to telephone reporting from New York, he struggled to write authoritatively about Washington. Moreover, he no longer enjoyed the give and take of talking to bureau reporters, who often gave him valuable material.

As the top editor Scotty sat at a desk in the vast New York newsroom, available to all. He was going to manage and edit the *Times*. The decision proved fatal. Scotty was not a working editor; he was a visionary. In Washington he had developed news analysis as a different form of journalism. It has enabled reporters to go beyond straight facts to interpret the news without wandering into opinions. As the bureau chief he sought to inspire reporters to extend themselves. The news editor developed the daily report.

In New York Scotty was the pipe-smoking professor inclined to philosophize about long-range goals at the regular 4 P.M. conference to decide on the next day's paper. The department editors at the table were confused; they wanted directions for putting out the daily paper. What did he like for the next day's lead story? Was the package of articles on the big bank merger complete? How about the picture of the victims of a Vietnam bombing? Reston tried to be the chief operating officer but spoke as chairman of the board of the news department and did neither job effectively.

He brought in Richard Mooney, a well-regarded financial reporter with experience overseas and in Washington, to help with details. The setup didn't work. Scotty never put a distinctive stamp on the job and after eighteen months he returned to Washington, turning the newsroom leadership over to Rosenthal, who had been pretty much running things anyway. The Washington bureau felt defeated, but Scotty said no one other than Rosenthal was capable of doing the job.

While Scotty was wrestling unsuccessfully with his new job in New York, the two major political parties held their nominating conventions. As the Washington news editor I made assignments at the conventions and edited the stories before sending them to New York. Harrison Salisbury was in overall charge.

The Republican convention in Miami Beach in early August was routine because Nixon had enough votes to win before it opened. I did have a scare the day before proceedings began. Betty collapsed in the lobby of the Fontainebleau Hotel while going for my lunch. Fortunately, Bill Blair, our logistics man, was nearby. He called for an ambulance. Blocked by clogged traffic in front of the hotel, the ambulance had to go the wrong way on Collins Avenue, but it made good time and a medical attendant soon knelt by Betty and started to kid her.

As it did for all big events, the *Times* planned for cardiovascular troubles among its staff. For Miami it made prior arrangements with the Miami Heart Institute. The ambulance took us there and Betty was put in intensive care. Punch was in Miami Beach, too, and offered to send Betty and me back to Washington in his private plane. But Dr. Seymour

London, who examined her, assured us that she had not had a heart attack or a stroke. She was suffering from tachycardia, a fast heartbeat, and there was no threat to her life. In two days she was out of the hospital and on Thursday sat in one of the *Times* seats on the platform at the convention and heard Nixon give his acceptance speech. I'm sure that the hospital gave her special treatment because of the *Times* connection. (Some at the hospital thought I was the top editor. I heard one of the nurses say, "He looks so young for such an important job." They couldn't have looked very close. My hair had turned gray and deep lines creased my cheeks.)

Three weeks later, the Democratic convention in Chicago erupted in violence. Demonstrators against the Vietnam War clashed with Mayor Richard J. Daley's police. As we did at all conventions, we operated out of two offices, one at the downtown convention hotel headquarters during the morning and early afternoon, the other at the convention hall in late afternoon and early evening for the official televised proceedings.

Our downtown office was high above the street in the Conrad Hilton Hotel. Day after day during that week of August 26 we could look down and see the protesters confronting the police who ringed the hotel. The brutal use of force against the youthful protesters turned many in the media against Daley; as a result, there was a gap in our coverage that I could never completely plug—the tactics the protesters used against the police. With their faces inches from the police, they would scream personal obscenities at them. Young women threw bags of urine at the police, daring them to strike back. Two times I sent reporters out to get the police side of the story but in each case the stories emphasized the protesters' side and didn't mention their provocations, a serious lapse in our commitment to balanced coverage. Neither reporter was among those injured by the police but both insisted that there was no police "side" to the story.

Ten days later in Washington, I sought to balance the report by interviewing David Ginsburg, director of the National Advisory Commission on Civil Disorders, which President Johnson established in July 1967 following major riots in Newark and Detroit. As an adviser to Senator Hubert Humphrey, who had been nominated as the Democratic candidate for president, Ginsburg had witnessed the violence in Chicago. In my article on page one on September 10, Ginsburg criticized all those involved except the black community and the National Guard—Mayor Daley, the police, the demonstrators, and the media. While he upheld the right of protestors to parade, he said there was no question that some of the demonstrators were "nihilists" seeking a confrontation with authorities and bent on "besmirching the city of Chicago, its administration and the United States Government."

> "Obscenity and profanity coupled with attacks—using weapons ranging from broken glass and rocks to lye—were used," he said.
>
> "The police undoubtedly overreacted but the media must also bear the burden of guilt in failing to portray the true nature of the organizations and the degree of provocations.
>
> "A balanced picture was not presented to the country. This was true of television and it was true of the [print] press as of the time. This isn't to condone the police overreaction, but it is to say that the country was not told what the police faced."

Months later, another group, the Chicago study team of the President's National Commission on the Causes and Prevention of Violence, issued an extensive report on the riots. Written by Daniel Walker, the team's director, the report placed primary blame on the Chicago police department, but mentioned the demonstrators' provocations.[1]

Before sending the text to New York on the *Times* private Washington wire I warned New York editors that it contained obscenities and graphic descriptions of the provocations. Rosenthal sent word that he wanted all the obscenities removed. The *Times,* he said, is a "family newspaper." I sent the unexpurgated version anyway, explaining that the New York editors should make their minds up only after reading the report.

"If you want to cut it," I said, "cut it."

Rosenthal's anger boiled over again. "I thought I told you I didn't want it," he screamed on the phone. He brushed aside my protest that the copy I sent was on our private line and no editor of any other paper and no reader could see it.

According to the Walker report, the demonstrators typically shouted, "Fuck you, pig" at the police and sometimes taunted them with jeers like "How would you like me to fuck your wife?" Women hippies screamed "cocksuckers" and "motherfuckers." Enraged police used similar terms. The study group said that "extreme obscene language was a contributing factor to the violence . . . and its frequency and intensity were such that to omit it would inevitably understate the effect it had."

The *Times* didn't publish the obscenities. Rosenthal thought readers could fill in the details from generalized descriptions. I believe that most *Times* readers never knew the degree to which the demonstrators provoked the police and the language the police used in retaliation. As far as obscenity was concerned, the *Times* published provocative advertising pages of women wearing brassieres and panties, but of course Rosenthal could not control the ads.

Shortly after Nixon's election, Reston disappointed me with a display of political considerations as an editor. I set up a meeting with him and James Goodale, the in-house counsel for the *Times,* to discuss the possibility of suing the government under the freedom of information law for release of Renegotiation Board settlements with private companies that had overcharged the federal government on contracts. I had written a number of stories about this little-known watchdog agency, which reported settlements and hailed the return of millions of dollars from contractors, many of them for military items. But the board refused to release background data, insisting that to do so would reveal business secrets. I wondered how good a deal the government had struck in the cases.

At our meeting, Goodale said he thought the *Times* could win if it sued. Reston, however, said that President Nixon, having recently taken office, would consider a court challenge a move against his administration. We should not give Nixon reason, Reston said, for considering the *Times* an enemy. Without Reston's support, my proposal died.

About the same time, Scotty, still executive editor, dealt a blow to my ambitions that halted my rise at the *Times.* Claude Sitton, a superb reporter who had covered the civil rights struggle in the South and who had succeeded Salisbury as national editor, resigned to become editorial director of the *Raleigh News and Observer* and *Raleigh Times.* I knew I was a likely candidate to replace Sitton because of my experience in New York as Salisbury's assistant and in the bullpen, as well as in Washington. This was the job I wanted more than anything. It would cap my career. My hopes soared when reporters in Washington, New York, and bureaus around the country called to say I was a sure bet. Betty and I talked about buying a house in Suffolk County, New Jersey, which would be more country than our previous home in Saddle River.

Scotty surprised everyone by choosing Eugene L. Roberts Jr., who had distinguished himself as a reporter in the South and as Saigon bureau chief in the Vietnam War. I was told that at a luncheon Scotty asked for suggestions about Sitton's replacement and one by one, as he went around the table, everyone said Bob Phelps. Then Scotty said he was going to appoint Roberts, a thirty-seven-year-old North Carolinian.

The appointment shook me. Salisbury flew to Washington to console me. Over lunch he said, "You're mad." I said, "No I'm not." He said, "Yes you are" and spent the rest of the lunch telling me how important I was to the *Times*. When I told Wicker of my disappointment he expressed surprise. His dislike for the New York office led him to believe I would never want to return. He, too, had backed Roberts.

Clifton Daniel, who was still managing editor, sought to assuage my feelings. Just before Christmas he wrote of being passed over twice for London bureau chief:

> I take the trouble to tell you this story, of course, because I imagine that you might be a little disappointed that you were not chosen as the new national editor. That does not mean, in my view or in the view of anyone else here, that your career on the *Times* has come to a dead-end. Your services in Washington are highly valued. Indeed, many of us think you can serve the *Times* better at this junction in Washington than anywhere else. You are really needed there in this transition period. There will be other jobs and other opportunities later, and you can be sure that all of us here, who are concerned with the health of this institution and the happiness of its staff, will constantly have you in mind.[2]

While I very much felt part of the *Times* I concluded I had neglected office politics; I had not ingratiated myself with my superiors, not even my mentor, Salisbury. I never buttered up to Rosenthal while working for him on the metropolitan desk or after he became managing editor. I was certainly not one of Scotty's Boys, like Tom Wicker, Max Frankel, Rick Smith, and

14. Gifted *New York Times* bureau chief Tom Wicker, right, one of Scotty Reston's Boys, doomed by office politics, conferring with relentless, creative but flawed reporter and editor Harrison Salisbury and me at 1968 Republican convention. Photographer unknown. Reproduced with permission by The New York Times Company.

Neil Sheehan. They were the reporters whom Scotty invited to his retreat in Fiery Run, Virginia, to talk in a relaxed atmosphere about the bureau, the Times, Washington, and politics. I never went to Reston (or to Krock) for advice. At the bureau I didn't choose sides, even though Daniel had sent me to Washington. I discussed problems with Wicker; he was my boss; I didn't go around him or any other bureau chief I worked under.

Perhaps I lacked the personality to insinuate myself with those in power. I never thought of trying to advance myself in that way and if I had tried I wouldn't have been capable of succeeding. Once, Wicker, pleading a previous engagement, did ask Betty and me to join Punch and his wife Carol at the Madison Hotel on a Sunday afternoon. Betty and Punch's wife had a pleasant conversation while Punch and I watched a football game. Others might have used that visit as an opener to try to develop a relationship with Punch. It just wasn't in me.

Eventually I realized that inability to participate in office politics was not the reason I didn't get the national editorship. The real reason, I concluded, was that Reston was looking for more dramatic changes in national news coverage than he thought I would deliver. In his mind I fit more in the style of an old-fashioned *Times* editor, ironically, more like Ted Bernstein, sound in judgment, steady and reliable, but not willing to try new ideas; in other words, not creative—a misconception based on my quiet personality, which to him worked quite well in getting out the daily Washington report but didn't suggest a much-needed innovator. He thought new blood was needed and it wouldn't come from anyone with New York experience.

Perhaps Reston was right, but if he had looked at my willingness to challenge ancient *Times* rules while a subordinate editor in New York and suggestions for bold changes in operating procedures in both New York and Washington he might have seen another Bob Phelps. Regardless, Reston made the right choice. Roberts expanded the national report beyond what I would have done.

Although expressing wifely sympathy for my setback, Betty, who knew me best, was happy with the decision. She did not want me to return to New York to work directly with Rosenthal. "You'll be spending all your time with a psychiatrist," she said.

# 11. Losing a Big Beat on the Vietnam War

**Max Frankel took** a firm hold on the bureau when he replaced Wicker right after the 1968 election. He moved with ease into Wicker's chair and held a staff meeting at which everyone understood that while he was still a friendly guy, he would be a more aggressive manager than Wicker. Although prodded by Reston to offer himself to the publisher as an alternative to Rosenthal for the top editing job, Max avoided confrontation. He wanted to restore morale in Washington without exacerbating strained relations.[1]

Max benefited from a change in scenery. The bureau had just moved from its scruffy, cramped room above a drugstore on Connecticut Avenue into spacious offices in a new building on L Street. *Times* executives in New York, convinced that journalists were incompetent in such matters, hired a high-priced architecture-interior decorating company to plan the layout. Naturally, I, as the least qualified, was designated to work with the decorators. I gave firm and clear instructions.

I did not want a school-room setup, with the editors sitting at a desk and reporters in rows facing them, like a classroom. Reporters were to be grouped in clusters according to their specialties. One cluster would consist of national security affairs reporters, another of urban affairs, a third for economic and financial reporters, and so on. This layout would give correspondents ready access to like-minded colleagues. Because of the need for speedy interaction we could not give the staff the private offices that other professionals enjoyed, but it was the best we could do.

The decorators took notes and, ignoring what I said, laid out the bureau with a school-room setup. The *Times* spent thousands of dollars to reconstruct that newsroom before we moved in but we got what we wanted and it worked.

Vital to the transition was the new national desk team. Gene Roberts proved an outstanding national editor. With bigger catfish to fry, he spent little time on the daily report, turning that over to his assistant, David Jones, who had been my chief assistant and thus understood the Washington bureau.

Roberts added reporters and opened new bureaus around the country. Unlike Salisbury, he widened the freedom of reporters in story selection and in writing. Reporters loved him for letting them ignore a lot of the routine breaking stories so they could pursue articles on important trends, articles that, as he said, oozed instead of exploded. Salisbury had introduced such stories into the national report; Roberts made them a staple.

He also knew how to handle the *Times* bureaucracy. At a New York lunch I saw Rosenthal erupt in anger when he discovered that Roberts had added to his staff by hiding an extra reporter on his organization chart. Nevertheless, in his deceptively casual way, he won Rosenthal's approval of his expansion of the national report. For example, he took Abe, a Manhattan boy who had starred as a foreign correspondent, but whose knowledge of his own country was limited to New York City, on a tour of the South, introducing him to cotton farming, catfish, and grits. Roberts's youthful experience as a door-to-door Bible salesman served him well in dealing with New York executives.

Roberts never sought changes in the Washington bureau, although it came under his jurisdiction. Occasionally he called me, but seldom did so regarding a specific story. He made the calls himself instead of playing the maddening game of telephone tag other New York editors usually played—having a clerk call me so that I was on the line first and they didn't have to wait. Much of the time I couldn't figure out why he was calling. After I responded to his cheerful, "Hey, Bob, how you doing?" he would often lapse into silence. Not just a few seconds, but minutes—and more minutes—of silence, and minutes can seem like an eternity as deadline nears. Sometimes he might ask my opinion about a reporter but often the call seemed to be just a friendly chat without a specific purpose.

Roberts chose wisely in selecting Jones as assistant national editor. I had spotted Jones's talents in Washington one Saturday when he filled in as a weekend editor. Instead of timidly acting as a temporary, he barked out orders. I soon made him my first assistant. He was ambitious. As a reporter he had a tough assignment covering the labor beat because he had crossed the picket line in making a token appearance at the Washington bureau during the second New York newspaper strike. George Meany, president of the AFL-CIO, ordered that Jones be barred from its building. When A. H. Raskin, a veteran *Times* labor reporter, appealed, Meany agreed to give Dave the courtesies of any stranger walking in the door but refused to talk with him. Frozen out, Dave had to cope as best he could. Reporters found it difficult to forgive him. I urged him to switch his efforts from the struggle between unions and management to stories about the workplace, a popular subject in the media today.

Max also benefited from the freedom to hire that Scotty's move to New York offered. With the memory of the Washington riots still fresh, one of the first staffers he hired was Paul Delaney of the *Washington Star*. Assigned to the urban affairs cluster, he was the first African American reporter in the bureau. Exuberant but thoughtful, Paul brought a new perspective on social issues. He thought of the poor in general, not just blacks. Editors liked him because he wrote clean copy, met his deadlines, and gracefully accepted suggestions for changes.

After living in the suburbs, he and his wife, Anita, decided that their children needed to experience urban black life before they grew up. It was back to the ghetto for the Delaneys, who threw a big party to celebrate their return to Washington. As Betty and I were talking to a group of the Delaneys' new neighbors, Paul asked how it felt to be surrounded by black faces. We laughed. We didn't feel threatened, but we understood the point; white faces surrounded blacks every day at work. Eventually Paul was transferred to New York as an assistant national editor and later became the *Times* Madrid correspondent.

With Paul's help (and an assist from Bill Beecher at the Pentagon) in recruiting candidates, Max and I developed a program for training blacks and Hispanics for reporting jobs. We thought that the *Times* had a duty to train minorities, not just steal them from other papers. Our program violated the newspaper guild contract because we hired and paid the trainees as clerks, but the union did not object.

I assigned them to stories and read their copy, often taking it home. After months of training, when they turned in especially good stories, I would give them bylines. The first time I gave Judith Cummings, a tall, talented black intern, a byline, she stormed into the office. "My name is Judith, not Judy," she shouted. Everyone called her Judy, but I had unintentionally violated the *Times* rule (waived for Tom Wicker) banning nicknames on bylines.

When a recruit seemed ready to go on staff we recommended him or her to the New York office. Some, smitten with the capital scene, balked at going to New York, but most of them moved to the home office. In the three years we ran the program four trainees became staff reporters. Unfortunately, some of them did not stay on the paper. Shawn Kennedy went to New York and stayed on. Judy Cummings served in Detroit but resigned after a few years.

Max also bolstered the staff by bringing in Jack Rosenthal from *Life* magazine, James Naughton from the *Cleveland Plain Dealer,* and Johnny Apple, then the national political correspondent, from New York. The bureau took on new life.

While very much in charge of the bureau, Frankel looked for opportunities to fulfill the other part of his job, as the Washington correspondent, the official title of the bureau chief at the time. He dived into many of the big stories. Thus he teamed up with Beecher in 1970 to report, despite administration denials, that the United States had renewed massive bombings of North Vietnam.

In 1972, when the White House, in a pique, refused to give the *Times* more than one seat on the press plane on Nixon's historic trip to China, Max used his rank to supersede Bob Semple, who had become the White House correspondent. Ordinarily the *Times* would have been allowed more than one spot and both Max and Bob would have gone on the trip. Max thereupon did two reporters' work, turning out daily spot stories, features, and news analyses in an awesome display of skill and stamina. For that 35,000-word coverage of what he modestly called "mostly superficial theatrics," Max won a Pulitzer Prize.[2]

To help solve the problem of underplaying articles that the Washington bureau felt belonged on page one, Max instituted a practice of sending a memorandum recommending our best stories before the afternoon meetings in New York where page one would be made up.

The memos broadened a long-time procedure regarding bylines. In New York, as well as in Washington, reporters were prohibited from putting their bylines on articles. Departmental editors in New York made the decision about who deserved them, presumably based on the merit of the stories, but the bylines were often given routinely to established reporters. In deference to the national, foreign, and business desks, the bureau sent its articles to New York without bylines. However, it did precede all but minor stories with the initials BLS—byline suggested.

Similarly, the page one memos were phrased as merely suggestions and therefore recognized New York editors' authority, a knee bending important to Rosenthal. The job of writing the memos fell to me. I would type up the list, carefully wording it so as not to push too hard, and would show it to Max for his approval before sending it to New York. The memos provided a civil way of communicating on a sensitive subject.

I overstepped myself one day when I suggested not only that a story deserved page one but also that it deserved a three-column headline. In nanoseconds Rosenthal called, heatedly denouncing me for trying to upstage him and other New York editors in making up the front page. I didn't explain that I was merely expressing an opinion, something I had done countless times as a substitute news editor in the bullpen. Certainly I knew better than to try to impose my will on the top editors. I swallowed and said I was sorry.

Generally, though, relations between the bureau and New York improved, and I wrote Rosenthal a note saying so. Abe answered August 10, 1970:

> It was just lovely to get your letter. I think you know I too feel that things are going just wonderfully between Washington and New York. I sense no feeling of tension at all and that makes me very happy. And I realize full well that this could never have been brought about if you and Max had not put so very much into it.[3]

One of our most difficult problems was convincing New York editors of the importance of Bill Beecher's stories. Bill had been hired as national security correspondent from the *Wall Street Journal*, where he had covered the Justice Department when Robert F. Kennedy was attorney general and the Pentagon when Robert S. McNamara was secretary of defense. With this background, he was not interested in doing routine daily stories. Before he accepted the *Times* job he checked with senior editors in New York and Washington to make sure they agreed that his role was to break exclusive stories on national security.

Although based at the Pentagon, Bill relied on many other sources, including White House and State Department officials, senators and congressional committee staffers, picking up pieces of information. He also effectively mined academic and foundation consultants who were privy to administration thinking. Unlike most other reporters, he carefully avoided looking at classified documents, even when they were offered to him. Bill was protecting himself from possible prosecution under espionage laws forbidding possession of national defense information. Nevertheless his wide-ranging reporting uncovered so many military and diplomatic secrets that the Nixon administration wiretapped his phones at home and his office.

Bill was outwardly apolitical and somewhat insensitive to the antiwar sentiment building up in the country as casualties mounted in Vietnam. To politically minded editors in New York and some Washington reporters this myopia raised suspicions that he was biased toward the Pentagon. As a result, his stories were sometimes underplayed.

Compounding this problem was the appointment of Neil Sheehan, who had been hired as national defense correspondent by New York editors on the basis of his reporting for United Press International in Vietnam. Sheehan's title obviously conflicted with Beecher's and none of us ever figured out the difference in their assignments. (A few years later New York editors, seeking a pre-retirement spot for Drew Middleton, who had spent much of his career in London and Paris, decided to send him to Washington as a national defense correspondent. Fortunately he retired before starting on the job or we could have had three reporters bumping into each other on the same story.)

Beecher spent little time in the bureau socializing with other *Times* reporters, who viewed him as a loner. Nor did he go out of his way to cultivate them. Yet, he willingly contributed and sometimes volunteered information to stories written by others. Bill worked long hours but preferred to go home to his wife and young daughters than hang around the bureau or join others at a bar.

Concentrating on long articles of wide significance, Bill sometimes didn't realize that some of his findings were so timely and newsworthy that they should be run as separate items immediately. When the Israeli Army invaded Egypt on June 5, 1967, he filed a memo to me, suggesting the material be included in someone else's story. The memo said that leading American military experts thought the Israelis would win the war in six days. I had him expand the memo and the story appeared on page one as a sidebar. It was right on target.

Sometimes, however, I failed to spot the news value of facts buried in Beecher's reports. On Friday, March 8, 1968, he reported, but didn't lead, with a request by General William C. Westmoreland, the American commander in Vietnam, for President Johnson to authorize 100,000 to 200,000 more troops for the war. In the stormy political climate of that presidential election year, I should have realized that such a request could fuel the debate over the war. No editor in New York called to ask why the troop request did not lead the article. The story ran on an inside page.

A few days later Sheehan and Hedrick Smith, working together, independently learned about the troop request, which they put at 206,000. Their story, with a three-column headline, led the paper two days later, Sunday, March 10. Neither I nor any other editor remembered that the figure had been in the Beecher story until he called my attention to it. To Beecher, the troop request was just one element of a wide plan to pursue the war. To Smith and Sheehan, it was a dramatic escalation of a war that was generating more and more public protests around the country. In short, the Johnson administration planned to send more American boys to the killing grounds of Vietnam.

When Bill wrote a story on July 22, 1971, giving the American fallback position in missile-reduction negotiations with the Soviet Union, editors expressed concern that the Pentagon might be using the *Times* to undermine a possible agreement by giving away U.S. secrets to the Russians. In fact, there were no such secrets; the American fallback position had already been given to the Russian negotiators. It was Congress and the American people who had been kept in the dark. To their credit, editors played the story at the top of page one.

The most egregious mishandling of Bill Beecher's copy came during the December 1972 Paris negotiations with the North Vietnamese. Dispatches from Flora Lewis, the *Times* diplomatic correspondent at the talks in Paris, had been optimistic but guarded about a possible agreement. Scotty Reston, who always seemed to be in the right place when a story was breaking, was also there and had been talking to Henry Kissinger, the president's national security adviser and chief U.S. negotiator. Scotty phoned editors in New York on Thursday, December 7, with the news that an agreement was near. He said Kissinger had told him so. About the same time Beecher phoned me from the Pentagon saying he had a big story; he didn't want to risk giving me the details on the phone but to get him three columns of space.

This was an unusual call from Beecher. He usually gave me a week's notice of one of his carefully reported stories. I knew, from the rare excitement in his voice, that Bill had a big exclusive tied to the news. While he caught a taxicab and raced to the bureau I called Jim Greenfield, who had quit during the Wicker affair but had been rehired as foreign news editor. Greenfield immediately expressed doubts about any long story on the basis that nothing could top Reston's information on a peace agreement because it was coming directly from Kissinger.

Arriving breathless, Beecher said that the Paris negotiations had broken up, that the failure would be announced on Saturday in Washington, probably by Kissinger, and that President Nixon was so angry he had ordered the resumption of bombing of North Vietnam on Saturday night. Beecher had Nixon expletives damning the North Vietnamese.

I filed a summary of Beecher's story. Greenfield called immediately, saying it could not be true; Beecher must be carrying water for generals opposed to ending the war. Beecher, I replied, had never, to my knowledge, been wrong on a major point of a story. Of course, I carefully acknowledged, it's up to New York editors to decide whether to use the story, but

I was going to file it. After receiving the story Greenfield called Reston, who said that the latest information he had from Kissinger was that the peace deal was all but signed. Greenfield informed me that he was holding Beecher's story out of Friday's paper, emphasizing that other editors in New York supported him. Meanwhile, would we fill a hole in the Beecher story? It didn't say what the South Vietnamese thought about the supposed breakdown in talks.

Shaking with anger and disbelief, Beecher went home, but came in the next day and wrote an insert on the South Vietnamese. We refiled the story. There was still time to get it in Saturday's paper, before the official announcement. But it was held again. Incensed, Beecher stormed off to his vacation home in Rehoboth Beach, Delaware. At a hastily called Saturday news conference in Washington, Kissinger, who had flown back, announced failure of the talks and denounced the North Vietnamese, thus confirming Beecher's story.

Greenfield called and asked if we could get Beecher to redo his article for the Sunday paper, leading with plans to resume the bombing, which still had not been announced, and making sure we included details of the collapsed talks. Still angry over losing his two-day beat, Beecher rewrote, but events overtook his story; the resumption of the bombing was announced in Vietnam before the edition completed its run and the *Times* switched to the story from Saigon. Thus almost his entire exclusive story was lost.

*Times* editors and many *Times* reporters didn't appreciate Beecher, often expressing doubts about his work. They didn't realize that his exclusives, based on multiple sources, drove the Nixon administration to some of its excesses. As early as May 1969, when Bill disclosed the secret bombing of Cambodia, Nixon, urged on by Kissinger, directed the FBI to tap telephones at the offices of his principal aides, at Beecher's office and home, and at the homes and working places of other reporters. Thus Beecher, doubted by some of his colleagues because he did not join in the antiwar chorus, became one of the first on Nixon's enemies list. This was two years before publication of the Pentagon Papers, the event that drove Nixon over the edge and led to the Watergate scandal.

# 12. The Pentagon Papers
### Never Trust the Government

**Like Bill Beecher,** Neil Sheehan balked at writing daily stories based on handouts and briefings by government public-relations officials. In 1971, unhappy with his Pentagon assignment and a brief spell covering the White House, Neil talked to a half-dozen editors about investigative reporting and got conflicting ideas.

Harrison Salisbury urged him to catch crooked Senators. Bureau chief Max Frankel advised him to avoid time-consuming investigations that led so often to dead ends. Spend a week or so studying members of a congressional committee, he told Neil, and write a story illuminating the personalities and forces that shape its deliberations. Then turn to another governmental unit, like a regulatory commission, and do the same thing. In no time, Max said, Neil would build a reputation as an investigator who produced results, unlike many reporters who spend months and come up empty-handed.

Max's proposal was sound but did not appeal to Neil. When Neil asked me for my recommendation I sided with my mentor Salisbury: look for a big story of wrongdoing and follow it through. That was exactly what Neil, the journalistic equivalent of an Irish cop, wanted to hear.

Sheehan made his reputation in Vietnam as a UPI reporter from 1962 to 1964. The news agency had sent him to Vietnam, partly because it didn't have to pay airfare from the United States to Japan (he was already in Tokyo) and he didn't command a top salary. United Press had added International to its name by buying Hearst's International News Service in 1958, but it was still the skinflint news service that hired me in 1942.

In Vietnam, Sheehan, as bureau chief, was bombarded day after day with "rockets," messages from UPI editors in New York demanding he match stories that Homer Bigart was filing to the *New York Times*. When a veteran UPI reporter arrived in Vietnam, Neil complained that he was spending most of his time chasing old stories. The UPI veteran told him to throw away the rockets and spend his time getting his own exclusives. Soon other reporters were getting rockets about Neil's stories. That's what drew the *Times*'s attention.

In his early days in Washington, Neil, like most newly hired reporters, struggled to find his place. Wanting to help, I asked him half jokingly if he wanted to write a book. His handsome face lit up. What did I have in mind? Remembering Red Ryder, the martinet captain at Okinawa, I showed him clips in which syndicated columnist Jack Anderson and members of Congress had castigated the navy for removing Captain Marcus Aurelius Arnheiter from command of the destroyer escort USS *Vance* while it was operating off Vietnam. Find the truth, I said.

Neil went to the navy and got a muster of the Vance crew. For months he flew around the country interviewing sailors who had been on the ship. His resulting story of Arnheiter's abuse of the crew was too long for the daily paper; sharply cut, it ran in the Sunday magazine. Neil expanded it into a book.[1]

As the coauthor of a libel handbook I was confident that Neil's article and book, dealing with a government official, Captain Arnheiter, were safe from damages. Arnheiter sued Neil and the publisher, Random House, but not the *Times*. Arnheiter's lawyers knew what they were doing: the *Times* would have mounted a strong defense against the suit. The *Times* never settled libel cases, a position that gave pause to individuals, public figures, and companies thinking about suing. Book publishers, prodded by insurance companies, often settle cases for tidy sums on the basis that paying the legal bills of trials is more expensive. Neil, operating alone, spent months getting the material for his defense. Eventually the suit was dismissed, with a court decision reinforcing the expansion of the media's right to criticize military figures on the basis that they are public officials.

Neil found his big story in the Pentagon Papers, the secret history of the Vietnam War that Secretary of Defense Robert S. McNamara had commissioned. Neil has never revealed his source, but Daniel Ellsberg, one of the authors, wrote in his memoirs that he readily showed the documents to Neil in March 1971.[2] He said he planned to give them to Neil but did not do so then. He did give Neil a key to his brother-in-law's apartment in Cambridge, Massachusetts, where the papers were stored.

In his memoirs, Ellsberg wrote that he was puzzled about what happened but referred to a chronology found in the safe of E. Howard Hunt, one of the Watergate burglars, who also broke into the offices of Ellsberg's California psychiatrist. According to the chronology, on a March weekend when Ellsberg was out of town Neil and his writer wife, Susan, removed the papers, copied them, and then returned the originals to the apartment.

This sequence sounds like the old trick of a source's covering up involvement in a leak by making the information available without doing so directly. Ellsberg knew he could be jailed for giving the top-secret papers to unauthorized people. Perhaps he wanted to reduce his risk. Or perhaps Neil suggested such a ploy to protect Ellsberg.

I didn't know about the papers until Neil took me outside the *Times* Washington bureau on a bright spring day for a walk around the block (we worried about wiretaps and bugs in the bureau). He told me about the Pentagon's Vietnam history, which I had never heard of, and asked if the *Times* would print all the thousands of documents. He said that his source wanted that guarantee before turning it over. I told him I doubted very much that the *Times* would guarantee to publish anything, no matter its length, without seeing it, but, with Frankel, the bureau chief, out of town, he should talk to Reston. Scotty expressed the same doubt but encouraged Neil to continue to seek the papers.

A few nights later national editor Gene Roberts got me out of bed with an angry call asking what Neil was up to. He said Neil had asked Bill Kovach, the New England correspondent, for thousands of dollars but wouldn't say what the money was for. I told Gene that because of fear of wiretaps, I could not tell him, but he should send the money. Although understandably irritated, he authorized Kovach to give Neil the money. Actually Bill used credit cards to pay for keeping photocopy outlets open all night while Neil and Susan copied the approximately 7,000 pages, almost all of the study, officially titled *History of United States Decision-Making Process on Vietnam Policy.*

An exhausted Neil returned to Washington and told Max and me that he had the papers. Max asked for a brief description of what they showed, but Neil shook his head and said he didn't know the contents; it was too massive. Okay, Max said, spend a few days looking it over and write a quick summary. When we came out of Max's office Neil said there was no way he could produce such a summary so fast. Max didn't realize the vast dimensions of the report, he said.

A little later New York editors, knowing that secrets don't stay secrets very long in any newsroom, especially when thousands of documents are concerned, decided to protect the exclusive story by setting up a clandestine operation in the Hilton Hotel in New York, away from both the Washington bureau and the New York newsroom. At first the staff included just Neil and Gerald Gold, a talented copyeditor. Soon, Hedrick Smith, E. W. Kenworthy and Fox Butterfield joined in the effort to study the massive pile of documents. The 3,000 pages of narrative history and 4,000 pages of documents—a total of about 4.5 million words—had to be organized and analyzed. Always careful, never one to rush, Neil meticulously examined every page. Plagued by a chronic back problem, he sent for his Washington bureau chair. We shipped it to New York by bus.

As weeks and then months passed, Rosenthal grew anxious. Word would certainly leak out and the *Times* would lose its exclusive, perhaps get beat on the story. Ellsberg might lose confidence that the *Times* would publish the story and slip the documents to another publication—a real danger because Ellsberg was shopping around for an outlet.

One night Neil called and said he was concerned that Representative Paul (Pete) McCloskey of California, an antiwar Republican, had the report. Would I check it out? The next day I called McCloskey, told him that the *Times* had heard he might seek the Republican presidential nomination (which was true) and asked if he would lunch with bureau reporters. Sure, he said, but he wanted to be the host. The day of the lunch, at the Republican National headquarters, I met with him a few minutes early to set the ground rules. Gingerly I asked McCloskey if he had ever seen a copy of the Pentagon's secret history of the Vietnam War. He showed no surprise, but said no, he had not. In fact, he said, as an ex-Marine, sworn to uphold the law, he wouldn't look at a classified document. "Well," I said, "if you do get a copy would you tell us about it? We certainly don't want The *Los Angeles Times* to beat us to it." He said he would.

Actually, Ellsberg had already given copies to McCloskey, a member of the House Foreign Affairs Committee, and J. W. Fulbright, chairman of the Senate Foreign Relations Committee. Both seemed excited about the secret history, but refused to act. With surprising blindness, Fulbright, the leading antiwar senator, who was proud of his erudition, replied, according to Ellsberg, "Isn't it, after all, only history?"[3]

Senator George McGovern was so unreservedly enthusiastic when informed about the study that Ellsberg pointed out the dangers his presidential candidacy faced if it used the documents. A week later McGovern told Ellsberg, "I'm sorry, I can't do it."

This refusal of congressional leaders to act persuaded Ellsberg to turn to the *Times*.

In May, more than two months after Neil received the documents, Rosenthal, who didn't take much to get agitated, was beside himself. Now managing editor, he was learning that just demanding a story would not automatically produce one. He asked Frankel what could be done. Max said that if anyone could get the story out of Neil it would be Bob Phelps.

Max was overoptimistic. I understood how Neil operated and had tried various ways to speed up his output, but with little success. He balked at giving me stories one page at a time because he was afraid I would put them on the wire to New York and he would lose a chance to revise. He wanted to be completely satisfied with the entire story before letting go. He was constantly rewriting in his head.

Once, on a routine story, he rolled paper into his typewriter, typed a Washington dateline and sat staring at it for close to a half hour. Then, without typing a single word of the story, he yanked the paper out, wadded it up, and threw it in the wastebasket, where I found it. Whatever had been in his mind had not worked.

When I walked into Abe's office in response to his call, he paced around, saying he didn't know what to do. Time after time Neil had agreed to a deadline, only to miss it. I didn't say so, but this was Neil's style. He would listen quietly to an editor's urgent pleas and softly reply that he understood the need. He never lost his temper, never answered anger with anger, a controlled calm that must have compounded Rosenthal's rage.

Abe said he didn't want to take the story away from Neil, but something had to be done. I said I would go over to the Hilton "to see what I could do." This was a risky phrase to use with trigger-tongued Rosenthal. I had uttered those same words years before when he had asked for a feature story from Washington and, drawing down his wrath, I had not delivered it. A few minutes later Abe called me in again and said I need not talk to Neil. They had had another talk and a new deadline had been set.

In the weeks that followed, while the publisher anguished over conflicting advice about publishing the secret material, Neil's drafts were rejected and Frankel rewrote the lead of the first story. I visited the crew at the Hilton to look over the clandestine newsroom. After all, I had been in on the takeoff of the story.

But I was not in on the landing; I never edited a single line of the Pentagon Papers. Neil, however, in giving me a copy of the hardcover book reprinting the articles, inscribed it to "a friend, a great editor, whose calm and sure advice helped bring us all through those grim months before the presses could roll."

The first stories were published on Sunday, June 13, with the page one headline using the erudite "Vietnam Archive." Max stood by in Washington, ready to write the expected Nixon administration's reaction. Top officials had taken the weekend off, some for Tricia Nixon's wedding, and didn't respond until Monday. Kissinger, then national security adviser, led the attack on the *Times* for what he termed violating national security. After the third installment appeared on Tuesday, the government won an injunction prohibiting the *Times* from continuing publication. The *Times* complied but Ellsberg, hiding out from the FBI and determined to get more of the papers published, gave them to the *Washington Post*. The *St. Louis Post-Dispatch* and the *Boston Globe* also followed with stories.

When the case reached the Supreme Court, I sat in the crowded spectators' section on June 26 to hear the arguments. Alexander M. Bickel, the Yale constitutional expert representing the *Times*, disappointed me when he indicated in his argument that there were situations when the courts did possess power to prevent publication of stories.

Hearing this, Justice William O. Douglas, who had been scribbling at his desk, interrupted Bickel. "The First Amendment provides that Congress shall make no law abridging freedom of the press," he said. "Do you read that to mean that Congress could make some laws abridging freedom of the press?"

"No sir," Bickel replied, "only in that I have conceded for purposes of this argument that some limitation, some impairment of the absoluteness of that prohibition, is possible."

"That is a very strange argument for the *Times* to be making," Douglas said, shaking his head, "the Congress can make all this illegal by passing laws."

"I did not really argue that, Mr. Justice."

"That was the strong impression that was left in my mind."

That afternoon, at a buffet lunch at the bureau, I asked Bickel why he didn't insist on absolute freedom of the press because of the flat statement in the First Amendment. Three justices had expressed that view in previous cases: Douglas, Hugo Black, and William Brennan. Thurgood Marshall generally agreed, but did not go quite as far as absolutism. Five were needed for a majority.

"You want to win, don't you?" Bickel replied. "I knew I had Douglas's vote, and Black's, Brennan's, and Marshall's. I was aiming at Potter Stewart and Byron White," two justices who might have voted either way. His strategy worked and the court, 6 to 3, with Stewart and White voting in the majority, lifted the injunction four days later. The *Times* completed the series and published it in book form.[4]

The *Times* nominated itself, not Sheehan, for the 1972 Pulitzer Prize on the basis that the publisher, Punch Sulzberger, showed courage by publishing the Pentagon Papers, thus risking the future of the *Times*. There was certainly merit in that position and the *Times* won the prize. Some of his most important advisers had recommended against publication, and Lord, Day and Lord, the *Times*'s law firm, had resigned the account over the decision to ignore its advice and publish. But, by definition, publishers are supposed to publish. It is the nature of the job.

Others besides Sheehan contributed mightily to the project. Frankel wrote a memo for the lawyers showing that every citation the government made regarding violations of national security was false. Other reporters also helped with analysis of the documents and writing sidebar articles. But the central fact remained that Sheehan obtained the Pentagon Papers. Without him the story would not have been so historic, even if another paper had broken it. No other paper had the capacity to publish so much of the study or the authority to proclaim its importance.

The Pentagon Papers revealed no secret strategies or plans. This lack of a smoking gun was what made the writing of the stories so difficult. No "gotcha!" document, order, memo, report, or anything else popped out on which to hang a shocker lead. What the papers did show was a pattern of deceit on the progress of the war. For years the Kennedy and Johnson administrations had withheld the truth from the public.

The night before publication I went to New York and dined with some of the Pentagon Papers crew at a small Italian restaurant, with the usual red-and-white checkered tablecloth and candles in squat Chianti bottles. While we waited for the first edition to roll off the press, I asked what the reporters learned in their months of looking at the documents. Rick Smith said it first—"Don't trust the government"—and all agreed that never again would they believe a government source without checking the facts thoroughly.

H. R. Haldeman, the president's chief of staff, saw the same impact and went even further. Recorded conversations of the Oval Office for June 14, the day the second article appeared, show he told Nixon:[5]

> But out of the gobbledygook, comes a very clear thing: [unclear] you can't trust the government; you can't believe what they say; and you can't rely on their judgment; and the . . . the implicit infallibility of presidents, which has been an accepted thing in America, is badly hurt by this, because it shows that people do things the President wants to do even though it's wrong, and the President can be wrong.

Haldeman saw what Nixon had not. In fact, the president was so gleeful the first articles had implicated Democratic presidents Kennedy and Johnson that he suggested that the government wait a day before moving to stop the *Times* from publishing to allow more revelations about his political enemies. Nixon did worry that eventually the material would deal with his administration.

The president had good reason to worry. Shortly after Nixon took office Beecher had reported the secret bombing of Cambodia. The next year Beecher and Frankel revealed the resumption of bombing of North Vietnam. In 1971 Tad Szulc wrote a number of stories based on the CIA's daily intelligence reports to the president and Beecher laid out the American fallback position on a missile treaty with the Soviet Union. Now the *Times* in publishing the Pentagon Papers, was revealing even more secrets. To the press, the revelations were in the spirit of informing the public.

To the president, obsessed as he was with secrecy, which he felt he needed to give him freedom to act, the government looked like a sieve. He gave orders to get his enemies. The White House "plumbers" unit, set up to stop the leaks, burgled the Democratic National Committee headquarters. The Watergate scandal broke, revealing widespread crimes by the administration and the president's attempt to cover them up. Facing an impeachment trial and certain conviction, Nixon resigned. Without the Pentagon Papers there might have been no Watergate scandal and the true nature of Richard Nixon might never have been exposed.

# 13. Watergate One
## How the *Post* Beat the *Times*

**I heard the news** of the break-in at the Democratic headquarters in the Watergate luxury apartment-office complex on a country-music radio station while driving into Washington to do some routine work on Saturday morning, June 17, 1972. I asked William Robbins, the desk editor that day, what he was doing about the story. He had not seen a short item that appeared on the United Press International Washington wire, but he fished it out and sent an intern, Nathaniel Shepherd, to look into it. Shepherd wrote a solid one-column article about the break-in and the arrest of five men, three of them Cuban exiles, which was played under a four-column headline on page thirty, deep inside the fat Sunday *New York Times*. Cautious, as always in those days, *Times* editors declined to play the story on page one.

I was not disturbed that the *Washington Post* displayed its lengthier story under a two-column headline at the top of page one, with a sidebar on the Cuban "plumbers," the group formed to plug leaks in the Nixon administration. The *Post* understandably viewed politics as the number one subject in the capital and often played prominently news that non-Washington papers considered minor.

Because of eavesdropping devices the plumbers carried, I, like everyone else, wondered whether the break-in was more than a burglary, so I called a Sunday meeting at my house in McLean, Virginia. Attending were Walter Rugaber, who had done some investigative stories and hoped to do more; Tad Szulc, a foreign affairs reporter who knew the Cuban exiles and Fidel Castro; Nat Shepherd, who wrote the original story; assistant editor John Hemphill; Bill Robbins, and, I believe, Robert B. Semple Jr., the White

15. Trying to rock away the tension during the Watergate investigation. Ashtray is for visitors. I did not smoke—ever. Photo by Mike Lien. Reproduced with permission by the New York Times Company.

House correspondent. Thus, from the beginning we saw the possibilities of Watergate as an important story, although certainly not in the dimensions that eventually surfaced. At that meeting we divided responsibilities. Rugaber would look into domestic political implications, whether the Nixon administration had been attempting political espionage; Szulc would check the Cuban aspects; Bob Semple would see what he could get out of the White House; Shepherd would cover the District of Columbia police department and district attorney.

For four days Szulc, eager to take over the whole story because he was convinced that the CIA (one of the arrested men said he had formerly worked for the spy agency), as well as the Cubans, were involved, rattled off page one stories. He implicated the White House, the CIA, and veterans of the Bay of Pigs disaster.

Szulc had impressed me right after he joined the bureau the previous year. He had become a legendary figure covering Fidel Castro and Latin America, as well as Poland, his birthplace. The legends sprang not only from his relationships with Latin American leaders—he could get them on the phone at all hours and talk to them in their language—but also from his scoops—Poland had expelled him—and his high lifestyle as reflected in his expense accounts. Clifton Daniel told me that when managing editor he spotted Tad having lunch with the Polish Ambassador to the United Nations at an upscale New York restaurant. "Who do you think is going to pay for that lunch," Daniel's companion asked him, "the *Times* or the Polish government?" "Both," Daniel replied.

In his first few weeks in Washington in the summer of 1971 Szulc came in the bureau regularly with a torn-up numbered copy of the CIA's daily intelligence report to the president that a government official whom he had met overseas had slipped inside a magazine. He didn't quote directly from the reports, which he taped together from the pieces; that was tempting but would have been foolhardy because the CIA could have quickly discovered the source of the leak. Instead, we would go over the report, select a subject, which Tad would check out with other sources and then write a story, sometimes, but not always, using the CIA information.

His article on June 22, 1971, disclosing that the United States was shipping military equipment to Pakistan after the State Department had announced suspension of such sales aroused particular concern in the administration. The article named a ship about to sail that day from New York.

We were not as clever as we thought. The Nixon administration had begun tapping phone calls of journalists shortly after it took over in 1969. It placed some of the first taps on William Beecher's phones after his May 9, 1969, revelation that American B-52s were bombing a neutral country, Cambodia, in support of the Vietnam War. Moved by the publication of the Pentagon Papers, the administration intensified the activities of the investigative unit in the Executive Office Building basement, next to the White House. Members of that group, who called themselves plumbers, tapped Tad's telephones. Reports flowed into the tappers at the rate of two or three a week. After a few weeks Tad's source, getting nervous—he was never caught—stopped feeding the CIA material to us.

Szulc's first Watergate stories were exhilarating, but he soon ran dry in his attempt to expand the CIA-Cuba links. By the end of the week Rugaber had begun writing the main Watergate stories. He summarized what we knew in 3,000 words that pointed to possible Nixon campaign and White House involvement and discounted the Cuban link. (Perhaps if Szulc had continued digging, he would have discovered what Oval Office tapes revealed later: the cover-up. The president wanted to use the CIA to block the FBI from investigating Watergate. Szulc, however, was convinced that Watergate was part of a CIA anti-Castro plan.)

At the *Post,* Bob Woodward was writing the daily stories, sometimes with Carl Bernstein, sometimes with other reporters; most of this material was also printed in other papers. Woodward, however, turned to W. Mark Felt, deputy director of the Federal Bureau of Investigation, who identified himself in 2005 as the *Post*'s anonymous "Deep Throat." Woodward, who had developed Felt as a mentor and a friend for two years, could not have found a better source. Felt saw everything that FBI agents were uncovering. However, Woodward's first conversations with Felt, by telephone, only days after the break-in, produced little. In late July, with their trail at a dead end, Woodward went on vacation to Lake Michigan and Bernstein was sent back to Virginia to cover politics.

It was the first but not the last time the *Post* eased up on Watergate. Managing editor Howard Simons remembered in a 1973 interview with the two reporters that "the story was getting away from us. It really was, we were drifting."[1]

Simons, the driving force of the *Post* investigation, thought Szulc's idea of a Cuban plot was "horse shit, just pure and simple." Convinced that there was a "hell of a lot more to it," he assigned Barry Sussman, the city editor, to oversee the two youthful reporters. Bernstein was twenty-eight, Woodward twenty-nine.

Rugaber didn't enjoy the luxury of advice from Felt; from the first he thought that the key to the case was a money trail. He knew where to start because five days after our Sunday meeting prosecutors told a judge at an open hearing in Washington that $89,000 from Mexico had been deposited in and removed from the Boca Raton, Florida, bank account of Bernard C. Barker, one of the "plumbers" arrested at the Watergate. That story, by staff reporter Agis Salpukus, ran on page one of the *Times* on June 24. Barker's attorney dismissed the transaction as a failed real estate deal. Rugaber was suspicious.

He flew to Miami on July 6 and, with the aid of George Volsky, a *Times* part-time correspondent who knew his way around town, met with Richard E. Gerstein, the Dade County prosecutor. Up to that point Gerstein had viewed Watergate as a Washington affair. Eager to piggyback on the investigative power of a prosecuting attorney, Rugaber urged Gerstein to look into the case. Even though the FBI had already been checking in Florida, he pointed out that it was a Dade County case, too. Barker lived there and money laundering at the Florida bank might be involved. Gerstein agreed and assigned his chief investigator, Martin Dardis, to dig into it. He subpoenaed Barker's bank accounts and telephone records that very day. Rugaber flew back to Washington with a clear understanding with Gerstein and Dardis that they would not release the results of the investigation until the *Times* published them.

On July 17 Rugaber flew to Miami again. Barker's telephone records showed numbers called from his office, but not the names of those called. To get those names Rugaber returned to Washington and with the help of John Crewdson, then an intern, checked the reverse-number phone books at the Library of Congress. A woman answered one of those numbers with these words, sweet to Rugaber's ears: "Committee for the Re-election of the President, G. Gordon Liddy's office." Rugaber's front-page story on July 25 reported that at least fifteen calls to the committee had been made from Barker's phone to the reelection committee.

To catch up with the *Times*, the *Post* ordered Bernstein to return from Virginia. He set aside the ethical question of privacy and called a source in the Bell system, who confirmed that the *Times* list was accurate. The source said he could not get other calls because the Miami district attorney had subpoenaed them.

That evening Bernstein telephoned Gerstein, who, according to *All the President's Men*,[2] said he would instruct Dardis to cooperate if the *Post* would not reveal it was dealing with his office. The book says that Dardis then called Bernstein and said he was willing to discuss Barker's telephone and bank records if Bernstein would fly to Miami.

But Rugaber had not only been in Miami again and inspected the bank documents, he had also flown to Mexico on July 26. On July 30 he filed a story detailing the $89,000 paid to Barker through a Mexican lawyer. Rugaber had beaten the *Post* again.

A sequence in the film *All the President's Men* shows Woodward and Bernstein looking at the story on the front page of the July 31 *Times*. The headline read "Cash in Capital Raid Traced to Mexico." That scene was a Hollywood touch. Actually, Bernstein grabbed a copy of the *Times* at the airport and read the story while flying to Miami to see Dardis. Robert Redford must have felt free to make such changes. His film contract with the reporters referred to *All the President's Men* as a "novel."[3]

When Bernstein checked into the Sheraton Four Ambassadors he asked for Rugaber's room number. The clerk said Rugaber had checked out over the weekend. On Sussman's advice, Bernstein stayed in Miami instead of hurrying to Mexico. That was a crucial decision. Instead of trying to match the *Times* story, the *Post* would try to get a better one.

Rugaber, however, was still in Miami, nailing down that better story, which was based on a $25,000 cashier's check payable to a Kenneth H. Dahlberg and deposited in Barker's account on April 10. This was in addition to the $89,000 from Mexico.

I did not know these facts when Rugaber called me that afternoon, July 31, and said he had a big follow-up story, but needed to tie up one point, which he would do the next day on his return to Washington. We were so worried about wiretapping in the Nixon years that Rugaber didn't mention names or details. The missing point was the identification of Dahlberg. If he were tied to the Nixon campaign it would be clear that the Watergate break-in had been financed with Republican funds. Rugaber felt confident that he could take the time to fly home because he had Dardis's promise to talk to no other reporter. A quiet, churchgoing Southerner, Rugaber believed that a man's word was his bond, even in journalism.

Meanwhile, a frantic Bernstein, camping out in the prosecutor's office, made no progress in seeing Gerstein or Dardis. (Woodward later wrote that Bernstein "ingeniously tracked down" Gerstein, who was sitting in his office only a few feet away.)[4] When Bernstein finally saw Gerstein three hours before the *Post's* first edition deadline, the prosecutor told him he knew nothing but said Dardis possessed some checks. Finally, according to *All the President's Men,* an hour or so before the *Post's* deadline, Dardis showed him the Barker folder with the canceled checks. Bernstein made drawings of the checks, including the one for $25,000. As soon as he left the prosecutor's office he called Woodward. In the next few hours Bernstein learned that Dahlberg had headed Nixon's 1968 campaign in the Midwest and Woodward found Dahlberg at his home in Minnesota. Dahlberg said he had turned the $25,000 over to the Nixon reelection committee.

The *Post* reporters had missed the first edition deadline, but the story ran in the second edition. That delay was fortunate for the *Post.* If it had appeared in the first edition the *Times* would have had time to get to Rugaber for its second edition, which went to most subscribers.

(Long before Watergate, I had a taxi driver pick up the first edition of the *Post* as it came off the presses and take it to my house in McLean every night. If the *Post* had a good exclusive story I would consult with the night editor or a reporter on how best to match it for the next edition. Katharine Graham, the *Post's* publisher, was incensed when she heard years later that I was getting a copy of the paper before she did.)

Not learning about the *Post* disclosure until its second edition, the next day, the *Times,* following custom, led its article with investigations into the $25,000 check, and credited the *Post* with breaking the story. Woodward and Bernstein took the lead with that exclusive, which widened the case beyond a burglary. It was the first important break in the investigation.

One other point: Bernstein says that Dardis gave him copies of the canceled checks. Dardis insisted that he lived up to the agreement with Rugaber and refused to release the material to Bernstein. He said that when he went to the bathroom Bernstein stole the material from his desk. Whatever happened, newspaper lore is filled with instances of sources' leaving material on their desk knowing reporters will look at it. I myself had done so in 1946 as a cub reporter for United Press in Harrisburg on a Pennsylvania Labor Relations Board order upholding a baseball union at the Pittsburgh Pirates.

Woodward and Bernstein used old-fashioned knock-on-the door reporting to get their second important exclusive. Working at night, they checked systematically from a list of campaign employees down to the secretarial level. They had doors slammed in their faces but Judy Hoback, a bookkeeper for the Committee for the Re-election of the President, and Hugh W. Sloan Jr., who had resigned as its treasurer, talked. Based on those talks but still using anonymous sources, the *Post* reported on September 29 that John Mitchell, when attorney general, controlled a secret Republican fund used to spy on Democrats. Unable to match the story, the *Times* used a UPI dispatch on page sixteen the next day, quoting the *Post*.

The *Post* reporters carried the story even further on October 10. The article was a sensational generalized report saying that the FBI had established that the Watergate burglary stemmed from a massive campaign of political spying and sabotage conducted on behalf of the Nixon reelection campaign. Based heavily on a four-and-a-half hour Woodward session with agitated Deep Throat Felt, the story attributed its sweeping findings to "FBI agents" and "information in FBI and Department of Justice files."[5] It said fifty people were involved in the disruption efforts, but named only one, Donald H. Segretti, in the eighteenth paragraph.

This lack of specifics worried the *Post* editors. They debated whether to lead the paper with it. "I think the question was how sure we were of the story," Simons recalled. Richard Harwood, the *Post* national editor, had been troubled for some time by the stories from anonymous sources. He told Simons he wasn't sure that he believed any of it. How, he asked, can you lead the paper with a story just taken on faith, without any facts? Simons replied, "Well, you know, we just trust Carl and Bob and we think we're right and time will tell."

After reading the *Post* article and checking with three sources, the *Times* published a page one dispatch in its late city edition based on its own reporting and crediting the *Post* for additional material. Instead of emphasizing the broad conclusions of the *Post*, the *Times* catch-up article led with the accusations against Segretti, the only saboteur mentioned in the *Post* story.

For months Simons kept bugging the two reporters to find the "other forty-nine" political saboteurs that Deep Throat had mentioned. He sent

Bernstein back to the West Coast. Segretti would not open up but Bernstein insisted the session had not been a failure; he told Simons he had made friends with the saboteur and was confident he would talk. A year later, in response to Bernstein's question of what he expected from the trip, Simons said:

"I didn't know what to expect. When you came back, however, and you were giving me that horseshit about buddy-buddy, and how you understood people, and you really think you've got him, you know, like you're making a check and you think you're going to score. All right. My expectations were, boy, old Carl, you know, he's got a way with women and now he's got a way with men. We're going to get it laid right out there. And you spent an awful lot of time with him, just talking to him as a friend . . . and you gave me all that bullshit . . . So my expectations were that, you know, just wait and it's all going to crack. And then it didn't happen. And then we just forgot about it, by the way. And that just got pushed aside."

Simons said he kept waiting but by 1973 the *Post* still hadn't really resolved the problem of naming the fifty saboteurs in one roundup article. Woodward reminded him that more than sixty names had come out piecemeal.

Some older hands at the *Post* regarded Bernstein, a college dropout, as a loose cannon, not to be trusted, and looked at Woodward, a Yale graduate who had been on the paper only a year, as an Ivy League snotnose and both as too inexperienced. Hearing such comments, I, too wondered whether Woodward and Bernstein were following a personal agenda.

To Simons, the two were "absolutely the odd couple." Woodward had more cachet with editors than Bernstein. He had, in Simons's words, "come on like gangbusters" in covering illegal drugs. Bernstein, on the other hand, was the enfant terrible in the newsroom, sometimes brilliant and sometimes lousy, inaccurate, overzealous, always late with his expense account. "Every once in a while you had to be spanked," Simons told him.

Because Bernstein openly told other reporters that he was a misunderstood genius and was constantly complaining about editors, while Woodward was a close-mouthed outsider in the newsroom who defended editors, the two decided that Woodward would do most of the talking and pitching for both with executive editor Benjamin C. Bradlee.

For a long time Simons worried that Watergate might be as unresolved as the 1933 fire that burned down the Berlin Reichstag as Hitler was coming to power. Germans still dispute who was responsible, the communists, the Nazis, or a mentally impaired Dutchman. Simons used that analogy openly in the newsroom.

Eight days after the first Segretti story Steven V. Roberts of the *New York Times* Los Angeles bureau provided further details. He did this with vital help from an eager young freelance photographer, D. Gorton, who heard about Segretti through Robert Meyers, the *Post's* West Coast part-time correspondent. Before the October 10 story, Bernstein had asked Meyers to find Segretti at his waterfront apartment at Marina del Rey, California. Meyers in turn asked his friend Gorton to accompany him to take a picture in case Segretti answered the door. No one was there.

Gorton, although determined to break the story for the *Times,* delayed doing anything more out of professional courtesy because the assignment had gone to Meyers from the *Post.* Meyers, working alone, staked out the apartment, found Segretti, who evaded his questions. When Meyers tried to take pictures, Segretti tussled with him. On reporting to the *Post,* Meyers was told to check Segretti's background; he did and produced instances of sabotage during political campaigns while Segretti was student at the University of Southern California, which were included in the inside pages of the October 10 story.

Because Segretti's phone exchange and answering service were the same as his, Gorton thought of getting the records. At Gorton's request, a neighbor walked into the phone company office in Marina del Rey, identified himself as Donald Segretti, and asked for his bill on the basis that he was leaving for a vacation. Without asking any questions, the phone company employee handed him a sheaf of papers listing three months of outgoing calls. Gorton hurried them to Steve Roberts, who saw on the first page the number 202-456-1414, which he immediately recognized from his Washington experience as a White House number. Among those called was Dwight L. Chapin, who was in overall charge of the "dirty tricks" operation.

Despite our efforts, the *Post* had run off three beats in a row—campaign money going to a burglar, Mitchell's control of a secret fund, and the national espionage campaign.

Given the pressure of producing Watergate stories after those first three Woodward-Bernstein beats, I wonder, tempting as it would have been, if I would have approved of what is now called pretexting to get the Segretti phone records. Certainly it was wrong. Today photojournalist Gorton, now based in Carbondale, Illinois, asks himself, "What really were my moral and ethical obligations?" And he answers: "I regret it. But I'd do it again."

Those three beats—Woodward later called the October 10 article "probably our most important story"—cemented the *Post*'s lead. From then on Watergate was rightly regarded as Woodward and Bernstein's story.

It didn't have to be that way. For a short time, we had our own leak in the FBI, but my dereliction and long-laid plans by Robert M. Smith, our Justice Department reporter, to attend law school held us back from printing anything. Here is what happened:

On May 3, 1972, before the Watergate burglary, Nixon appointed L. Patrick Gray III, an assistant attorney general in charge of the civil division, as acting FBI director, replacing the long-time director, J. Edgar Hoover, who had died. Smith wrote a long page one story on the appointment, giving Gray's background and noting he was a long-time Nixon friend. Bob followed up the next day with another page one story in which Gray said in a telephone interview that Nixon had directed him to run the FBI in a totally nonpolitical way.

A week later, Bob expanded the relationship, interviewing Gray in person and calling in *Times* bureau photographer Mike Lien to take pictures. Gray laid out his plan for wide changes, including hiring more blacks, Hispanics, and women as agents. One of the questions Gray said he wanted to address was who would police the police. "I want to open the window a little," he said. The long article, with a two-column Mike Lien picture of Gray in shirtsleeves, started on page one. Another picture, of him and his staff, was printed on an inside page. Elated by the display, Gray called Bob and asked for a copy of his picture, which Lien provided.

This was heady stuff for the new FBI chief, three page one stories in the *Times*. Naturally, then, Bob wanted to sound out Gray on Watergate. On August 16, he had lunch with Gray at Sans Souci, a posh restaurant popular with officials and the media. As Bob recalls, he was amazed when Gray opened up about Watergate. He dropped the name Segretti. With the lunch off the record, Smith couldn't take notes, but he remembered Segretti, whose name had not yet appeared in the Watergate stories, by using the mnemonic "spaghetti—Segretti." In response to Smith's questions, Gray hinted, without saying directly, that the White House and former attorney general Mitchell were involved in Watergate. Smith needed no mnemonic to remember those points.

Because he had to leave for Yale Law School the next day, Smith didn't have time to check out Gray's leads. He did the next best thing. Within minutes on returning from the lunch, with the conversation still fresh in his mind, he spoke into a recorder sitting at my desk in my little office while I debriefed him.

There we were, with leads from the acting director of the FBI that a man named Segretti, former attorney general Mitchell, and the White House, perhaps Nixon himself, were involved in Watergate, long before the *Post*'s revelations. Clearly we couldn't rush into print. We thought Gray might be trying to use us, as public officials regularly do, for some political or personal purpose. That's what Felt was doing with Woodward, who, with Bernstein, checked out his tips before publication. Woodward was lucky that the source he had begun to develop as a young naval officer turned out to be so well-placed to divulge Watergate secrets, but in no way should that serendipity detract from the hard work he and Bernstein did to confirm their stories.

Similarly, we had to check out the Gray tips and see where they would lead us. But Smith, the reporter in the best position to follow through with Gray, was off to New Haven and the start of a career that would take him to San Francisco, London, and Paris as an internationally respected mediator in resolving business disputes and a facilitator in business mergers.

We never developed Gray's tips into publishable stories. Why we failed is a mystery to me. In fact, while I can still picture the debriefing, my memory is fuzzy on the crucial point of what I did with the tape. Betty and I flew to Alaska the next week and vacationed there for a month. If I followed my usual practice I would have given the tape to one of my assistant editors or to one of the Watergate reporters. Some logical recipients on the staff have died; none of the others remembers the tape. Regardless, there is no point in placing blame on any member of the staff. I could have screwed up completely and tossed the tape into a drawer and never thought about it again. That is inconceivable. Certainly one of the first questions I would have asked on returning from Alaska would have been about the tape. The fact is that I bear major responsibility for our failure to follow up on our best opportunity for an early Watergate breakthrough. We had more than a month to work on Segretti even after I returned from vacation, before Woodward and Bernstein heard of the man and before the *Post* published the story on the massive spying operation on October 10.

I should have circulated Smith's debriefing to all our Watergate reporters. It would never have been lost with all those ears hearing it. What is clear is that Gray's mention of a big fish like Mitchell seemed more important than that of a minnow like Segretti. Mitchell was more likely to lead to the biggest fish of all, the president. (The *Post* must have reached the same conclusion when it buried Segretti deep in its article.)

Lacking confirmation, we would, of course, hold back publication of the tips about the White House and Mitchell's involvement even though the material came from such a high source. Gray, on the job only a few weeks, was higher, but probably not as knowledgeable, as Felt, who had spent decades at the FBI and was looking at all documents on the investigation.

Many editors talk of demanding double or even triple sourcing, but the temptation to use a single anonymous source is often too great on a story involving the president, especially if the president is disliked and is antimedia, as Nixon was. Our credibility was too precious to sacrifice, even for a beat of such proportions. As a guardian of that credibility—the *Times* had become my substitute for religion—I was not going to commit the cardinal sin of betrayal.

As I sought to make clear, the lesson of the Pentagon Papers went beyond distrusting government sources. Whistleblowers should also be distrusted and should be checked just as vigorously, because they almost always want to advance their own agenda. I told a panel on government secrecy at New York University's Center for International Studies on February 24, 1973, that since the Pentagon Papers the press tended to believe dissident information and play it up without adequate checking.

We will never know how far Gray, who is dead, would have gone in speaking to Bob Smith. Gray's son, Ed Gray, checked his father's records and confirms the lunch with Smith at the Sans Souci, but insists that he would never have leaked any secrets. "That I would not do," Patrick Gray says in the book his son Ed Gray put together from his father's writings.[6]

Patrick Gray was committed to Nixon even to the point of giving FBI files to White House counsel John W. Dean and of destroying documents taken from the White House safe of E. Howard Hunt Jr., another member of the dirty tricks group. The files, which the Gray book says he did not read but insists they did not concern Watergate because he glanced at them to make sure, were at Gray's Connecticut home when he lunched with Smith. Perhaps, knowing what was going on, he was weighing his options. It was not until months later, in December, that he burned the documents with the family's Christmas trash.

Since Felt disclosed that he was Deep Throat I have speculated over a situation in which the two top FBI officials were both leaking on Watergate, Felt to the *Post* and Gray to the *Times,* each for his own interest, Felt perhaps in revenge for not getting appointed director, or, as Woodward thought, to protect the FBI, and Gray perhaps to protect his legacy after he found out the White House involvement in the cover-up. Patrick Gray does say in the book that he and Smith "had become quite friendly" but does not disclose what they talked about.

Would Felt and Gray leaks have dovetailed? Would they have found each other out? Hollywood could make a drama—maybe a comedy—out of the possibilities. What I am certain of is that Gray would never have been able to mislead Bob Smith if he had tried.

Years later, Robert Redford asked me at a *Boston Globe* lobster lunch at the Ritz (he paid) why the *Times* had not done better on Watergate. Woodward and Bernstein, he said, had feared Walter Rugaber more than any other rival. Without mentioning the Gray lunch, I told him that the *Times* lacked a tradition of investigative reporting and that our staff had little experience in breaking off from their regular beats for team reporting. That was not a complete answer.

A better answer is that from the top editors on down we all shared in the blame. A particular reporter or editor was not the goat—not Walter

Rugaber, not Bob Semple, not Max Frankel, not Gene Roberts, not Bob Phelps, not Abe Rosenthal. The basic reason for our poor performance was institutional. Our reporters and editors were assigned to Washington to cover national and foreign affairs, not crimes. (Note that the *Post's* national staff, its counterpart to the *Times* Washington bureau, pooh-poohed Woodward and Bernstein's stories. The two *Post* reporters were outsiders; they had to be continually briefed on how government worked.)

Moreover, controlling us all at the bureau was a reluctance to take any risk that would damage the *Times's* credibility.

It is true that we also had operational dysfunctions. Except for Rugaber, our reporters were working the story part time in 1972, giving priority to regular coverage. After his initial flurry, Szulc returned to the diplomatic beat. Semple was too busy with day-to-day coverage of the White House to devote much attention to Watergate. New reporters were finding their way around the Justice Department. Seymour Hersh, who wrote a number of exclusives about Vietnam in mid-1972, says he nearly quit when Frankel, then bureau chief, rejected his proposals for Watergate stories. Denny Walsh, who had recently joined the bureau and had excellent FBI sources, responded as investigative reporters usually do in such cases: he wanted to develop his own stories on other subjects and not follow another paper's lead. In addition, nobody at the bureau wanted to impinge on Rugaber. Individual responsibility was the maxim.

Moreover, most of our reporting was by phone at a time when fear of eavesdropping permeated Washington. It is a weak excuse to say that I prodded reporters to try to talk to White House staffers and Justice Department officials at their homes at night, arguing that with wiretaps so common, no one wanted to speak confidentially at their office or over any phone. I could have pushed them harder to ring doorbells, perhaps by ringing some bells myself. And, we did not have Felt. As a result, we were outsourced.

Significantly, I didn't devote myself sufficiently to the story. I spent too much time on other news and other problems. I tried to do it all. As a result our coverage lacked the leadership it needed. While I was in daily contact with the reporters and knew what they were doing I should have been constantly going over the information we had, thinking of leads, engaging in a constant dialogue on Watergate. The *Post* moved Sussman from the city desk to do just that and it paid off. It was understandable why an experienced editor should hold the hands of two inexperienced reporters. At the *Times* I did not think veteran reporters would have accepted hand-holding.

Despite our problems, the *Times* could have beaten the *Post* on all three key revelations that marked Woodward and Bernstein's superb work in 1972—Nixon campaign money going to a Watergate burglar, attorney general Mitchell's control of a secret fund to spy on Democrats, and the massive effort to sabotage the Democratic campaign. With more sustained and passionate leadership from me, a little luck, and tougher reporting, we might have broken through in the fall of 1972 and Woodward and Bernstein would have been following the *Times*, instead of vice versa. The accepted conclusion about the *Times* coverage of Watergate is that we just "blew it." I would not dispute that insofar as the fall of 1972 is concerned. The *Post* certainly deserved its 1973 Pulitzer Prize for Woodward and Bernstein's work. There is no question that the *Post* opened up the case, and, of vital importance, kept it open with story after story.

The next year, however, tells a different story.

# 14. Watergate Two
## How the *Times* Beat the *Post*

**As important as they were,** the 1972 Watergate revelations did little to damage President Nixon's popularity. Voters believed the Republicans were doing what both major parties had done for years, just trying to disrupt their rival's campaign. To the public, all the *Washington Post* brought to light were political tricks by Nixon's campaign forces in an election year. People seemed to think that the tactics were reprehensible, but understandable because the Democrats were just as bad. The hints of White House involvement extended only to the president's advisers; there was no proof that Nixon knew what was going on. Granted, sometimes in their exuberance, political operatives went too far, but, Nixon, with his vast responsibility as president, could not be expected to know every detail of his campaign for reelection.

Except for diehard supporters of the Democratic ticket, Senator George S. McGovern for president and Senator Edmund S. Muskie for vice president, few seemed upset by the Republican tactics. Nixon maintained a 60 percent share of public opinion polls right through late summer and fall, with little variation despite the *Post* revelations. A *New York Times*/Yankelovich survey published two weeks before the election found that Watergate did not appear to swing many voters to McGovern. Asked whether either candidate had conducted a "dirty and unscrupulous campaign," slightly more respondents chose McGovern than Nixon. The president's landslide victory confirmed the ineffectual impact of the Watergate findings up to that time. In fact, postelection polls showed that 36 percent of Democrats deserted their party to vote for Nixon.

Shortly after the election, the New England Society of Newspaper Editors invited me to speak to counterbalance a talk by Charles W. Colson, counsel to the president, known for a remark he probably never made— that he would walk on his grandmother's grave if it would help Nixon. He was never charged with any Watergate crime but spent a short time in prison for planning the burglary of the office of Daniel Ellsberg's psychiatrist, an offense he volunteered to the prosecutor. Colson's short time in prison led to his conversion to evangelical Christianity and the devotion of the rest of his life to helping prisoners.

In his speech on November 11 Colson denounced the *Washington Post's* Watergate stories as "election year smears." In the maddening style of Nixon and his supporters, Colson said that the tragedy of the *Post's* handling of Watergate "is that public confidence was probably eroded 'somewhat' not just in the *Post* but also in the institutions of government." Speaking at a different session, I noted administration efforts to block reporters' efforts and expressed dismay, in the aftermath of the election, that when the press did dig out the truth it had little impact. "Readers do not believe us."

Just before the election Woodward and Bernstein had played into the hands of doubters with a serious error; Simons later called it the "only blemish" on their record.[1] Their article on October 25 reported that grand jury testimony listed H. R. Haldeman, Nixon's chief of staff, as one of the officials in control of the funds to sabotage the McGovern campaign. The major source for the story, which took the sabotage campaign dangerously close to the Oval Office, was former campaign treasurer Hugh W. Sloan Jr., who publicly denied its accuracy. The White House roundly condemned the *Post* and the two reporters worried that they might have to resign.

Disturbing to Simons was Bernstein's trick to confirm the Haldeman story before publication. When a Justice Department official said in a phone conversation that he could not comment on the report, Bernstein said he would count to ten. If the official thought the story should be held he would hang up before the count reached ten. If he thought it was okay he would stay on the line. He stayed on the line and Bernstein gave thumbs up to the editors. However, the official had mixed the signals, thus indicating there was something wrong with the story. The *Post's* image had been damaged even though *Time* magazine a few days later confirmed the basic charge, that Haldeman had authority to make payments from the fund, while noting that the *Post* had erred only in saying that the information had come from grand jury testimony.

To some, the error, even though technical, supported their doubts about the reporters and it certainly added to mine. As Simons recalled, "I think people were waiting for us to fall on our face and I think that's why we were so cautious." Specifically, executive editor Bradlee and managing editor Simons told *Post* publisher Katharine Graham of their fears that the administration might be setting them up for scandals based on income tax returns, phone tapping, computer searches, even kidnapping children, selling dope, or getting compromised sexually.

The 1972 election put a damper on the press. The people had spoken. Why should a spiteful press not allow the president a chance to carry out the mandate of his awesome victory instead of hampering him with nitpicking questions about the campaign? Let the justice system handle that "third-rate burglary," as the White House called it. Caution set in. For nearly six weeks Woodward and Bernstein did not write an exclusive Watergate story. Critics were saying that the lack of new disclosures proved that the *Post* had really been working for McGovern. Thus Watergate was over. No one was going to talk. Once more Simons worried not just that the truth would never be known but, "My God, what happens if we're wrong?"

Feeling the pressure, Bradlee would not give up, urging the two reporters to produce new disclosures. Finally, on December 8, they broke the dry spell with a story about a secret White House telephone billed to the Arlington, Virginia, secretary of the plumbers. *Post* editors did not think much of it, but Bradlee, who graded it as B-minus, put it on page one in an attempt to get the pot boiling again. He kept reminding the reporters "this is the hardest hardball that's ever been played in this town."

He pushed too hard. In early December, Woodward, under pressure, surreptitiously obtained the names of Watergate grand jurors from court records. With Bradlee's reluctant permission[2]—"No beating anyone over the head, no pressure, none of that cajoling"—Woodward and Bernstein attempted to get a half dozen jurors to talk. One juror told the prosecutors, who informed U.S. Judge John J. Sirica. The *Post*'s high-powered attorney, Edward Bennett Williams, succeeded in persuading Sirica not to send the reporters to jail for trying to get grand jurors to violate their oath of secrecy. Fortunately for the two, none of the jurors talked.

A few days later, however, prosecutors informed Williams that a potential witness had complained that Woodward had posed as an FBI agent, possibly violating Sirica's ban on talking to witnesses. Probably acting on Williams's advice, Bradlee ordered the reporters to stop digging new ground. It was the first time since summer that they had been called off the hunt.

Up to this point the *Post* had not asked lawyers for advice on the articles, which is strange because so many of the stories cited anonymous sources and lacked documentary evidence. "That's the difference between Watergate and the Pentagon Papers," Simons told Woodward and Bernstein. "Pentagon Papers was wow, damn, you had the lawyers involved the first day . . . Nothing like that here . . . Katharine [Graham] was informed but more informationally. Are we doing right, or are you nervous about this? And, you know, we never called the lawyers and said . . . what's the legal view of this?"

To Simons, the *Post* just slipped into the story by increments, one article after another. "It's like being in a bathtub where, scientifically, you can turn the [hot} water [up] a little bit at a time and burn yourself to death without realizing it because the increments are so small that the body doesn't understand."

At a lunch on January 8, 1973, the first day of the trial of the burglars, Katharine Graham asked Woodward what was going to happen. "I mean, are we ever going to know about all of this?" Despondent, Woodward replied that he and Bernstein weren't sure the truth would ever come out.[3]

Who had persuaded Bradlee to put the reporters on a leash? Was it Williams? Had Graham raised serious questions about going too far? Or had the hardball editor lost his nerve? Would another miscue ruin the fine work Woodward and Bernstein had done in the autumn and give Nixon the opportunity to escape only slightly scathed by the scandal? Was this one of those times when the *Post* invoked what Simons called its "code of responsibility" to call a truce with the Nixon administration and "go out of our way to prevent bloodshed?" Perhaps Bradlee shrewdly concluded that the best policy was to let the rest of the media carry more of the load. Safety in numbers provided more legitimacy for the *Post*. If the past was any guide, he could count on Washington reporters eventually to follow their herd instinct. So far the instinct had barely kicked in.

As Simons noted, Watergate was the only time a big story in memory had failed to set off the pack. To Woodward, who had worked night and day for every development, the reason was simple: the story was too hard to get. The *Post* had outsourced the competition. That was true even though we did not know of the existence of a Deep Throat. Simons thought that negative tittle-tattle from *Post* reporters about Woodward and Bernstein served to warn competitors off. He singled out me, as a harbinger of the *Times*, which all Washington news bureaus read, "peeing on the story," apparently because of criticisms I had made of the *Post*. I had said it was the editor's job to make sure the stories were sound. I was especially concerned about the anonymous sources and lack of documents and specifics. We wondered when the *Post* would publish documents to support its charges. As the months went by and it didn't, our suspicions grew.

We do not know why the *Post* eased up in the winter of 1972–73, but by spring, with an ever-leaky Congress gathering facts on Watergate, the herd was in stampede. Simons used another metaphor, referring to the period as the "shark frenzy," with much of the media tearing pieces from the big fish the *Post* had wounded. Leading the attack in late winter and early spring was Seymour Hersh of the *Times*. In effect, he practically took the story away from the *Post*.

Convinced that Clifton Daniel, the new *Times* bureau chief, would support him where he felt Frankel had not, Hersh had been writing Watergate stories for months. To start him off, the London-tailored Daniel had given the khakis-and-sneakers Hersh a box of Brooks Brothers shirts and sweaters.

For weeks Hersh wrote exclusive stories about the scandal. On January 14 he disclosed that four of the five defendants in the first Watergate trial were still being paid. The next day he reported that the four were under great pressure to plead guilty. On January 29 he wrote in a page

16. Clifton Daniel, who bounced back gracefully to become Washington bureau chief after losing the top editor's job, chatting with me at a party at Columbia University, where I received an alumni award. Photographer unknown.

one story that Dwight L. Chapin, head of the Republican espionage effort, was being forced out as Nixon's appointments secretary. The following day he revealed that the FBI had failed to fully investigate Segretti's sabotage operations although it knew of some of his activities within weeks of the Watergate break-in. On February 7, a page one story reported the first direct link between a White House official and the undercover intelligence operation. On February 8 another Hersh page one story said that the FBI had learned that a Nixon aide had told the president's personal attorney to pay Segretti for his sabotaging of Democrats. And on February 9, Hersh had still another front-page article; this one told of a new prosecution move to discover high-level involvement in the case.

Hersh stayed on Watergate and in a remarkable display of investigative skill, produced significant stories while still reporting on such other events as attempts to discipline American prisoners in Vietnam who opposed the war. As Denny Walsh, another *Times* investigative reporter, marveled at the time, "Sy walks the razor's edge day after day and produces good stories without once getting even nicked" with an error.

This was a period when the *Post* reporters felt especially low. "The more we've written, the more we've found our role is lessened," Woodward told Simons. "That's unfair," Simons admonished him. "Don't diminish your own role. Don't be so enamored with the idea of being good guys . . . That guy at the *Star* is good and those guys at the *Times*, they're really good. Some are not." He then gave this appraisal of Sy Hersh: "Sy Hersh is good but not good. I mean there's the good side and the bad side. Sy does some things that I wouldn't tolerate on my newspaper. Blackmail. And, you know, I just wouldn't. That's not my idea of what professional journalism is all about. And yet I like Sy and I've liked him for a long time."

Conceding that "we were hurting" from revelations by the competition, Simons quickly added, "If you had removed Hersh from that goddam scene entirely you [Woodward and Bernstein] wouldn't be that bad. I don't know whose nose he had a ring in, but"—and never finished the sentence.

By April 1973, increasingly frustrated, Woodward and Bernstein sought help from an unlikely place, the rival whom it had bested the year before, the *New York Times*.

Through an intermediary, they invited Hersh to dinner April 8 at the Post House, a hangout for reporters and editors. Curious, but also careful, Hersh brought along John Crewdson, the intern who had become a staff reporter in February.

At the dinner, the *Post* reporters said that they needed more competition if they were going to convince their editors that the story wasn't over; a lot of questions remained unanswered. Crewdson, who soon wrote some important Watergate articles, was astonished that *Post* reporters would make such a blatant appeal to a competing paper.

According to *All the President's Men*, the discussion turned to witnesses and principals in Watergate, with all those at the table taking care not to be too candid.

In the 1973 interview with Simons, Woodward said he and Bernstein had had "a couple of dinners" with Hersh (who remembers only one) in the previous months. He said they had not exchanged information and characterized the discussions as "a very subtle sort of, well, what do you think of that story, what do you think of so and so." He added, "and it's been helpful."

As the April 8 dinner ended, Bernstein kiddingly asked Hersh what story they would read when the list of the *Times* front page stories arrived at the *Post* that night.

"Just a little something," Hersh said.

That "little something" was a story the *Post* team had vainly tried to get: James W. McCord Jr., one of the burglars, had testified that the Committee for the Re-election of the President had paid the conspirators to keep silent.

It's difficult to believe that in the intensely competitive atmosphere of Washington journalism that Woodward and Bernstein had arranged the dinner to ask the *Times* to push harder. More likely, they were on a fishing expedition, not passing up any possibility of a tip. They certainly knew from reading the competition that the *Times* had not stopped seeking Watergate answers. How much competition did Woodward and Bernstein want?

If I had known about the Woodward-Bernstein invitation to dinner, I would have been disturbed. I did not believe in sharing information except of a most basic kind, like the spelling of a name. Apparently neither Hersh nor the *Post* reporters shared any vital information. Nevertheless, the meeting smacked of ganging up on the administration. I did not believe in that.

Neither did Simons. When Bernstein asked Simons if he saw any way that pooling would have been justified, the editor replied: "Well, it so goes against the sharp edge of what it's all about, which is competition, that I would have been dead set against it." Bernstein persisted: "Well, we would have been, too," but noted that the administration had been lying. Asking, "Is your responsibility to the truth?" Bernstein said that if he, Woodward, Hersh, and Sandy Smith of *Time* magazine had pooled their information "we probably could have really broken the whole thing." Simons said that the revelations come out without pooling because of the cumulative effect of one publication's building on another.

Sometimes New York editors refused to print Hersh's findings. Once while I was in New York Sy flew up and we worked out of Tom Wicker's office. Managing editor Rosenthal refused to run the story, which was based on unnamed sources in the prosecutor's office and the Cubans' lawyers. Abe said he wanted better sourcing. For two days I watched close-up while Sy worked that story. Whipsawing his sources, he would get the defense lawyers on the phone and tell them that the Cubans were going to be railroaded unless he got more information. Then he would call the prosecutors, inform them, "I was just talking to the slime," and prod them for more material. This was not blackmail to me. In that instance, Sy could not come up with a story that Abe would run. Abe wanted not just two sources, but three.

As Hersh sipped a martini and I my usual Campari on an Eastern Airlines shuttle returning to Washington, he said, referring to his exclusive 1969 story on American massacre of Vietnamese civilians at My Lai, "You know, Bob, when I walked into that barracks and that guy [Lt. William Calley Jr., later convicted in the killings] started talking, I knew he was telling the truth. I didn't need second and third sources. I just knew. And I know this story is right, too." Weeks later parts of the rejected story ran elsewhere.

Sy and I worked well together. Even on the rare occasions when I edited his stories hard he was more interested in the finished product than in retaining his exact wording. On one occasion, working in my office, I was cutting up his story so much that I sent it to my assistant, Dana Little, in the newsroom for retyping before putting it on the wire to New York. From time to time Sy leaned over Dana's shoulder, reading the final version. He wanted to make sure I had not written errors into his copy. Suddenly Dana, beautiful, prim, and Vassar-educated, burst into my office, Sy closely following.

"He said I fucked up," she said, eyes blazing.

"She did," Sy answered.

I was so startled to hear Dana, so proper in manner and appearance, use such language that I wanted to laugh. I had told her she would have to marry a diplomat to meet her high standards. To settle the dispute, I said that my editing scratches and arrows were to blame. (I was right about Dana; she did marry a diplomat; retired, they live in San Miguel de Allende in Mexico.)

Other *Times* staffers were also doing good work. Daniel showed his continued interest by inviting Leon Jaworski, who had taken over prosecution on the case, to a lunch at the F Street Club. Jaworski told us his plans for indictments. Rugaber was covering the trials of the burglars and writing lucid perspectives putting developments in context. James Naughton, Christopher Lydon, and others were keeping watch on Congress. Russell Baker wrote some humorous columns on the scandal, including one on March 19 titled "Feeling C.R.E.E.P.Y." in which Nixon supporter "Titcomb Barnes" moaned that he felt like the only person in America who had not contributed $200,000 to the president's reelection campaign. Even Scotty Reston had gotten tough.

Although he was still a cub reporter, Crewdson plowed new ground on the scandal with a series of articles, beginning May 11 on the Nixon administration's wiretapping. He tracked down a senior FBI official directly involved in arranging the wiretaps and funneling the reports to the White House. The official, who had retired, revealed that for two years beginning in 1969 the agents had tapped telephones of reporters at the *New York Times*, the *Washington Post*, and the *Sunday Times* of London. The wiretap targets also included six members of the National Security Council and three high-ranking Foreign Service officers. Later Crewdson found that the surveillance also involved officials without access to secret information.

In early June, Crewdson and Lydon obtained a copy of the top-secret Huston plan, a proposal to expand domestic intelligence gathering. The story said that Nixon had approved the plan in 1970 although cautioned that parts of it were clearly illegal. Nixon said he had rescinded his approval five days after he ordered it put into operation because J. Edgar Hoover, then FBI director, had opposed it. The broad outline of the plan had been published earlier; Crewdson laid out the details, including burglary, electronic surveillance, and opening of mails, the targets being foreign embassies, college students, and left-wing protest groups.

Crewdson and Lydon had no trouble in getting the document. They flew to Indianapolis, interviewed Tom Charles Huston, who had left his job as a presidential assistant to practice law. When they asked for a copy of the plan, he shrugged, pulled it from his files and handed it to them. As they left the office, the reporters looked at each other and said, almost simultaneously, "Did he just do what I think he did?" After celebrating at an ice cream parlor—they were not grizzled reporters—they flew back to Washington, where Crewdson wrote the story the next day. We took pleasure in reading the *Post* version of the story, which quoted the *Times*. It began on page one with a two-column headline and continued inside for four columns. The next day the *Post* picked up excerpts of the plan from the *Times*.

In July, Crewdson, with the aid of six other *Times* reporters, produced two lengthy articles pulling together the elements of the sabotage programs run by Donald Segretti and Jeb Stuart Magruder. Segretti had been mentioned in previous stories, first by the *Post*, but the resourceful Crewdson talked a top-ranking FBI official into giving him several thousand pages of the agency's Segretti investigation. These stories provided an extraordinary account of the most extensive attempt in American history by a political party to subvert its opposition through covert attacks. Terrified that security guards might check him, he walked out of the J. Edgar Hoover building with his briefcase stuffed with the documents. A few hours later he returned the files to his source at a prearranged place outside the Justice Department.

Thus the *Times* completed the Segretti story that Simons said the *Post* had never finished.

Following up his May report on wiretapping, Crewdson learned in early August that the Nixon administration had ordered a wiretap on the telephone of William Safire when he was a speechwriter for the president. This disclosure cleared Safire, who had been hired as a columnist by the *Times*, of suspicion within the paper that he might have known about or even been involved in the Watergate cover-up. While still in the White House, Safire complained to Simons about the *Post*'s Watergate coverage. They had lunch at the Cantina d'Italia the day after Nixon's big election victory. Here's Simons's account as he told it to Woodward and Bernstein in 1973:

> Bill . . . just took my head off on what the president was mad about and what he implied what he was mad about and what the White House was mad about and how could we, The *Washington Post*, attack, just destroy

such a sweet nice guy like Dwight Chapin, who was just a nice, innocent boy. And how could we do that to Ken Clawson, who is suffering from diabetes. It sort of destroyed him and what kind of a newspaper were we? These were honorable people.

Chapin, the president's appointments secretary, had hired Segretti to disrupt the Democratic campaign. Clawson had been named by the *Post* as the author of a fake letter accusing Democratic Senator Edmund Muskie of making disparaging remarks about French Canadians.

Safire retired as an op-ed columnist in January 2005 after writing more than 3,000 columns and winning a Pulitzer Prize.

Without taking any credit from the *Post* a proper perspective of the first year of Watergate coverage must include, in addition to the *New York Times,* the *Los Angeles Times* and *Time* magazine. On October 4, Jack Nelson and Ronald J. Ostrow of the *Los Angeles Times* had the first interview with Alfred C. Baldwin III, who operated electronic eavesdropping devices as part of the Watergate operation. A former FBI man, Baldwin was a key government source. Sandy Smith of *Time* magazine scored a number of beats on FBI findings. He wrote the article correcting the Haldeman story that the *Post* had messed up.

The *Post* locked on to CREEP's secret fund to disrupt the Democratic campaign in 1972 and stayed on politics. The "dirty tricks" did not violate the law in the opinion of legal authorities. Not one of the *Post*'s exclusives that broke open the case and for which it won its Pulitzer Prize dealt with a subject involved in the three counts of impeachment drawn up by the House Judiciary Committee—obstruction of justice, especially the cover-up; abuse of power, including wiretaps; and contempt of Congress by refusal to give the Oval Office tapes to the House Judiciary Committee.

As late as April 18, James Reston noted that none of the disclosures had actually tied the president to the scandal. He wrote in his column:

Everything is suspected here now, but nothing has been proved. The distinction is important. It is ten months precisely to the day since the five men were arrested for burglaring and bugging the Democratic headquarters at the Watergate, and ever since then, the admitted crime has been political instead of judicial.

These observations are not designed to undercut the *Post*. Woodward and Bernstein excelled in the hardest kind of journalistic detective work, digging into the executive branch, which, in its effort to cover up the crimes, imposed strict secrecy on officials and repeatedly lied about what had gone on. The *Post* reporters broke through this stone wall to produce their key articles in the fall of 1972.

Moreover, the *Post*'s relentless beating on Watergate, with Bradlee cheerleading, undoubtedly placed the scandal on the national agenda and kept it there, even when there were no important developments, and led to stories by others in the media and to congressional investigations.

These conclusions conform to the *Post*'s own Watergate chronology as posted on its Web site. Not until June 3 do the 1973 entries indicate a major *Post* exclusive. That was the story that John Dean, when White House counsel, had discussed the cover-up with Nixon at least thirty-five times. Walter Rugaber reported the same story in part the same day in the *Times*. These conclusions do show that the *Times* led the field in Watergate in 1973. We didn't "blow it" the second time around; we did better than anyone else.

Having staked out that claim, I would not dream of contending that we deserved a share of the 1973 Pulitzer Prize for Watergate. The *Post* was in a class by itself. The year before, however, the *Post* asked to be named co-winner with the *Times* for the 1972 Pulitzer Prize for publishing the Pentagon Papers. The attempt failed. The *Times* broke the story five days before the *Post* published its excerpts.

As most who have studied the scandal generally agree, none of the media, not the *Post*, not the *Times*, not any other journalistic outlet, can take credit for bringing about the first presidential resignation in history. The big break came in mid-March 1973, when James McCord, one of the Watergate burglars, agreed to talk. The American governmental system did the rest. The Senate Select Committee to Investigate Campaign Practices headed by Senator Samuel J. Ervin held hearings that brought out the administration's crimes, the House drew up its three impeachment counts, and, facing certain conviction in the Senate, Nixon resigned on August 8, 1974.

In a letter to Woodward and Bernstein thanking them for inscribing her copy of their book, Katharine Graham said "we must all concede" that "we didn't bring him down." The courts, grand juries, and congressional committees did. But she added: "It was still an extraordinary, gutsy, hard, brilliant piece of journalism."[4]

Both the *Times* and the *Post* might have scored beats on another important development. In late winter of 1972–73 or early spring of 1973—the exact date is uncertain—Daniel summoned a number of us to his office. There, bureau photographer Mike Lien, who had become friendly with the Secret Service while taking pictures of Nixon, and Nick Chinetti, a young New Yorker who was Lien's assistant, said one of the agents told them that the president's conversations in the Oval Office were tape-recorded. Hersh debriefed Chinetti in Fran O'Brien's, a noisy Irish singles bar on L Street. Hersh then sought out John D. Ehrlichman, Nixon's assistant for domestic affairs, and other high officials, but could not break through the wall of secrecy.

We were not surprised, then, when John Dean told the Senate investigating committee on June 25 of his suspicion of Oval Office taping. For the next three weeks neither the *Times* nor the *Post* nor anyone else could confirm Dean's suspicion, although we all understood that tapes could prove either that Dean was lying about the president's involvement or they could provide the "smoking gun" that would bring him down.

Senator Ervin's committee, with its subpoena power, did what the media could not do. On July 16 Alexander Butterfield, a deputy assistant to the president, testified that the Oval Office was taped.

The *Post* also came close to getting that story earlier. In *All the President's Men*, Woodward wrote of learning about the taping "strictly off the record" two days before Butterfield's testimony, but Bradlee, still in his hold-back stage, discouraged aggressive pursuit. "I wouldn't bust one on it," he advised Woodward, in another indication that the legendary hard-charging Bradlee was worried that the two reporters were going too far.[5]

Important to understanding the situation, however, was the circus atmosphere pervading Washington at the time. Every day new facts, new rumors, new revelations, new charges, new counter-charges boiled up from Congress, from the White House, from prosecutors, from lawyers, from every part of the political establishment. Journalists are trained to decide which of the multitude of possibilities should be pursued. All of us tried and all had many near-misses.

Simons, of course, faced the same problem as the rest of us. He told the two reporters he wanted to follow up everything, knowing they couldn't. "The fact that we had all these goddamn leads and which do you follow, so that the string doesn't end half-way up the mountain?"

Caution certainly clouded my view of *Post* stories. Over the years I had learned to distrust some of its reports, especially in the Style section, too often based on rumors at cocktail parties and anonymous sources. I didn't want the *Times* to get caught out on a limb with a series of shoot-from-the-hip false stories accusing the president of the United States of criminal behavior. The *Times* had always valued its integrity more than the scoop mentality that motivates some journalists.

Of course I worried as Woodward and Bernstein churned out their exclusives. It was difficult to be patient. On two separate occasions in 1972 I asked *Times* veterans to check with their *Post* counterparts to see what they thought of rumors that the two unproved reporters were off base. Word came back to me that experienced *Post* reporters were concerned that Woodward and Bernstein were leading their paper into deep trouble. In other words, senior *Post* staffers doubted the accuracy of the disclosures. With such doubt in the *Post* newsroom, I was especially cautious. Looking back, I realize that the sources we checked were reporters from Richard Harwood's national desk who thought they, not two city desk men, should be handling the story.

As late as February 1973, I was quoted as speaking critically of the *Post*'s Watergate coverage. In an article in the *Washington Monthly* Barbara Raskin wrote:

> Strained or restrained by Rosenthal's conservative centralized government, Phelps claimed the *Post* was making "bridges" between the evidence they gathered and the implications they drew and printed from it. "The editors at the *Post* should have stopped the Watergate reporters from going on too long without hard facts," Phelps said. "That's the editor's job."[6]

That same article described me as sitting at the front of the newsroom "gazing at the scene like a Norman Rockwell grandmother serving Thanksgiving turkey to her family." Her description of me may or may not have been accurate but I know how constantly worried I was that the *Post* would break another story. In particular, I remember walking through the newsroom mumbling "murder in the White House" after hearing a rumor that a young woman had been found dead there. Neither the *Times* nor any other newspaper could discover any truth to that rumor.

The *Washington Monthly* was wrong regarding Rosenthal pressure. At no time did Abe restrain our investigation; in fact, he seldom called me. Nor did Max Frankel, the bureau chief, nor Gene Roberts, the national editor, show special interest. My chief contact was with David Jones, the assistant national editor. My strongest critic was my wife. On sheer instinct, Betty read truth into phone calls to reporters from John Mitchell's wife, Martha, hinting that administration officials were lying about Watergate. Bob Semple talked to Martha but got no real tips, let alone solid information. He did get a feature story.

When New York editors did complain about the *Post* beats, I said I would welcome any help we could get. Metropolitan editor Arthur Gelb sent Nick Gage, an investigative reporter, to Washington. After writing a good story based on tapes of Nixon excoriating deputy attorney general Richard G. Kleindienst, he returned to New York and told Gelb that the Washington bureau didn't even have the phone number of the Washington police, a statement of ridicule patently untrue. Gelb wrote in his memoirs that Rosenthal had thought of sending him to Washington to run the investigation. Gelb also said that Rosenthal thought he should have removed Frankel as bureau chief. Either move would have set off an uproar in the bureau similar to that during the Wicker affair.[7] This was our counterpart to the *Post*'s national desk-city desk rivalry.

In idle moments, I have sometimes wondered whether the *Post* would have covered Watergate as vigorously as it did if Scotty Reston had accepted an offer in 1964 to be its editor. In that year the recently widowed Katharine Graham made a personal appeal to Scotty and his wife Sally:

> I have thought hard about our talks. They have been indefinite only because I wanted to work out what was best for you, since what is best for us is to have you here advising me and advising us, and being part of the *Washington Post* . . . I am arguing hard that you can be with us; that

we have always wanted you and want you even more now that we are
without Phil.[8]

Philip Graham had tried a number of times to lure Reston to the *Post*. In
fact, the Grahams were so close to the Restons that they had "willed" their
children to them in case of death. The widow-in-distress's plea touched
Scotty.

Moreover, Scotty's role model, Walter Lippmann, had urged him to
join the *Post*. Lippmann argued that the *Times* had long been recognized
as the country's best newspaper. All Reston could do was carry on the tradition. He could make a larger contribution, Lippmann said, by going to
the *Post*, which was just on its way to becoming a great newspaper.[9]

After much anguish, Reston's affection for the *Times* and the Sulzberger family won out. "I just can't do it," he wrote Graham.

She then appointed Bradlee to the job. Bradlee was diametrically
opposite Reston in style, interest, and substance as an editor. Much earlier,
when Bradlee was writing for *Newsweek*, he had been mentioned to Reston
by a *Times* reporter as someone the *Times* might want to consider hiring.
Having heard of Ben's high-flying life, the Calvinist Reston replied that he
had heard that Bradlee was a cad.

What if Reston had accepted Graham's offer? Certainly the *Post* would
have been a different paper. Bradlee opened up the writing and reporting,
giving free play to rumors. He was tough but sympathetic on Woodward
and Bernstein. I doubt that Scotty, who listened to conservative old-timers,
would have kept Woodward and Bernstein as lead reporters on the story.
The man who blocked my request to file a simple Freedom of Information
case because it might anger Nixon would hardly have permitted a hard-
charging anonymous-source attack on the president.

As a result of Watergate, journalism changed, not just in Washington,
but also throughout the country. Inspired by Woodward and Bernstein's
exclusives, reporters used investigative techniques every day, not just in
long undercover operations. Young journalists especially emulated the
two reporters, seeking the "real story" behind the news. Their aggressive
approach raised standards.

Unfortunately too many editors and reporters failed to extend the
Pentagon Papers lesson—don't trust the government—to nongovernment

sources, particularly to dissidents. Confrontation became an accepted style; reporters began to argue with sources, as I discovered at the *Boston Globe.*

At the *Times,* some editors vowed never to play catch-up again. While they were in charge no paper would beat the *Times* on an important story. They did not realize that, to a great extent, the *Times,* in its moves to become a national paper, had forced other papers to devote more resources, hiring better reporters and editors, to meet the competition. For many reasons some of the best people preferred the *Chicago Tribune,* the *Wall Street Journal,* the *Los Angeles Times,* the *Philadelphia Inquirer,* and the *Washington Post.* These journalists made the *Times* goal of never getting beat impossible to achieve. Often overlooked is that a significant number of them left the *Times* because of wider opportunities elsewhere.

Gene Roberts is the prime example of how the *Times* fed talent into competing papers. He resigned as the *Times* national editor to take over the *Philadelphia Inquirer* in 1972. In the two decades he ran the Inquirer it won seventeen Pulitzer prizes with the aid of former *Times* people, especially James Naughton, who became managing editor. Bill Kovach left the *Times* to run the *Atlanta Journal-Constitution* and within two years had earned two Pulitzers. Al Shuster became foreign news editor of the *Los Angeles Times.* John Crewdson moved to the *Chicago Tribune,* as did editor-reporter Douglas Kneeland. I did my bit at the *Boston Globe.*

For decades Watergate myths have induced some *Times* editors to push reporters to take chances, to write stories relying on inadequate reporting, in effect, to lower standards. Reporters abandoned responsibility in a rush to be first—not just first with the major facts, but also first with the minor details, first with color, first with the best quotations. As a result, the *Times* lost credibility. Thankfully, it has acted to restore those standards while moving more swiftly on breaking stories.

# 15. Imperial Editor— Or Partner Editor?

**In September 1972,** Betty and I went to Alaska on vacation. We had a wonderful time, but midway in the trip, as we returned to Anchorage from a visit to the oil fields of the North Slope, the *Times* Alaska stringer met our plane and said that I had an urgent call from Dave Jones in New York. Gene Roberts had resigned as national editor to become executive editor of the *Philadelphia Inquirer* and Jones had been named to replace him. For the second time I had been passed over.

I thought about this a great deal in the next few months. My career seemed blocked. I had had no quarrel with Roberts and certainly no quarrel with Jones. I saw how much Roberts had improved national coverage and realized the key role that Jones had played as his assistant. But why had I been passed over again? Eventually I heard that when Roberts resigned he had told Rosenthal that if Jones were not appointed national editor he would take Jones with him to Philadelphia. Looking deeper, I concluded that Roberts's warning had been unnecessary. Rosenthal would never appoint me national editor.

Rosenthal was an Imperial Editor. From a business point of view, he was chairman of the board, as Catledge had been, setting the general direction of the paper and shaking up underperforming departments. He was also chief operating officer, as Bernstein had tried to be, deciding each day the content and appearance of the paper. Moreover, at times he also attempted to be the head of every department, intervening to change coverage and the way stories were written. Thus Rosenthal sought to impose his will on every aspect of the editorial process, from setting the direction of the news department to rewriting headlines in the composing room.

He talked about delegation of responsibilities but kept the strings of control tight, an executive style that made it impossible to win the affection of reporters and other editors.

Like so many despots, Abe wanted to be loved. Most *Times* people respected him, but no one ever told me they loved him. Arthur Gelb, his no. 2 man on the metropolitan desk, came closest. No wonder that Gelb said he felt betrayed when Abe, just named as managing editor, appointed Seymour Topping as his assistant managing editor.[1]

Rosenthal's inquiring mind searched everywhere for improving the paper. A good example was religious coverage. He wanted more than routine stories about conventions and contests for church offices. Intrigued, perhaps, by Vatican II's widespread changes in Roman Catholicism, Rosenthal hired John Cogley, editor and columnist of the liberal Roman Catholic magazine *Commonweal,* as religion news editor in 1965. Before this stunning advance, the *Times* approached religious news timidly, fearful, for example, of digging deeply into contentious issues like birth control. Its stylebook gave the Catholic archbishop of New York equal footing with the president of the United States and the governor of New York as persons whose first names and middle initials did not have to be used in first references in articles.

One reporter, George Dugan, covered all religions except Jewish organizations. Because New York City was one-third Jewish, that job fell to Irving (Pat) Spiegel, who was more than a little embarrassed of the beat. He did not want favorable treatment for Jews. When I was working the day national desk he would call in from a convention and timidly ask if he could get a few paragraphs into the paper. For *Times* editors it was easier to run those short items than face a barrage of complaints from Jewish organizations, which, unlike most other religious groups, knew and used the power of protesting to editors.

Without disturbing Dugan and Spiegel, Cogley tackled the big issues, especially those roiling his faith, Roman Catholicism.

Rosenthal maintained a deep interest in religion. At an AP convention in Oklahoma, years after I left the *Times,* he passed up the regular proceedings to interview Oral Roberts, the evangelist. Although a fervent supporter of Israel, he did not, so far as I could see, let his feelings affect *Times* coverage. He told David Shipler, in assigning him to Jerusalem, that it was time for a Jew to cover Israel. Shipler is said to have replied, "But Abe, I'm a Protestant." Shipler won a Pulitzer Prize for his book on Arab and Jewish prejudice.[2] Later, when Abe was a belligerently pro-Israel columnist at New York's *Daily News* and I was editor of *Nieman Reports,* the journalism quarterly at Harvard, I asked him to write an article on the impact of Judaism on him as a journalist. He declined, explaining that he wanted to do that in his memoirs (which, if he wrote them, were never published.)

In all my days in New York and Washington I never once heard anyone at the *Times* complain about religious bias by reporters or editors, except for a jocular protest about South Bend datelines for articles about the University of Notre Dame. The rule at the time was datelines had to be based on a post office and Notre Dame had its own post office.

Sometimes Rosenthal's instincts failed him, with regrettable results. That was true of the "Blood Brothers" story. Junius Griffin, a reporter hired to bring a black perspective to local coverage, wrote about a gang of militant black youths calling themselves "Blood Brothers," who were roaming Harlem streets planning to kill whites. Neither the police nor any other newspaper could find the gang, leading to widespread doubts of its existence.

Despite—perhaps because of—his imperial style and his explosive temper, Abe produced a far better newspaper than the one he took over. His sharp mind, inexhaustible energy, and unwavering determination didn't merely revive the *Times,* he recreated it while stoutly safeguarding the newspaper's ethical standards.

The cost in human terms of this soaring advance was immense. He degraded editors by second-guessing too many of their decisions. He insulted some veteran reporters by constantly ordering rewrites of their stories. The staff began to doubt whether the price to work for the best paper in the world was too high, and some, like Earl Mazo, hired from the *Herald Tribune* Washington bureau to be a top political reporter, left.

Reporters could not be sure where they stood. Murray Seeger, a new reporter from Cleveland, proved himself on general assignment and was transferred to the labor beat. I handled many of his stories on negotiations between the New York newspapers and the printer's union in 1965 and was impressed by his ability as a newcomer to the city to cover such a sensitive story flawlessly. Top editors and management searched his stories every night for suspect passages, but there were few quibbles. As prospects for a strike gained, Rosenthal took Seeger for a walk around the newsroom and assured him, "We want to make sure you come back."

Within a few weeks, Seeger says, "Abe came storming to my desk to announce: 'This is not working out.' He said I was welcome to look for a job elsewhere in the *Times* but I was finished with him. He turned on his heel and left." *Newsweek* quickly hired Seeger and assigned him to Washington. Later, Eileen Shanahan, a *Times* Washington reporter, passed on to Seeger this message from Rosenthal: His treatment of Seeger was one of his "greatest mistakes."

Others learned how to work around Rosenthal. In fact, it was the business department that proposed one of his lasting improvements, expansion of the daily into four sections. At first Rosenthal and Gelb resisted, fearing loss of control to advertisers. Walter Mattson, a senior vice president (later president), and John Pomfret, assistant general manager (later general manager and executive vice president), knew better than to try to force such a change by just arguing economics. Like other newspapers, the *Times* suffered in the severe recession of the 1970s. Mattson and Pomfret had to talk journalism first—how a four-section daily would open up coverage in areas like science, medicine, computers, and the arts.

Rosenthal didn't have to be talked into the nirvana of extra space and a bigger staff. But he and Gelb worried that the news department would lose its independence if it cooperated with the advertising department. That's where Mattson and Pomfret, veteran diplomats in dealing with unions, performed their magic and persuaded Rosenthal to embrace the extra sections. After all, Adolph Ochs, who took over the *Times* in 1896, established the tradition of expansion instead of contraction when faced with a bleak financial outlook.

Rosenthal and Gelb presided over the expansion, which remains perhaps their greatest accomplishment, especially in the age of the Internet. While some *Times* veterans still consider much in the extra sections fluff, circulation and advertising (with a timely assist from the economy) increased and laid the basis for the national paper of today.

From Rosenthal's perspective, I understood why he didn't view me as an ideal editor. I didn't inspire confidence in him. My low-key approach, my quiet manner, indeed, a sphinx-like quality, made him uneasy that I might not be on top of things. Underlying this doubt lay my independence, first demonstrated when I rejected his offer to be an assistant metropolitan editor and continuing through the Wicker affair and conflicts on individual stories. At one of the national political conventions I told him that he and Gelb as visitors had to wait for floor passes until working reporters had finished talking to delegates. They stormed off and went back to New York.

Rosenthal seldom called to ask about stories we planned for that day. Once when he did I ran down the list and asked if he had any suggestions for changes or additions. No, he said, he just wanted to make sure we were on top of the news.

"What do you want me to do?" I said, in a show of irritation that I usually kept to myself, "Jump up on the desk and shout orders as if I were in the movies?"

More substantively, I differed with Abe over the fundamental question of how much leeway to give reporters in choice and writing of stories. I was a Partnership Editor. My way was to discuss ideas, whether from a New York editor or me, with a reporter and come to an understanding about its priority in relation to his or her own ideas. Rosenthal always wanted me to give his ideas priority and the reporter would have to give up or postpone work on an article he or she wanted to do. To me that was not only demeaning the reporter, it was also dangerous in that it often substituted an editor's judgment for that of a reporter specializing on a subject. Of course an editor's idea often did deserve top priority and in such cases, after a discussion, the reporter, although annoyed, would usually agree. Sometimes reporters became so close to their sources that they wrote for insiders and not the general reader. My job was to recognize that tendency and view stories through the eyes of Everyman. On that basis we could usually agree on story ideas. Most New York editors understood how I operated. Unfortunately, Rosenthal did not.

The problem remained throughout the nine years I spent as editor of the Washington bureau. Early in my tenure, at a dinner with five or six Washington hands at the Federal City Club, John Finney, a standout reporter who could cover almost any subject, put the problem this way to Rosenthal, as I remember the conversation:

"Abe, we reporters think we know our beats better than anyone. We think we know which stories we should write and when to write them. Now, Wicker has some ideas, and Bob may come up with a suggestion or two, and the foreign editor and the national editor and you ask for certain stories. We can't do them all. What are we supposed to do?"

Abe's answer was a quick nonanswer: "I'm greedy; I want them all."

Moreover, as I learned while on the metropolitan desk in New York, Rosenthal's unwavering concentration on his own ideas extended to how a story was written, further denigrating the reporter. Thus reporters were constantly in danger of becoming mere extensions of him or Arthur Gelb. My operating philosophy was to let the reporter write the story in his or her own fashion as long as it told the news with clarity and didn't violate *Times* standards. Of course I would draw attention to problems of organization, grammar, and syntax. Of course if I saw holes in the articles I would ask for inserts. If I saw a better way to write an article I would say so, but I insisted on adopting my way only in cases of violation of logic, ethics, and *Times* standards. I was a partner in the process, not the micromanaging sovereign.

On one of those occasions, when I was an assistant metropolitan editor in 1965, Gay Talese brought me his lead about a parade. He had written it as a feature because parades are usually color stories and he was a graceful writer. But demonstrators had turned the parade violent so the lead had to reflect that fact. Talese tried a number of times but could not write a straight lead. He finally fed his material to a rewriteman, who wrote the story.

Over the long haul, I believed, the Partnership Editor approach produced a better news report because discussions usually led to solid news judgments. Rosenthal, on the other hand, insisted on personally intervening to make every day's paper the best in his view. Undoubtedly, his ideas were often superior.

In a way, our difference was the journalistic equivalent of the contrast between Detroit and Japan over how to make automobiles in the 1990s. As an expert on quality control explained, Detroit manufacturers, when confronted by better-built Japanese imports, instituted a multitude of checks to eliminate bugs as cars were assembled. But they still could not match Japanese in quality. They didn't understand that Japanese companies, particularly Toyota, began by teaching suppliers how to make better parts. As a result, the Japanese required fewer assembly-line checks and built better cars.

Rosenthal was running around the newsroom like the Detroit checkers; I, in my subordinate role, depended on the quality of the reporters but remained alert for problems. The partnership system raised reporters' morale; the imperial system undermined confidence. Nevertheless, an Imperial Editor like Rosenthal can, through sheer brilliance, improve almost any story.

Frankel, who succeeded Rosenthal as executive editor, was for the most part, a Partnership Editor, dishing out material to reporters like Bernard Gwertzman that Max obtained from his special relationship with Henry Kissinger.

Shortly after Max took over as bureau chief, John Finney tested him. We were moving into new offices on L Street, with color-coordinated desks, chairs, and file cabinets. In a memo, Max told the staff that all old furniture would be thrown out. Disregarding the memo, John took two old bookcases into the new offices. Max walked over to John's desk, sat down and explained that for aesthetic reasons he didn't like the old bookcases, that the new furniture provided all the space he needed for his books. John dug in and Max, realizing that the issue was not important, let John keep his old bookcases.

I experienced first-hand as a reporter Max's partnership quality when I began researching an article on the Israeli lobby in the spring of 1970. This was an article I had long thought should be written. Jewish reporters, in New York as well as in Washington, shied from the assignment, but urged me to do it and suggested sources to contact. Arab diplomats doubted that the *Times* would print a fair report, but welcomed the opportunity to talk. Not long after I began making my calls Jewish organizations began to protest to Max. "Who's that Nazi you have there?" was typical of the remarks. Max assured the callers that the article would be fair. Not once did he ask me to back off. Shrewdly he suggested that I work

17. Ambitious Max Frankel, another of Scotty Reston's Boys, who eventually held every top editing job at the *Times*, whooping it up with Betty and me at a Manhattan party. Photographer unknown.

something into the article about the oil lobby, which often was pro-Arab. That addition was designed to provide a balanced approach that would be difficult to attack as unfair. The half-page article, which began on page one on April 6, was scarcely an exposé, although most readers would conclude that the Israeli lobby had far more influence than the oil lobby. In any event, it stimulated more response than anything else I wrote in Washington, with the exception, perhaps, of my final article, in the *Times Magazine*, on increased bird population, four years later.

As executive editor, Max demonstrated his willingness to work with a former rival by appointing Arthur Gelb as managing editor. This move surprised the staff because of Gelb's long close friendship with Rosenthal. Following the publisher's request, Frankel, who said he would be "not Abe," restored morale in the newsroom.[3]

I had long left the *Times* when Howell Raines became executive editor at the turn of the century, but evidence indicates he acted like an Imperial Editor in his twenty months on the job. Convinced, like Rosenthal, that the staff didn't leap fast enough or hard enough on stories, I am told, he brushed aside subordinate editors and dealt directly with reporters. Eventually an inexperienced reporter, Jayson Blair, cracked under the pressure and turned to fabrication, which led to Raines's resignation.

The logical conclusion that I drew from my differences with Rosenthal was that I should leave the *Times*. The publisher might ditch Rosenthal for Reston, but certainly not for a subordinate editor. It was not logical, however, to leave the job that I often said was the best in American journalism—running the day-to-day coverage of the Washington bureau. Second in command, I was not bogged down with the demands on the bureau chief, who was primarily a writer. I could write but only when I pleased. Unlike the bureau chief I was free of social obligations in a town where social events cemented news sources and often provided news tips. Betty and I could travel when we wanted to and had a built-in travel network in the correspondents around the world.

Important to me was the fact that I had an impact on the Washington news report. Day after day other newspapers, the wire services, and the broadcast networks followed the *Times* in what Reston called the "multiplier effect" of its coverage. If we printed a story other media quickly followed. Overall, my job was more important in shaping Washington news than that of almost any editor at any other news organization.

But how long could I hold this ideal job in view of Rosenthal's doubts? The more I thought about it the more certain I became that in a year or two Rosenthal would call me to New York, say I had done a fine job in Washington but I was needed for something else, like editing the news service, which would remove me from directing coverage. In my mid-fifties, I would be back where I had started at the *Times,* merely processing what other editors had edited. Betty and I concluded—I was more certain than she—that perhaps I should look around to see if other newspapers would be interested in hiring me. Over the next year I thought about what to do and I let a few friends know that I was available if the right position came along.

It's nearly impossible to keep a secret in a newsroom, but I did for a few months. Then one day early in 1973 Russell Baker asked me to lunch and said he had heard I was thinking of leaving. He expressed sympathy for my situation and, startlingly, in view of his national prominence, compared my problem to his. As I remember the conversation, he said, "You and I have done our jobs well but there comes a time when we wonder what else we can do. I can continue my column and I can continue to give lectures for thousands of dollars, but to what purpose?"

I had no ready answer, finding it difficult to equate myself with him. Although he had not yet won his first Pulitzer Prize—that would come in 1979—he was as famous as a journalist gets. Readers all over the country read his "Observer" column. I was one of a score of second-in-command editors. Russ solved his problem by moving his base from Washington to New York, continuing his column until 1998 and winning a second Pulitzer Prize for his biography, in 1983.[4] From 1992 to 2004 he hosted PBS's *Masterpiece Theatre*.

Some Washington friends suggested I try the *Washington Post*, saying they were always in the market for good editors. But I could not see myself working for a rival paper. Wanting to stay at the *Times*, I decided to talk to the publisher. I went to Punch and proposed that I be the editor of all the smaller papers the *Times* had purchased over the years. He shook his head and said, something like this: "Bob, I couldn't do that. Do you know how much I make from those papers? Thirty, thirty-five, forty percent a year. You would want to spend money to improve them. No, you stay in Washington and continue to do a good job."

As an alternative, I suggested that when he promoted Frankel to a New York editorship, as rumored, he should consider making the editor of the bureau the bureau chief. That would give the editor more power to direct the bureau and free the chief correspondent to spend all his or her time on writing. Punch nodded but said nothing. Years later he made both these changes. He created the job of editor of the smaller papers for Seymour Topping, who spent money on the papers and improved them, and made the Washington editor, Bill Kovach, the bureau chief.

On another visit to New York, Rosenthal asked me into his inner office, a cubicle off his main office, for a drink. He had never done this before. On my guard, I asked for a Coke. After awkwardly pouring Scotch for himself and spilling a little, he said he had heard that I was thinking of leaving the *Times*. In the warmest session I ever had with him he urged me to rethink the matter and pointed out that I would be giving up "the impact of the *Times*." No matter where you go or what you do, he said, it cannot match the significance of what you can do at the *Times*. I thanked him for his thoughts and explained that if I could not get the job I wanted at the *Times* I would have to consider going elsewhere. Abe didn't respond then or later to this obvious feeler about possible jobs.

Still searching, I went to John Pomfret, the former White House correspondent, who had become general manager of the *Times*. I had worked with Pomfret in Washington and with his boss, Walter Mattson, then a senior vice president, in my stints as a substitute news editor in the bullpen. They offered me a job working with them. It was tempting. I liked both of them and would be free of Rosenthal. But it would be the end of my editing career. Regretfully, I declined the offer.

The ideal position, I thought, would be to run a metropolitan paper in a vibrant city. That meant two requisites: a willingness on the part of the owner to commit the resources to publish a great newspaper and a city that could produce the news that such a newspaper could report. I confided in Salisbury, who, with Abe in power, was out of the chain of command. He encouraged me especially in my choice of New Orleans as a city that needed a better newspaper and had the kind of community that deserved one. Perhaps I could convince S. I. Newhouse, the newspaper chain owner, that he ought to build the *Times-Picayune* into a great newspaper as another legacy to journalism in addition to the communications school he had underwritten at Syracuse University. My other choice was San Francisco, but Wally Turner, who in his years as the *Times* West Coast chief knew the *Chronicle,* discouraged that approach. The owners of the *Chronicle,* he said, thought they already had a great newspaper.

I didn't forgo the idea that so many editors harbor of running a smaller paper in a small town. Ever since my navy days, when I wrote hometown stories at Okinawa, I had seen the impact of the local press. Of the contacts I made, however, it became clear that small dailies were not paying the salary that I demanded. Media General, which owns the *Richmond*

*Times-Dispatch*, the *Tampa Tribune*, and the *Winston-Salem Journal*, heard of my availability and invited Betty and me to Richmond. While I met with executives at a long conference table, Betty was taken on a tour of the city's cultural attractions, a strong indication of interest. They wanted to convince my wife that the South would be a fine place to live.

Their interest quickly evaporated when I answered their first question: How could the *Times* justify publishing the Pentagon Papers, revealing wartime secrets and thereby imperiling American security? I insisted, of course, that we had not given away any secrets, that every example cited in court had been published before, often by the government. The Southern gentlemen, polite but firm, did not agree. We went on to other subjects, but they didn't suggest a further meeting and offered no job. As we returned to Washington I told Betty how difficult it was going to be to find a paper with the resources and willingness to report the news aggressively and objectively. We might be stuck at the *Times*. That didn't sound like a bad future to Betty.

# 16. Clifton Daniel
## Luring Sally Quinn

**For weeks after** Clifton Daniel replaced Max Frankel as bureau chief we consulted almost every night over dinner, talking about bureau procedures and the strengths and weaknesses of the reporters. His wife, Margaret Truman Daniel, was still in New York with their children and he was a little lonely. One night as Clifton and I came out of a restaurant, he said he had a package for Betty. From the trunk of President Truman's old DeSoto, he took a brown paper bag. When Betty opened it she found three bottles of fine Rhone wine, her favorite red, and a note apologizing for taking me away from her for so many evenings.

We often ate lunch together, too, and, to my surprise, he told me a little of his personal affairs. Margaret was so busy, he said, that he had to shop for clothes for their sons. Close friends called him E-C (His full name was Elbert Clifton Daniel Junior). I called him Clifton.

Enjoying social life, Daniel wanted to expand the bureau's coverage to social affairs, particularly gossip. In New York he had hired Charlotte Curtis to write about society, treating the wealthy not with veneration, but with candor. She would whip out her notebook at parties and in full view take down their words exactly as spoken, often making the rich and the famous look stupid, a fact that didn't stop them from talking to her. Curtis would fly to Washington for major social events, like presidential inauguration parties, but spent most of her time in New York.

Daniel was intrigued by the *Post*'s Style section, which, with loose standards, reported rumors and prattle at social affairs. As managing editor he had urged the bureau to get similar stories. I could not interest anyone in the bureau to spend their evenings on amorphous happenings at dinner parties, passing on back-stabbing comments. Throughout his career, especially in London and New York, Daniel sought out society news, defending such stories as important because, even if untrue, they affected events as politicians responded to them. Indeed, his memoirs reflect this interest.[1]

He boldly struck at the *Post*, offering a job to its best-known Style reporter, Sally Quinn, the girlfriend of managing editor Ben Bradlee. In a secret meeting with Daniel, Quinn expressed doubt that the *Times* would let her write as freely as the *Post* did or at the lengths she was used to. Her stories often ran on for four columns or more, which *Post* staffers attributed to her close relationship to Bradlee. To ease her fears Daniel had her meet secretly with me.

I had met Sally once, at an annual dinner of the White House Photographers Association. I was late in arriving—still socially shy after all the years, I didn't like to mix in the predinner cocktail whirl—and there was only one seat vacant at my table. I introduced myself to Senator George McGovern on my right, then turned to the pretty blond woman on my left and, as I remember, the following conversation ensued:

"I'm Bob Phelps of the *New York Times*. Who are you?"

"I'm Sally Quinn."

"Oh, and what do you do?"

"I'm a reporter for the *Washington Post*."

"And what do you cover?"

Not quite sure whether I really didn't know she was a well-known figure, she said, simply, "society."

Then I laughed and she knew I was kidding.

At the luncheon to discuss the *Times* offer I told her the obvious, that I didn't have the clout to change *Times* rules but that if Daniel set up an understanding with the New York editors it could work. The best I could do would be to flag her on passages that might upset New York editors. Lured by the wide national audience of the *Times*, Sally accepted the offer but when she told Bradlee about it he invoked his power as her lover and she stayed with the *Post*. That was the last serious attempt the *Times* made in my tour to make Washington gossip a regular part of the bureau's report.

(Later, Dana Little, who had been my assistant, sought to strengthen the "Notes on People" column, in one instance asking Bradlee when he was going to make an "honest woman" out of Sally. He and Sally eventually married. Barbara Gamarekian, who had been secretary to bureau chiefs for years, took over the society beat full time after Daniel retired.) She died in 2004.

Daniel let me run the bureau pretty much my way. He didn't change the operation significantly, but he made life easier for me by fending off many calls from New York. Although he had been sent to Washington in another attempt to get control of the bureau, he didn't push us hard; in fact, he became the bureau's defender. For months he didn't try to write any story of his own, and on his first attempt I took it back to him, saying it was not strong enough for a bureau chief's first dispatch. He flushed but didn't object. In time he did write, but not very often. Usually his articles were news analyses.

Clifton did express the wish that I spend more time talking to older reporters about their writing. Noting that I always seemed to find time to work with younger reporters and interns, he said that the older reporters could benefit, too. E. W. Kenworthy was a good example.

Rumpled, lovable Ned placed no value on traditional newspaper rules or values. With a background as an English teacher and a government public information officer, he learned journalism as a freelance writer for the Sunday Week in Review section of the *Times.* In those days review articles summarized the news chronologically. Ned was in his late 40s when he joined the bureau in 1957 and, unless he had infinite time, used that same story structure. Despite space limitations—he was always told how many words he could write—he usually wrote chronologically after his first summary paragraph and continued until he had exhausted his notebook. The editor had to hold the story until it was finished and cut it himself to fit the allotted spaced. That practice suited Ned and no discussions changed him.

As I had been advised when I went to Washington, you could tell the importance of Ned's story by his dress. Jacket off was run-of-the-mill; an unbuttoned collar and loosened tie was moderately important; all those plus a flapping shirttail was page one. Ned didn't read the paper closely and sometimes would bustle into the bureau complaining that the *Post* had an exclusive story. When someone pointed out that the *Times* had run the story the previous day he would laugh and say the paper was too big. "You can write for it or read it, but you can't do both."

I was reluctant to chastise experienced reporters openly. I avoided generalizing a reporter's weakness in dealing with a daily story. It was more effective to deal with the specifics to put the article in shape and tackle the recurring problem in a private conversation. For example, if a reporter constantly used clichés, I would not throw the article on his desk and demand, "Why do you always write, 'the all-powerful House Rules Committee?'" Instead I would delete the offending phrase and talk about the problem when no deadline was looming.

While I did not make time for such talks often enough, I did seek to help even experienced reporters in our talks before they began to write. Jim Naughton, whose clean, crisp copy required little editing, explained my style in an interview in 2002, on retiring as president of the Poynter Institute, the Florida journalism school. After years of outstanding work in the *Times* Washington bureau Jim asked for an editing job. The *Times* refused and Jim accepted the national/foreign editorship at the *Philadelphia Inquirer*, where he was central to the winning of a string of Pulitzer Prizes. In the interview, he said the best advice he ever got was, "Use your head." He told the institute's house organ "About Poynter" that he got that from a lot of people, but especially from Bob Phelps in Washington, explaining:

> When I would come back from an assignment [Phelps] had the most con-
> genial way of seeming to just be curious about what I had discovered.
> He was so collaborative. I remember vividly one of these chats that I
> thought were just chats but were very purposeful. [He] would say, "You
> know, on your way back to the office in the cab, be thinking about what's
> my lede?" I valued that. When Bob Phelps retired some years later, I sent
> him a note thanking him for that, but telling him he screwed up my
> whole life because I couldn't write a lede without being in a taxi cab. I
> think what he was saying was "Use your head."[2]

I did enjoy working with young people filled with the romance of news-papering. In New York I had taught at the Columbia School of Journalism as an adjunct professor one day a week for years; in Washington I would take a student or two into the bureau for a week and let them work on minor stories.

One of my courses at Columbia was news judgment. I stressed values, with human life the most precious. As an example I cited an event that often occurs in big cities: A commuter throws himself in front of a subway train; tens of thousands, sometimes hundreds of thousands of passengers, are delayed a half hour. What should the headline say: "Thousands Delayed in Subway Suicide" or "Youth Dies in Subway Suicide?" Does the first headline value the irritation of thousands more than the loss of one life? I surprised the students by saying I would choose the delay headline because the loss of a half hour to each of tens of thousands commuters adds up to a greater loss of life than that of one individual.

Reston's interns were, in some ways, my interns, too. Assigned to stories that otherwise wouldn't be covered, they responded enthusiastically, usually turning in professional-grade stories and eagerly accepting criticisms and suggestions for changes. Among them were Steve Roberts, Craig Whitney, Iver Petersen, David Shipler, Linda Greenhouse, and William Hamilton. All became outstanding journalists.

Their desire for reporting often exceeded their sense of duty to Scotty. One of their chores was to read through Reston's mail and write drafts of letters in response. Unknown to me and I believe to Reston, James Sterba, a 1967–68 intern, sometimes threw the letters in the trash and rushed out to my desk for an assignment. He became a *Times* reporter and covered the Vietnam War, where, in a magazine article he helped popularize the term "grunt" to designate GIs fighting in the jungles. He has spent most of his career at the *Wall Street Journal*. In recent years he has turned to writing books.[3]

When I hired John Crewdson as a copy boy I gave him the usual warning that he had to make coffee runs and, above all, had to jump at the call of "copy" from a reporter. Like other copy boys before and after him, he openly disregarded my instructions as he turned out one good story after another. Unfortunately he left the *Times* a year later to attend Oxford University. He returned to Washington a day after the Watergate break-in and I immediately assigned him to the Watergate story to help

Walter Rugaber. His keen mind and his dogged pursuit were ideal for chasing that story, as shown in 1973 when he became a staff reporter and began getting bylines. In subsequent months he disclosed the extent of Nixon's plans to spy on "enemies" and Kissinger-inspired wiretaps. Later he won a Pulitzer Prize for stories of Mexican immigration, and then left to work for the *Chicago Tribune*. From Washington he exposed the theft by an American scientist of an AIDS virus developed by the French.[4]

During the Watergate investigation I agreed to edit the memoirs of Charles E. Bohlen, the retired diplomat and expert on the Soviet Union. In accepting the job I violated my best instincts. When reporters got book offers, I would warn them of what they were getting into. In those days the *Times* seldom gave leaves of absence to write books; reporters had to do their research and writing on their own time.

After cashing his advance, I said, the thrilled reporter would decide that he needed a quiet place at home to work. That meant renovating the attic or the basement for an office. The office would require a new desk, a comfortable chair, file cabinets, another telephone, and perhaps one of those new word processors to replace the old manual typewriter. All this would eat up the advance and more importantly, take six months to complete. If the contract called for delivery of the manuscript in a year, half the time had gone by without any significant start on either research or writing. Some, like Bob Semple, who planned a book on Nixon, eventually gave up.

I made the same mistake of underestimating the time it would take to edit the Chip Bohlen book. My guard dropped when I talked to him. He really needed help and his book was important. Bohlen, who spoke fluent Russian, was Franklin D. Roosevelt's interpreter at the World War II conferences with Stalin and Churchill. His career put him in superb position to write a significant book but he had not kept any diaries, letters, or documents, as Reston had urged him. His memory was excellent, but hardly sufficient on which to base a book, especially one that could be checked by historians. In addition, Bohlen could not type. He had no organizational concept for the book.

We worked out a plan under which Bohlen, starting from his childhood, would dictate chapter by chapter to a recording machine, from which his secretary would type the manuscript and send it to me. I would read the manuscript, make notes and then meet with Chip, and ask him to write inserts and make changes by dictating into the recording machine. When these were typed I would put them in the proper place in the manuscript. In this way we eventually built a huge file, which became a book.[5]

Reviewers liked the book, but one exception, and an important one, was Christopher Lehmann-Haupt, in the daily *New York Times*, who conceded he might be unfair. He wished that Bohlen had used the book to denounce the Vietnam War instead of sticking to his forty years in the Foreign Service.

But the book bug had bitten me. The give and take with prominent Washington figures would keep my mind stimulated, the subject matter was substantive, and the slower pace of editing a manuscript would provide time to reflect on editing decisions. Book editing would be a satisfying change of career.

PART THREE • **The *Boston Globe***

# 17. *Boston Globe* Offer
### Quitting the *Times*

**In 1973,** Richard Halloran, the *Times* Tokyo correspondent, invited Betty and me to Japan. We accepted and decided to go to Hong Kong too. When I mentioned the trip to Clifton Daniel, he suggested we go on to Vietnam and Thailand. Before the conversation ended we had decided on an around-the world trip, with stops in India, Iran, Israel, and Ireland, at the *Times* expense.

All went well until our KLM pilot said, without explanation, that traffic controllers were diverting our New Delhi to Teheran flight to Beirut. As we landed on October 6 he told us why: Egypt and Syria had attacked Israel; another Mideast war had erupted.

In the van on the way to the St. George Hotel, Betty said we should return to the airport, board the KLM plane, which was going on to Belgium, and get out of the war zone fast.

"I can't do that," I said, "I have to call New York and offer to help cover the war."

When Juan de Onis, the *Times* Beirut correspondent, and I met he expressed his concern that I might be taking over the story, or at least dictating coverage. It was the traditional reporter's protection of his territory. Of course it would have been foolish of me to play the big foot, as some well-known journalists do. I offered to help on secondary stories, leaving the best one to him.

Every morning for the next few days Betty and I ate croissants and sipped coffee on a balcony of the lovely St. George Hotel while Israeli jets screamed over the blue Mediterranean. Then Juan and I would meet to discuss story ideas and we would go our separate ways. Evenings we dined with the de Onises.

221

My first story was my best. It tried to answer the question everyone was asking: How had the Egyptians succeeded in defeating, at least so far, the vaunted Israeli war machine? I talked to the best sources I could think of, the military attachés at the embassies. They agreed that the Israelis had become arrogant and overconfident; the Arabs took advantage of Yom Kippur to catch them napping. Luckily for me the attachés spoke English because my French, while adequate for simple travel situations, was not good enough to converse about the war. My story, with an eight-column headline, led the inside pages the second day of the war.

While I was reporting, Betty went to a hospital to check on a pain in her chest suffered when she fell in a ditch in India. X-rays showed she had three broken ribs. Nevertheless, she toured Baalbeck and the Bekka valley, viewing their Roman ruins while Syrian and Israeli jets roamed overhead. When regular *Times* reporters streamed in, Betty and I flew to Ireland for a little rest.

On returning to Washington I intensified my hunt for a publisher eager to build a great newspaper. Through various sources I learned the names of people close to S. I. Newhouse. In December 1973, I was preparing to try to set up appointments with them when Thomas Winship, editor of the *Boston Globe*, called. Christopher Lydon, a *Times* reporter who formerly worked at the *Globe*, had told him that I might leave the *Times* for the right job. Would I go up to Boston to talk to Winship?

Lydon briefed me on the charismatic Winship, who had inherited his job from his father and who had, through the force of his energy, raised the *Globe* from a lazy no. 3 paper to the largest and best paper in Boston. Tom was driven by his love of Boston and his liberal political leanings, both of which colored his journalism. Winship pointed the way and the staff, much of it young, joyfully followed with little editorial discipline.

On December 31, I flew to Boston and talked to Winship. One of his first questions was what I knew about the *Globe*. I knew that the *Globe* published material from the Pentagon Papers after the court had enjoined the *Times*. (I did not know that Daniel Ellsberg had told Thomas Oliphant, a *Globe* reporter, about the Pentagon Papers more than a week before he talked to Neil Sheehan and had written an article about it.[1]) Aside from that, I said, using a line that Bob Smith, who had also worked at the *Globe* before joining the *Times,* had suggested, I thought of the *Globe* as a giant rocket, almost ready to take off, but needing something additional to propel it. That was what Winship wanted to hear. What did I want to do at the *Globe*? Edit the magazine? Run the National Desk? I turned the questioning around. What do you need most of all? I asked. Well, Tom said, the real need was for someone to take charge of the coverage of Boston school desegregation, which was scheduled to go into effect soon.

The meeting didn't last long and Tom called Bill Taylor, son of the publisher, in to look me over. All went well, and Tom said I would be hearing from him soon. Betty seemed happy about Boston—or was she happy that someone wanted me? For the first time we thought we really might make a move.

A week passed and I heard nothing. I called the *Globe* and learned that Winship had gone to Kenya on safari, so I settled back and waited. But on January 14 Robert Healy, the *Globe*'s executive editor and chief political columnist, who often worked in Washington, asked me to dinner, where he said that Tom had not persuaded the publisher, Davis Taylor, to approve my hiring. "The old man," Healy explained, "isn't going to put an outsider over people who were loyal to the *Globe* in the lean years." I could understand that and admired Davis for feeling that way. I went home and told Betty we were not going to Boston. She was not upset. She had come to like her life in McLean and had developed good relationships with people in the bureau.

In a week or so I received a hand-scribbled confirmation note from Winship, who had returned from the African safari, saying that he had gone to the well twice, using "every ounce of my persuasive ability," but Davis is "dead set against hiring such a good man in a high spot who is over 50." I reached for the phone to call Tom and to thank him, but before I could pick it up it rang. It was Winship. "I got your note," I said, "and was just about to call to thank you." "Throw it away," Tom said, "the old man has changed his mind. Can you come up here and talk to him?"

Later I learned that a long letter from Chris Lydon changed Davis's mind. I was surprised that Lydon would go to such lengths to help me. True, we had a good relationship, but he had trouble in meeting deadlines and many nights I had to harangue him to get the copy moving. I tried various tricks, including putting a sign on his desk, "Hasten Slowly," but he continued to increase the blood pressure of the desk editors. He was a superb reporter, excellent at interrogating sources, and the extra time he took in writing paid off in elegant prose. Thus I gladly supported him when William M. Magruder, the director of the program to build a supersonic airliner, complained of his articles. On one occasion Magruder called to urge that I remove "that un-American" from the SST story. When I asked why he called Lydon un-American, Magruder replied that Chris had dirty fingernails (which was true). In his letter to Davis Taylor, Lydon wrote of me:

> Professionally, his strengths are rooted in the good, gray disciplines that the *Times* perhaps overdoes and the *Globe,* I think, still misses: thoroughness and fairness about reporting, and a certain intellectual rigor about weighing the news. He also has a powerful, un-gray zeal about prose style and about stretching the boundaries of "news." He has all the old-fashioned virtues without being in any way conventional.
>
> Personally, and most extraordinarily, he is a man of rock-like calm and, I take it, confidence—and almost friction-proof character in a business full of egomaniacs. There are many people, theoretically at least, who could match Bob Phelps for experience and judgment, but I can't imagine any others who could assume authority in a humming establishment like the *Globe* and not upset the personal rhythms of the place even for a moment.[2]

In early March, when I saw a day clear, I flew to Boston and, as directed, went straight to the publisher's office. There I met Davis and his cousin, John I. Taylor. Bill Taylor was there, too. After the introductions Tom said Dave would like to hear a little about me. An hour and a half later I had reached only high school when I stopped and said perhaps I was going on too long. "No, no," Dave said, "it's exactly what I want to hear." I finished by noon. Dave shook my hand and thanked me for coming, then left the room, closely followed by Bill. John I., Tom, and I chatted a bit until Bill returned. "What did he say?" Tom asked. "He's all for it," Bill, said with much relief. We quickly agreed to terms. I would be assistant managing editor for metropolitan news. I said I wanted the opportunity for advancement. Tom said, "If you do as well as I think you will we will take care of you." As for salary, I said I didn't want to make less than I was making at the *Times,* which was about $45,000. We agreed but Bill said that my regular salary would be less because, except for Tom, no editor was making that much. I would be given a bonus to make up the difference.

(Years later, when Betty told Davis Taylor how glad we were that he had changed his mind about hiring me, he told her in an overstatement, excusable since he was talking to my wife, that "it was the best thing I ever did.")

Bill Taylor and Tom Winship were impressed when I told them that I would fly to New York, see Punch Sulzberger and resign from the *Times* that very day. I was not going to use the *Globe* offer to wangle more money from the *Times.* I called Betty to make sure everything was okay, and then flew to New York. From a pay telephone in the lobby of the *Times* I called Clifton Daniel and told him where I was and that I was about to see the publisher and resign to go to the *Globe.* Testily, he said, "You didn't see fit to inform me of your plans, but let me give you some advice. Don't do what is good for the *Globe.* Don't do what is good for the *Times.* Do what is good for Bob Phelps." Sound advice, but nothing to change my mind because I thought I was doing exactly that.

About 5 o'clock I went to the publisher's office where I talked with Punch, Pomfret, and Sidney Gruson, the publisher's closest confidant. Believing that Daniel was my problem, Punch apologized, saying he had no other editor to send to Washington. Apparently he had forgotten that I had suggested that the way to solve the Washington problem was to make the editor the bureau chief. I told him that Abe, not Clifton, was my problem and that we were different kinds of editors. Punch made no comment. He had settled on Abe as his managing editor and was not going to change, nor did I expect him to.

A half hour and two mammoth scotch and sodas later, I said goodbye and Punch told Pomfret to make sure that I received the best possible retirement deal. It wasn't much of a deal. I opted to retire immediately. Pomfret was a friend, but, after nearly twenty years of service, I received an annual pension of only $5,000 (later bumped up by $10 a month!), to carry over to Betty after I died—and a set of Tiffany glass tumblers with the NYT logo.

Standing on 43d Street, under the *Times* clock, I finally realized what I had done. I had turned my back on nearly two decades of productive work at the best newspaper in the world, about half of it in what I had long described as the best job in American journalism, to step down to an assistant managing editor's job on a lesser newspaper. Had I lost my mind? Would others think I had been forced out? Once more I had taken a backward step. This was far more significant than quitting United Press to return to college and riskier, at age fifty-four, than leaving public relations to go to a lower-paying job at the *Providence Journal.*

Messages and phone calls soon came in from foreign and national bureaus and New York. Scotty Reston, who was overseas, phrased his note with words that surprised and puzzled me because he had never praised me or expressed any friendship beyond the courtesies of the newsroom: "That is very sad news for me personally. I'll never go away again." (He did.)

In the midst of these calls Clifton Daniel telephoned Betty and said "I hope that this move will be as good for you as Bob says it will be for him." No one else thought of doing that. In that one call, in one sentence, Daniel epitomized my career, as I learned a quarter-century later.

A few days later, at a party at Daniel's house, a tipsy Turner Catledge asked me why I had decided to leave the *Times* for the *Globe.* He didn't say so, but it was obvious he was curious why I would step down. A little tipsy myself, I said, "Because I want to help make it a great newspaper." Catledge, who had once left the *Times* to become the first editor of the *Chicago Sun,* shook his head and said, in words that frequently returned to my mind while at the *Globe,* "You don't have time, Bob, you don't have time."

Tom Wicker, my first boss in Washington, noted, however, that I was not only embracing an opportunity at the *Globe,* but also accepting rejection by the *Times.* In a handwritten letter, received after I started working in Boston, he wrote that I was not only a fine editor but, more importantly, an honest man.[3]

My last day of work was April 12. Betty and I flew to Harbour Island in the Bahamas for a week's vacation. The final act was a party Sunday, April 21, that Betty and I gave for the bureau at our house in McLean.

18. Reporter Anthony Ripley, dressed as Big Bird, enter-
tained the crowd at my retirement party. Photographer
unknown.

Reporter Tony Ripley dressed up as Big Bird, the *Sesame Street* character.
The *Times* gave Betty a beautiful serving dish with a blue bird motif and
gave me the rocking chair in my office, adding the inscription. "Stolen
from the *New York Times*." In the closing scene I sat in the rocking chair on
the lawn and paid homage, one by one, to all the members of the bureau,
my voice slowly dropping off until at the end I could hardly be heard.

While I never regretted my decision to leave the *Times*, I also felt that
from the standpoint of prestige, my nineteen years, eight months, and
four days there would remain the high point of my career. The *Boston
Globe* would be a coda. Personally, the *Times* had been a way of life; it had
consumed me like a religious faith.

Day after day revolved around the paper. I would drop everything to rush into the office when news broke. I was on the phone with the late editor in the bureau or with a New York editor, often both, almost every night. I usually ate lunch with reporters or editors, sometimes with interns. I succeeded in eating dinner with Betty most of the time but we also took visiting *Times* people to restaurants.

The *Times* was central even on our vacations. While careful to pay our full way, I didn't hesitate to use the *Times* name to get reservations at hotels and resorts. I accepted rides for Betty and me on a British Petroleum plane to fly to the North Slope of Alaska to see the northern terminus of the Alaska pipeline because I wrote a check equivalent to the commercial airfare.

Eager to participate in one of the biggest birding events of the year, the Christmas bird census, I asked a *Times* reporter if he could persuade the noted ornithologist Allan Cruickshank to take Betty and me on his championship team in 1963. Cruickshank didn't want to handicap his team with a couple of dilettante bird watchers, but took us because of the *Times* connection. The team did well, spotting 195 species in the one-day count. Betty proved her worth by identifying a sandhill crane through shimmering heat on a grassland thousands of yards away.

I sat with a happy Betty in the front row in 1971 as Leonard Bernstein conducted the premiere of his "Mass: A Theater Piece for Singers, Players and Dancers," commissioned for the opening of the John F. Kennedy Center for the Performing Arts. At a reception we joined congressmen and high government officials crowding around Elizabeth Taylor. Sadly, she did not cast her violet eyes on me.

Betty and I enjoyed our occasional rides on the press plane accompanying the president, drinking the endless cocktails and participating in the pastime of rolling a tennis ball up the aisle to see how far it would roll back before hitting a seat leg. (It was a good vacation deal; the *Times* paid my way and I paid $55 for Betty.) I took the pampering for granted, with presidential press aides registering for us at hotels, handing us our keys and sending our bags directly to our rooms.

I felt like a real Washington insider at briefings at the Central Intelligence Agency in McLean, not far from our house. After the *Times* group

19. No trouble spotting this bird. Betty was the expert.
I got the credit. Photo by the author.

registered and were given passes, the public information officer, musta-chioed Angus MacLean Thuermer, would lead us through halls to a small unwindowed room with a sofa, a few chairs and a silver coffee set on a small table. In a few minutes the briefing officers would enter and we would hear what the agency wanted us to hear about the Vietnam War, the Mideast or the Soviet Union, whatever subject we had asked for. The information was for our guidance only; we were free to ask questions but could not quote the CIA.

The briefings impressed me although I should have known better after I learned that CIA Director Richard Helms lied in response to a direct question I asked him at an off-the-record luncheon at the bureau. He looked me straight in the eye and denied any CIA involvement in the coup that overthrew President Salvador Allende of Chile in 1973. Documents eventually released showed that the CIA planned and abetted the coup. The CIA always defended its lies as necessary to protect national security.

In truth I enjoyed the panoply and perquisites of the Washington equivalent of a royal court even though I operated only on its fringes. For that pleasure I could thank the *Times*.

I had come a long way since that day in November 1954 when I told Betty that there was so much talent at the *Times* that I should be quite happy if I just stayed on the national desk as a copyeditor. Success had inflamed my ambition and my ambition had exceeded my grasp. The *Times* had given me much but had denied me the fulfillment I sought despite my good work and loyalty. Would I run into the same disappointment in Boston?

# 18. School Integration
## Pulitzer Gold Medal

**The *Globe* staff** received me warmly, in contrast to the coolness of the first few months in Washington. I attributed a great deal of this warmth to respect for the *Times*. In the newsroom, John Driscoll, Winship's chief assistant, and Matthew Storin, the metropolitan editor, whom I was succeeding, were especially friendly and helpful.

Instead of staying at a hotel, I was booked through Davis Taylor into the Union Club, which was started during the Civil War by Boston leaders supporting President Lincoln. My room overlooked a burial ground for colonial figures. I felt a little out of place eating breakfast with tottering old men, but I did enjoy the genteel atmosphere, white tablecloths, heavy silver, and quiet waiters.

Soon after I arrived in Boston Winship asked me to speak to a conference of selected *Globe* executives and reporters to discuss ways to improve the paper. I saw it as an opportunity to present my ideas for covering metropolitan news and offer some thoughts about the *Globe* in general. I made some notes, but spoke extemporaneously. Here are the points I made:

• I believed in strong editing.

• I didn't read the editorials in the *New York Times* and I wouldn't read them in the *Boston Globe*. I didn't want to know the official view of the paper.

• I didn't believe reporters should also act as editors.

• The *Globe* should offer stories balanced among various views. Only in that way would Bostonians know what was happening.

• The *Globe* was rising to a new level.

231

When I finished, Dexter Eure, the *Globe*'s liaison with the black community, grumbled about my emphasis on balanced coverage. He said he had not heard anything about the rights of minorities. I replied, to applause, that I was probably more of a minority than he was, because I was part American Indian. Dexter, who became a valuable adviser to me on Boston neighborhoods, muttered that Indians owned lots of oil wells. The audience laughed. The speech was a good start, as far as I was concerned. Winship and Bill Taylor seemed to think so, too. Bill played the piano to close out the evening.

My final introduction to the *Globe* came at a meeting of the board of directors of the parent company, Affiliated Publications, at the exclusive Somerset Club. When Chris Lydon heard about it he said, "They wanted to meet the *Globe*'s newest acquisition." Most of the directors were old men. Ill at ease at the paper's liberal position on issues, they asked what I thought of the *Globe*'s endorsement of George McGovern over Richard Nixon for President. I repeated what I said at the staff conference, that, as an editor in charge of news, I had not and would not read the editorials. The old heads nodded in approval. Winship, who believed in using all the *Globe*'s strength to push his liberal agenda, held his tongue.

At the *Times* I had adopted its high standards as a substitute for religion; at the *Globe* I quickly realized that I needed to make converts because so many were nonbelievers in objectivity. The ethos of the *Globe* newsroom was a driving determination to change the world according to the latest progressive thought. What dismayed me more than anything was the fact that many of the *Globe* reporters had been actively taking sides in controversies. Education reporters were advising black leaders on fighting school segregation. The mental health reporter was known as "Miss Mental Health" because she was so close to the group advocating more government aid. And so it went throughout the newsroom.

Reporters who argued with guests at *Globe* luncheons troubled me. To me, the best way to deal with a source, at a luncheon, a news conference, or a private interview, was first to listen sympathetically to get a true understanding of his or her view, and then shoot the hard questions in a neutral tone, like, "How do you answer those who criticize your environmental program as easy on business?" Not, "You're letting business pollute the Charles River." The reporter should not assume the role of a defense attorney or of a prosecutor, but of a judge, making sure all questions are answered. Objectivity extends to a reporter's relation to sources, not just to writing or editors' decisions on how prominently to display articles.

Nowhere was this bias more true than at the state house bureau. Following Winship's lead, reporters covering the governor and the state legislature sided with liberal politicians. Not long after my arrival I read a page one story about a bill up for passage. Dismayed that the story carried only quotations from its liberal sponsors, I asked the reporter if any opponents had spoken against the bill. "Yeah," he said, "but they didn't make sense. You wouldn't be interested." I speedily corrected him.

My job was to convince the staff that many old practices now conflicted with the new *Globe*. This task was especially difficult because Winship had praised the old ways. But he had promised to give me a free hand and I moved quickly.

The *Globe* needed a good dose of discipline, but not in a way that would destroy morale. The *Globe* was known as a writer's newspaper. I wanted to show that high standards were more than compatible with good writing; they often improved stories. On March 22, even before I arrived in Boston, I spoke of the need for strong editing with the *Globe*'s Washington bureau at a lunch. David Nyhan, one of the freewheeling Washington reporters, smiled and said, "So the Dr. Spock era at the *Globe* is over."

One of my first moves was to remove reporters from the editing process. Like most metropolitan papers, the *Globe* grouped reporters according to specialties, such as science, education, and politics. A lead reporter was designated as the group editor to read all copy before it was sent to the metropolitan editor. The new job gave me the chance to put into effect an idea that had intrigued me. For years I had been convinced that a major problem at newspapers, especially at the *Times*, was that too many editors dealt with the same story.

When Reston went to New York to become executive editor I wrote him a letter saying that the best thing he could do to eliminate hostility between Washington and New York was to institute a one-on-one relationship in the editing process, one editor dealing with one reporter. In

20. Tom Winship, the *Boston Globe*'s top editor, and I writing headlines on 1976 elections. Photographer unknown. *Boston Globe* photo; reproduced with permission.

Washington either one of my two assistant editors or I was the only editor who talked to the reporter about his story. But when the story arrived in New York it had to hurdle a half dozen editors, some insisting on overruling a previous editor and talking to the reporter. The result was conflict and anger. Reporters threw up their hands and asked the editors to make up their minds. To Reston I suggested that all ideas by New York funnel through one editor in Washington who would deal with the reporter. Reston never replied.

Given a free rein in Boston, I established the one-on-one system. Like other papers at that time, the *Globe* was hurt by a recession that cut deeply into advertising, which resulted in a ban on new hiring. So I chose four young *Globe* reporters, made them assistant metropolitan editors, gave each a team of reporters and put them to work. What a joy that was. What a contrast to the cumbersome decision-making at the *Times*. The four story editors and I worked long hours and made the system work. We talked a lot during that first year and I tried to guide them into my ideas about journalism, especially about objectivity and ethics.

We were soon tested. In June federal Judge W. Arthur Garrity ordered desegregation of Boston public schools. Because the plan he accepted called for transferring black students to white schools in such close-knit communities as South Boston, civic leaders feared violence. At a meeting of city officials with representatives of the media before I arrived in Boston, the *Globe* half-promised that it wouldn't report acts of violence so as not to encourage further troubles. When I arrived I told the group that the *Globe* would report whatever happened, whether violent or not. We wouldn't report predictions of violence but we wouldn't bury incidents that occurred. Withholding the news would damage our credibility.

Just before the first day of desegregation I drafted a "Memo to All Hands" setting guidelines of coverage. Distributed with Winship's blessing, it stated that the best job the *Globe* could do for the community was to be as even-handed as possible. The thirteen guidelines created no new journalistic procedures. Some who read them guffawed that they were platitudes: We talk to all sources dispassionately, keeping our views to ourselves. We do not print rumors; we check them out. Editing must be with the utmost care. Headlines must be written with delicacy. We do not suppress news because it doesn't fit our views. We do not carry predictions of violence, but if there is violence we print it. The memo concluded:

"Above all, we must remember that the *Boston Globe*'s credibility is at stake. Our news columns must be believed—not just by those who agree with our editorial policy, but by those who disagree. Our aim is to convince all that the *Globe* is committed to the goal of seeking the truth."

Yes, these were clichés, but in view of the *Globe*'s history of taking sides in the news columns, of some of its reporters and editors, including Winship, advising news sources, of the paper's aggressive advocacy of liberal policies, of its triumphant voice proclaiming victory, I thought it necessary to signal the staff that times had changed. The *Globe* news columns on school integration would be even-handed in contrast to its earlier reporting on the civil rights drive in the South, the Vietnam War, Richard Nixon, women's rights, the youth culture—issues that had won plaudits nationally but had undercut the paper's credibility with many conservatives.

That memo remained our guide throughout the year although it didn't please either the pro- or anti-busing sides. At a luncheon at the *Globe* black ministers decried balanced coverage. The *Globe* should be on the side of what is right and moral, they said.

While I sympathized with them, I also sympathized with the blue-collar whites whose lives were being disrupted. On one of our visits to a South Boston home, a man told Jack Driscoll and me that he was not against the blacks. "I papered these walls, I put in our furnace," he said. "Now you are going to take away the life we have worked to build. All I'm saying is that blacks should work to build their own."

Although I stressed objectivity, I understood that perfect objectivity was not possible because as humans we are unable to compartmentalize our feelings. Unlike many editors, however, I believed that a reasonable measure of objectivity was not only possible, but also necessary for papers like the *Globe,* which dominated their territory.

The *Globe*'s story on the first day of desegregation drew strong criticism from the national media because the lead said that most schools had integrated without serious incident, adding in the third paragraph that there had been violence at South Boston High School. (The *Boston Herald* and the local broadcast media used a similar approach, but the *Globe,* as the leading paper, took the brunt of criticism.) The wire services, national newspapers, and television emphasized the violence.

At a session at Harvard discussing media coverage, I accused John Kifner, a friend who wrote the *New York Times* lead, of losing perspective. "The real story was that 79 out of 80 schools integrated peacefully," I said, warmed by a few drinks, "but you focused on the one that had trouble." Kifner insisted that the *Globe* had downplayed the violence.

"Look," I said, "if the Pentagon fired a dozen experimental rockets for the first time and one or two fizzled but the rest flew fine, what would your lead be?" He said the situation was not comparable. I believed it was.

Kifner quickly replied: "If 3,000 jets take off in a single day and all but one land safely, you don't write '2,999 airliners arrive at destinations,' you write 'jet crash kills 200.'"

I responded: "But airliners land safely every day. This wasn't a routine event; it was an important test. If you test 100 missiles and 99 of them

21. Reporter Richard Knox and I check on police deployment the first day of Boston school desegregation, September 1974. Photographer unknown. *Boston Globe* photo; reproduced with permission.

perform adequately, you don't write 'one missile fails,' you write '99 percent hit targets.'"

In the months that followed, violence erupted in a number of areas, which the *Globe* reported thoroughly and prominently. Throughout the nation, heavily Irish South Boston symbolized resistance to busing. To some, the *Globe*, which a half-century before had refused to carry classified help-wanted advertising with the words "no Irish need apply," had turned its back on the community. A *Globe* truck was hijacked. Shots were fired at the *Globe* building (missing me one night as I was crossing the parking lot). The next day bullet-proof windows were installed. The anti-busing leaders noted that *Globe* editors lived primarily in the suburbs and had little sympathy for inner-city ethnic Bostonians. Sensing this anger I wrote a note to Dave Taylor: "We really do not know what goes on in South Boston and all the other neighborhoods. We are part of an establishment that has lost touch with the people."

This was a problem we never overcame.

Six months into desegregation I was amused when the *Phoenix,* an alternative weekly with a national reputation, ran a cover story on the most important people in Boston. In journalism, the *Phoenix* said, it was Bob Phelps. In sophomoric journalism style it said that Tom Winship had more authority but "Bob Phelps has the power at the *Globe* for one simple reason: he decides what the news is.[1] *Globe* staffers chuckled. Winship, who never felt threatened, shrugged it off.

The *Globe* won the 1975 Pulitzer Prize Gold Medal for community service, the highest newspaper award, for its balanced, comprehensive coverage of Boston school desegregation in 1974. As was the custom, Winship, a member of the Pulitzer committee, didn't participate in the vote, but Pulitzer awards often reflect the board's close ties. Nevertheless, the *Globe* deserved the prize. Editorials were not mentioned in the award, but part of the credit should go to the editorial department because of its unwavering insistence on upholding the court's desegregation orders. Winship gave me full credit for winning the award; I told my four story editors they deserved much of the honor and I thanked the staff.

While daily coverage was important, I also wanted a historical record of this important development in Boston's history. Before the start of desegregation I had Richard Knox break away from his job as chief medical reporter to do a reconstruction of events, which would run at the end of the first year. Later I added other reporters and on May 25, 1975, the *Globe* published a special section, "The first year: an account of Boston school desegregation—the students, the officials and the public."[2]

Winship had been cool to the idea and instead of offering to push it had me broach it with the publisher. Davis Taylor agreed, saying it was the *Globe*'s responsibility because no one else would do it. As we neared publication I told him that we would need more than the eighteen pages he had allotted. "How much?" Twenty-four pages, I said, and without another question he said okay. His willingness to print twenty-four extra pages—150,000 words plus pictures—at a time when the *Globe* had lost thousands of readers because of a boycott by antibusing forces and an increase in subscription rates endeared him to me. After the special section appeared, he sent me a note in red ink that said: "Sunday documentary one of very best pieces ever done for *Globe*. You and your team deserve tremendous credit for a great journalistic feat. Please thank your excellent team for me personally."

From Washington, Dave Nyhan wrote: "I have never seen anything quite like it. Congratulations. I think that effort was worth more than the [Pulitzer] prize that preceded it."

I thought so, too, and it remained my proudest production in Boston. It was comparable to *Common Ground*, J. Anthony Lukas's book published ten years later. His book, on the lives of three families caught up in the Boston desegregation struggle, won a Pulitzer Prize.[3]

As a reward for winning the Pulitzer, Winship promoted me to managing editor of the flagship morning paper. This position gave me the opportunity to improve all aspects of the *Globe* except the editorial page, which did not interest me.

My first priority was to build the editing staff. When I started at the *Globe* a great deal of the copyediting was performed by part-timers. Some were suburban weekly editors, some graduate students, some writers looking for a way to get a foothold at the *Globe*. It was impossible to set editing standards under such conditions. In 1976, Winship and Bill Taylor agreed to let me hire full-time copyeditors on a gradual schedule until there were no part-timers.

Thomas F. Mulvoy Jr., whom I had snatched from the sports department and made news editor, selected the candidates. In only one instance did I reject his choice and that rejection created a myth.

In chatting with one of the candidates, Chris Brooks, I asked the title of the latest book he had read. After a long, awkward silence I asked him another question. Eventually I asked whether he planned to make editing his career. He said no, he was studying criminal justice at Northeastern University and planned to make that his career.

After he left my office Mulvoy asked my opinion. I said not to hire him because he was using the *Globe* to finance a career in criminal justice. It was not surprising that the word got around that I hadn't hired him because he could not remember the title of the book he was reading. That was too good a story to let the real reason get in its way. After I retired, Mulvoy hired Brooks because of pressure from Winship, who knew the

Brooks family. He stayed at the *Globe*, never advanced beyond copyediting and never went into criminal justice.

In building up the desks, Mulvoy selected copyeditors from the South, the Midwest, Philadelphia, and New York City, as well as New England. The result not only improved the editing, it also advanced another goal, breaking the incestuous atmosphere at the *Globe*. Blood lines flowed throughout the building. Employees in advertising, circulation, typesetting, and the pressroom, as well as the newsroom, alerted their relatives and friends when openings developed.

The opportunity to reach out further for reporters came when Winship consolidated the separate staffs of the A.M. and P.M. papers under my direction. Instead of hiring a talented intern, Marguerite DelGiudice, I selected Curtis Wilkie, a Mississippian with an accent as broad as his voice was deep. To emphasize the move, I assigned him to City Hall, one of the coveted beats, much to the irritation of long-time *Globe* staffers who thought that any new reporter should pay his dues by working the night shift, preferably on weekends, as they had. (Eventually the *Globe* hired DelGiudice, who did outstanding work before leaving to join the *Philadelphia Inquirer*.) Wilkie proved to be one of the best political reporters in the country, covering the White House and Presidential campaigns. He twice rejected offers from the *New York Times*.

More difficult for me was the question of Eileen McNamara. An honors graduate of Barnard College with a master's degree from the Columbia Graduate School of Journalism, McNamara had turned down an offer from the Associated Press for a reporting job in the South to become my secretary because she wanted to work at the *Globe*, her hometown paper. A spitfire with an acerbic tongue, she kept me vigilant to women's rights.

One of her first days on the job I asked her to get me a tuna fish sandwich on whole wheat bread. She shot back: "Fine, and tomorrow you'll get my lunch." I pointed out to McNamara that in Washington, my assistant, Dana Little, would serve my lunch on a tablecloth in my office, with china, real silverware, glass stemware, a cloth napkin, and a red rose. Even though that clever riposte was true I knew I had lost. From then on I got my own lunch.

McNamara also protected me from annoying phone calls and was aware of the goings-on in the newsroom. She wrote like a whiz, as demonstrated by the letters she would draft for me. She deserved a beginning reporter's job and she had earned my loyalty with her good work. Yet I had opposed hiring of favorite subordinates.

I proposed to Winship that McNamara write obituaries for six months and, if satisfactory, go on the general assignment staff. He refused. I should have fought harder for her. Thankfully, Jack Driscoll got her a job at United Press International. She toiled there for a short time until the *Globe* hired her. She proved herself during years on a wide variety of assignments, capped in 1997, when she was a columnist, with a Pulitzer Prize for commentary and the American Society of Newspaper Editors award for writing. She retired in 2007 to teach at Brandeis University.

It didn't occur to me for some time that in broadening my search for new talent I was running counter to the system that had made the *Globe* one of the best papers in the country. Publisher Davis Taylor had succeeded his father and turned the job over to his son, William O. Taylor. In the newsroom, Tom Winship inherited the editorship from his father. Nepotism sometimes did produce the best. Moreover, when it didn't produce the most talented, it did create loyalty, which, except in unusual circumstances, was more important in the long run. I was bucking a system that had worked. But they let me go ahead and, thankfully, most of the new people worked out fine.

To guide the staff I also started "Glass House View," which was similar to in-house publications put out by editors at other papers, most notably "Winners and Sinners" by Ted Bernstein at the *New York Times*. In this every-once-in-awhile sheet I laid out guides for writing and editing, with an emphasis on ethics. In separate memos I offered tips on writing profiles and news analyses. While I thought that my news analysis memo was clear (I had written a similar one for the *Times*) Winship said he was puzzled; he could not see the difference between an analysis and an opinion. He must have been right because the staff seemed paralyzed. No one wanted to analyze. They were too used to sliding opinions into their stories.

I was pleased in 1979 when I was promoted to executive editor, but soon learned that the title carried far less authority than the managing editorship that I had given up. This was the first move to find a replacement for Winship, as editor, the top title in the *Globe*'s hierarchy. Being a year older than Tom, I could not hope to succeed him. While I would have loved that job, I never had any pretense that I would get it.

Others were not so sure. At a party at the Winship house soon after I joined the *Globe*, Tom's wife commented that I might replace him, but stopped in mid-sentence when she realized what she was saying. Years later, a long-time Bill Taylor confidant called and told me that I must have lunch with him that day; he had important news and it wouldn't wait. At that lunch he said that Bill had told him that he had become fed up with Winship and was going to name me to replace him. Not for a moment did I believe the story, even though my confidant talked with Bill almost daily.

Bill Taylor did get angry with Tom, but the Taylors, father and son, owed too much to the Winships, father and son, to kick Tom out as a result of a Bill Taylor pique. Tom had built the paper into one widely respected by publishers and editors around the country. Pushing Winship aside would violate the Taylor sense of loyalty. My luncheon host never brought the subject up again and I never asked him about it.

When I was appointed executive editor, Bob Healy, who had been told that he would not succeed Winship, gave up the job graciously. He still enjoyed his freedom to write about politics and to travel where he pleased.

I looked around to see what role I could play. I latched on to some special projects, none of which was notable, set up some political polls, oversaw the Spotlight Team investigative team and spent a lot of time on journalism ethics.

Winship invoked my new title to involve me in the editorial page. I had carefully kept my pledge not to read the editorials. While this practice drew wide praise, it did not achieve its goal of insulating me from the *Globe*'s official position on issues. Winship was so forthright about his views that everyone in the building knew what he thought. He did not even pose as an objective editor in conversations with sources. I was in his office in the fall of 1984 when he took a phone call from Senator Walter Mondale, the Democratic candidate for president, and gave him tips on how to run his campaign in New England.

As executive editor, I was free, he said, to read drafts of the editorials. Anne C. Wyman, the editorial page editor, reacted kindly and we got along smoothly. Winship upset her, though, when he asked me to supervise a series on the energy crisis in 1979. He hungered for any Pulitzer, but the one that he craved the most was for editorials, which represented his views. The *Globe* had submitted editorials year after year without success. With a wan smile to Anne, I set up interviews with academic experts and brought in Tom Oliphant, who had been transferred to Washington, to do the writing and, with my approval, some rewriting of Wyman and Bruce C. Davidson of the editorial staff. We did what publishers and editors always deny: we sought to win a prize, not just inform our readers. When the prizes were awarded in the spring of 1980 it was time for a wan smile from Wyman. The *Globe* was nominated as a finalist, but no paper was judged good enough to win.

One role I wished Winship had given me was monitoring the columnists, especially Mike Barnicle. Street smart, with close ties to the police, Mike wrote colorful stories about ordinary people. Even in my early days at the *Globe* I doubted many of his columns. He quoted people although he had not been present and offered no source for much of his material. Because readers loved his column editors gave him wide latitude. One column told of two old people arguing at their breakfast table. In colorful, direct quotes one of them accused the other of marital cheating. It ended with the husband shooting his wife dead. Where did the quotes come from? The two were alone in their apartment. The editor I asked just smiled and said, "that's Barnicle." All it took to save that column was a sentence on the source: "Here is what the police say happened."

No editor fixed that column nor did they save many of his other defective pieces. In Chicago, Mike Ryoko accused Barnicle of copying a number of his columns. The *Globe* had to settle two libel cases, one by Harvard lawyer Alan Dershowitz and the other by a gas station owner. In 1998, long after both Winship and I had left, a former editor of *Reader's Digest* told the *Globe* the *Digest* had concluded that a 1995 Barnicle column was untrue. The column reported that a white boy and a black boy, both suffering from cancer, had become friends. The *Globe* forced Barnicle to leave.

Barnicle is a prime example of tremendous talent wasted because of poor oversight. He was doing what was common in Boston journalism—not just at the *Globe*—when he started as a reporter decades before. A strong editor could have reined him in and showed him how he could use his talents to tell stories in his special voice. It would have been so easy to save him.

Winship lived up to his commitment to let me run the metropolitan staff without interference, but we differed on important matters. This difference didn't mean that we didn't work well together; in fact, we complemented each other. He once said to me, "I wish I was as smart as you." I shot back, "I wish I had your instincts."

He continued to send me "tiger notes" long after the novelty of having me on the *Globe* had worn off. In 1980, the year the *Globe* won three Pulitzer prizes, he wrote me: "You should feel pretty smug. Compare a *Globe* six years ago to today's." With his personal touch, which I envied, he even sent notes to Betty. In 1984 he sent Betty a picture of me taken at the *Globe* with a note asking: "Do you accept this person as your lawfully wedded husband? He looks like a deadbeat truck driver to me!" Betty responded: "It doesn't look like the man I married, but since his mother's not around I'll have to keep him."

Tom never apologized for crusading in the news columns. He realized, he said, that he sometimes overstepped the line. It was my role to tell him when he did so.

Although quickly acclimated to Winship's favoritism, I was taken aback one morning to read in the *Boston Herald* that the principal speaker at the dedication of the *Globe*'s new auditorium would be Mayor Kevin White, who was going to present his vision of the future. The *Globe* and White had sent out joint invitations to civic leaders. It was an obvious effort to push White's campaign for reelection. Trying to control my anger, I confronted Tom, who was on his way to his regular morning meeting with the publisher.

"Is this true?" I asked, pointing to the Herald.

"Yes," he said, "What's wrong with it?"

"You are helping him campaign," I said, shaking my head in disbelief that he didn't see the obvious.

"I don't see anything wrong," he replied as he wheeled and left.

An hour later Tom returned to the newsroom. The mayor wouldn't speak at the dedication; the invitations would be withdrawn.

"Help me be ethical," Tom said.

"How can I," I replied when you don't tell me what you're doing?"

Tom did not always confide in me, partly, I think, because he was used to running his own show and partly because he was concerned that I might balk at some of his pet ideas.

Mayor White must have detected some change in the *Globe* because he told aides that I was out to get him. Perhaps my detached manner in dealing with him, in contrast to Winship's enthusiasm, led to this conclusion. I was neither for him nor against him. In any event, he said he would get me. I didn't take the threat seriously.

When faced with the choice between his political leanings and his editorial integrity, however, Tom's journalistic values prevailed, sometimes with great anguish. In 1978, when the Spotlight Team uncovered Senator Edward Brooke's misuse of his mother-in-law's funds, Tom uttered objection after objection to the wording, but his real reason for opposing the story was that he didn't want to discredit Brooke, the first black person elected to the United States Senate by popular vote and the first since Reconstruction after the Civil War. Eventually he turned to me, hoping I would find a fatal flaw in the story although I had not been involved with the Spotlight Team at the time. I said the exposé should run with minor tinkering of the first few paragraphs.

Gerard M. O'Neill, the Spotlight Team editor, made the clinching argument: that the journalistic reputation of the *Globe* would suffer irreparable harm if the word got out, as it was certain to do, of suppression of the story. As he left the newsroom after finally giving the go-ahead, Tom said, "I hope you guys know you are bringing down the only black in the Senate."

In the end Tom prized the *Globe* more than his political goals. He was right regarding its impact. Brooke was defeated for reelection.

I was not immune from making unethical decisions at the *Globe*. My most serious involved a story on March 26, 1976, regarding the last few days of the Nixon presidency.

*Newsweek* released in Washington excerpts from the book *Final Days*, by Woodward and Bernstein, the *Washington Post* reporters who had outdistanced everyone else in the first months of covering the Watergate scandal.[4] The *Globe*'s story on the book led with Nixon's praying hysterically with Secretary of State Henry Kissinger the night before the President resigned. Other details followed: Nixon's weeping, his drinking, his family's worry that he might kill himself.

It was a good story because it revealed so many things about the crumbling presidency. There was no question that it would go on page one. I read deep into the copy, wallowing in the disclosures. Then I came to this paragraph:

> The President became increasingly isolated from his family. Mrs. Pat Nixon, the book reports, wanted a divorce in 1962 when Nixon ran unsuccessfully for governor of California. According to one excerpt recounted by *New York Daily News* columnist Liz Smith, Mrs. Nixon confided to someone in the White House physician's office that she and the President had not had sexual relations for 14 years.

That last sentence disturbed me. I had only a little problem with running the report on Pat Nixon's desire for a divorce. Yes, it was personal and, yes, spouses sometimes do express such thoughts in the heat of anger without ever really intending to go through with them. But, like many other politicians, Nixon had used his wife in campaigning; therefore, their relationship was fair game for public reporting.

The sexual relationship gave me pause. Wasn't that going too far? I asked other editors whether we should kill the passage. The response (of course there were predictable bad jokes) was divided, but most of the editors favored printing the entire passage. I still hesitated. There was also the question of trusting the authors. Woodward and Bernstein had proved right on Watergate when seasoned reporters, including some on the *Washington Post*, had insisted they were wrong. What I overlooked was the odd attribution of the sentence on the sexual relationship to Liz Smith, the gossip columnist. Actually Liz Smith went too far. *Newsweek*'s excerpts from the Woodward-Bernstein book said this regarding Pat Nixon's relationship with the President:

> She and her husband had not really been close since the early 1960's, the First Lady confided to one of her White House physicians. She had wanted to divorce him after his 1960 defeat in the California gubernatorial

campaign. She tried, and failed, to win his promise not to seek office again. Her rejection of his advances since then had seemed to shut something off inside Nixon. But they had stuck it out.[5]

Eventually I decided to let the sentence run. Never before had we had a presidential resignation. Any light that could be shed on that presidency, that could offer clues to the failure of the man as a leader, was justified.

The next day, on reading the story in print, I concluded that I had made a serious mistake. I had let my feelings about the evils of the Nixon presidency override professional ethical standards that should protect the personal privacy of every individual. The relationship between the Nixons was based on sheer rumor. In the case of the sexual relationship, the report had come not directly from the *Newsweek* excerpts but from what a gossip columnist had heard about the excerpts. There was no evidence to support the statement, no evidence that even if true, the absence of a sexual relationship had any effect on Nixon as the key Watergate figure or as president. I regret that I let that passage stand.

Neither Winship nor any other editor at the *Globe,* nor, as far as I can remember, any reader protested about this breach of ethics. We didn't run a correction or even an explanation. I did recount my error in *Drawing the Line,* a booklet put out by the American Society of Newspaper Editors in 1984. It's a safe bet that few *Globe* readers ever saw that skinback.

Interestingly, Katharine Graham, the *Washington Post* publisher, held no such reservations. In a letter from New York to Woodward and Bernstein, she wrote:

> Hey, what's the big to-do about sex between Nixon and Pat when a story just as juicy could be written about FDR and Eleanor! They quit having sex when their son John was born and didn't FDR have sexy sessions with another lady for many years. And how about a really sensational book about Jack Kennedy, our most prodigious stud. Bathing nude in the pool with call girls and taking two of them to bed for extra kicks! . . . So let's have a big, snoopy book about FDR and JFK, much more interesting, yes? And when you and your wolves stop having sex be sure and let everyone know about it in a book! There's nothing so exciting as invasion of one's most intimate privacy.[6]

Sy Hersh also admired the book. After reading excerpts in *Newsweek*, he dropped a note to Woodward saying, "I wish I had written it (which . . . is the ultimate compliment anyone can get from me . . . )" [ellipses are his].[7]

A decision I made on another story embarrassed the *Globe* nationally. In my first year in Boston, when I was metropolitan editor, one of my assistant editors informed me that his wife, a nurse in the Dana-Farber Cancer Institute, had told him that Premier Leonid Brezhnev of the Soviet Union was going to be admitted to the hospital the next day as a patient. This didn't make sense. While Brezhnev was thought to be suffering from cancer, Moscow would be reluctant to concede the West's medical superiority. Dana-Farber was internationally recognized as a major treatment center for cancer, but it seemed incredible that Brezhnev would give up on Soviet medicine. We checked the Boston Police Department, Logan Airport and government officials in Washington to see if they had been alerted to the Soviet premier's arrival. All we got were negative responses.

We realized that for security reasons officials wouldn't tell us in advance so we didn't accept the negatives as definite. We went back to the nurse, who told her editor husband that she had seen a computer printout of the admissions for the next day and Brezhnev's name was on it. Then someone mentioned that a *Globe* telephone operator had a personal relationship with a high official in the police department. At my request, she called him and reported back that the rumor was true. Reluctant to run a story on such fragile evidence, but concerned about missing a big story in our own territory, I had a short item written that there were rumors that Brezhnev was flying to Boston for cancer treatment but federal and local officials were denying any knowledge of the trip.

We played the story under a small one-column head at the bottom of page one. The rumor was false. We learned later that someone at Dana Farber had put Brezhnev's name on the computer printout of admissions as a practical joke. How much better it would have been if I had not run the story but had staked out the airports and Dana Farber the next morning just in case the rumor were true.

My interest in ethics led to my appointment to the ethics committee of the American Society of Newspaper Editors. Maybe that was a consolation prize for coming in next to last in an election for directors of the society. Using that committee job I won a grant from the Markle Foundation to put on a series of ethics seminars around the country. Philip Meyer, while working at Knight-Ridder, had developed the concept of precision journalism, the use of computers to spot trends in social issues. He joined my group and surveyed editors and publishers on ethical views. With these findings we held workshops in half a dozen cities to offer editors solutions to ethical problems.

At a session in Sacramento I complained about newspapers that, in my opinion, overplayed findings of "tiddly-assed" corruption. My comments were aimed at big headlines exposing government officials who rewarded small-scale contributors with minor greasing of the bureaucratic machine. Katharine Graham, who sat in on the seminar, scolded me. Newspapers, the *Washington Post* publisher said, had a duty to expose all public corruption, minor as well as major. To me, reporters should not spend undue time checking out minor misdeeds, but concentrate on larger violations.

One of my last attempts to change the *Globe* was to develop a wide-ranging code of ethics. When a number of ethical infractions developed in other newspapers, I broached the idea to Winship. In particular, Janet Cooke, a young *Washington Post* reporter, had won a Pulitzer Prize for a story about a young boy as a victim of drug abuse. There was no such boy, she eventually admitted; he was an invention, a composite of young boys she had seen in her reporting. She had to forfeit her Pulitzer Prize. About the same time a reporter for the *Daily News* of New York admitted that he had made up people caught in the conflict between Catholics and Protestants in North Ireland. Because this was a national journalistic issue, Tom enthusiastically supported my proposal.

Using those cases as a springboard, I delved into other ethical problems. Obscenity, exact use of quotations, moving quotes from one part of an interview to another and masking a reporter's identity were a few of the subjects. At meetings the staff raised many objections. To my surprise some of the best reporters brought up the strongest objections. They wanted the freedom to change quotations, insisting that they wouldn't alter the meaning; by straightening out garbles, they said, they were actually helping sources make sense. They wanted the right to move quotations from one part of an interview to another, which, in my mind, could easily distort its meaning by placing it out of context.

Sports editor Dave Smith presented this problem: Professional athletes routinely use obscenities in everyday speech. If you ask a pitcher how he struck out the side in an inning he is likely to say, "I took the fucking ball, threw a fucking slider, then reared back on my ass and burned my fucking fast ball past 'em. I got all the fuckers that way, a fucking slider, a fucking fast ball."

I suggested that the reporter tell the pitcher it was a great quote and ask if he could take the obscenities out, So it would read: "I threw a slider, then reared back and burned my fast ball past 'em. I got all of them that way, a slider, a fast ball." Or he could explain to the reader that he was doctoring the quotation to make it fit for a family audience. Or he could substitute "obscenity" for "fucking." Otherwise, I said, he would have to use fragmented quotes. I also proposed that the reporter have a general understanding with a team that the obscenities would be deleted, treating them like speech interruptions, such as "you know" and "uh uh."

The best investigative reporters said they would be severely handicapped in checking on wrong doing if some suspects knew they were reporters. They wanted to pose in other roles—what is now called pretexting. They wanted to spy on subjects through peepholes in vans.

On the basis of these discussions I drew up a long proposed code of ethics but before I could even attempt to push it through I was put in charge of a special project for the *Globe*. Moving out of the newsroom to offices by the Massachusetts Turnpike, I turned the draft of the code over to Jack Driscoll, who had become managing editor, and urged him to adopt it. He said that he planned to include it in a revised stylebook, but that never happened. Thus, one of my most ambitious goals at the *Globe* died aborning.

I enjoyed my time at the *Globe*. The Taylors and Winship gave me opportunities not open at the *Times*. But Turner Catledge, the former editor of the *Times*, had been right when he told me I didn't have enough time to make the *Globe* a great newspaper. At fifty-four, I had placed my hope in transforming the paper by raising editing standards and thereby establishing objectivity and fairness alongside the *Globe*'s enthusiasm for helping the weak and exposing the corrupt. We made progress, but the job was unfinished when I left the newsroom, as it is at every newspaper at any time. Ethics is a day-by-day job for reporters, editors, and, we must not forget, for publishers, too.

# 19. End of Journalism
### Transcendence—A Love Story

**My journalism career** was not over. In fact, the project I headed offered an opportunity to pioneer in the new world of the Internet, a term not then in wide usage. Knight-Ridder, the newspaper chain, was developing a technology called Viewtron, to distribute news and other information on a computer-like screen. We became the first newspaper to sign an agreement, giving us the right to the Knight-Ridder Viewtron technology in New England. Our staff of eight put together a business plan to provide national, international, local, even neighborhood news, plus banking, brokerage, chat, advertising, and many of the other elements of what is now on World Wide Web sites today.

Excited by the possibilities, I pushed the project hard. With strong support from publisher Bill Taylor, we were ready in two years, to open Viewtron New England as a commercial business at a cost to viewers of $10 a month. Knight Ridder, however, would not pledge to keep the technology going because its trial in the Miami area had failed to sign up many viewers. We were not surprised. Knight Ridder made fundamental errors in its nearly $50 million effort. Instead of rolling out the service in a high-technology area like the Silicon Valley, where it had a natural market, it chose Miami, with demographics heavy in unlikely customers, old people and Hispanics. Instead of keying service to personal computers, it required customers to buy a special $800 AT&T receiver, good only for Viewtron.

Without the Viewtron technology we were dead. As we shut the office down in 1985 I told Bill Taylor that I was retiring. He offered to find something for me to do in his office, as long, he said, as "you retain your

22. Sitting for a portrait at the desk of General Charles Taylor, the first of the Taylors to run the *Boston Globe*. Photographer unknown. *Boston Globe* photo; reproduced with permission.

marbles." But, at sixty-six, I said I was ready to leave and, within a few weeks, retired.

I decided to study acting. For two years I attended classes at Brandeis University, only a few miles from our house. Then I tested the market. After uncounted hours at auditions, to be told time after time, "Lovely, lovely, you'll hear from us," almost always followed by endless silence, I faced up to the truth. My laid-back style proved fatal as an actor. (I'm still puzzled. It worked for Jimmy Dean. Why not me?)

It was back to editing. I spent a decade at Harvard University putting out *Nieman Reports*, the oldest journalism quarterly in the country, in a persistent effort to nudge newspapers and broadcasting stations toward more responsible behavior.

With this detachment from daily journalism, Betty and I were slowly discovering a new intimacy. It was not sex in the fullest sense, but it did involve more touching. Betty always enjoyed massages of her back and especially her feet, although she often complained that I was rough. She also liked to have her scalp rubbed. Just as we had on our wedding night, we nestled together again as we fell asleep. We also were hugging each other more, sometimes briefly during the day, longer at bedtime. If she had a particularly difficult day, I would listen to her problems and comfort her. And if I had troubles I would tell her and she would hug me.

During this period Betty made her only request in our half-century together that I consider becoming a Catholic. She had heard from young friends of a Catholic renewal movement called Cursillo. Founded in Spain in 1944, the Cursillo method spread rapidly around the world. I readily consented, but it was a bad choice for me, a nonbeliever, because of its focus on reconversions through what seemed to me to be manipulation and tricks.

I attended a three-day weekend meeting at Stonehill College, south of Boston. Almost everyone there had been born Catholic and had fallen away from practicing their faith. For many participants it did renew their faith; for me it was a disaster. The half a hundred men (no women allowed) were divided into groups of about eight and assigned to tables. After an introductory talk by a priest, a man at an adjoining table asked if he could speak. It seemed like a spontaneous response but it quickly became clear that he had been a plant and his speech had been well prepared. Each of the tables was asked to draw in colored crayons on a big cardboard the meaning of the speech. Then an individual, obviously chosen in advance, explained to the entire group what the cardboard signified.

After that we were handed the English lyrics of the Cursillo song, Colores, which we sang as we marched to the dining room. Throughout the meal individuals would jump up and tell smutty jokes, some of them quite raw, a shock to me considering the nature of the sessions. (The reason, I was told, was to show the participants that they could be masculine and still be Christian.)

This was the procedure of the dozen or so talks. On the final evening we went, one table at a time, to the chapel, crawled under the altar where our leader uttered a short prayer, kissed a crucifix and handed it to the next person, who did the same. When it came to me I merely handed the crucifix to the next person. Then we marched to the dining room for our final dinner. As we finished, the doors burst open and our sponsors rushed in to congratulate us. Betty, who wanted to attend, was not allowed in because she was not an official sponsor; one of her friends was. The exclusion embittered her because she, of all people, wanted to be present if I had become a Catholic.

The sessions had not appealed to me in any way. Far more persuasive for me was Hans Küng, a Swiss theologian, whose books ran afoul of the Vatican.[1] To me those books offered a Christianity that did not violate science and modern biblical findings. Betty and I had visited Küng in his house in Tübingen, Germany, on a trip to Europe. He served us sherry as we chatted on his veranda. If the Vatican had followed his lead I might have been convinced.

We were happily entering retirement, keeping fit by swimming, treadmilling, and weight lifting at a health club, enjoying the Trinity Theatre in Providence, gardening our little acre in Lincoln. But we soon faced a terrible threat. Betty was fighting a second battle against cancer.

Surgery and radiation had beaten bladder cancer in the early 1990s. Now she had to fight lung cancer, a tougher opponent. She didn't say so, but she needed me. She had needed me throughout our half-century of marriage, as I had needed her, but she had almost always sacrificed for me while I gave up much less for her.

In 2000 I quit my job at *Nieman Reports*. Gradually I assumed most household tasks—cleaning, laundry, ironing (yes, I did my shirts), and even preparing dinners. Before long I boldly cooked for guests. They may have been apprehensive to see me in an apron but they usually— our guests were kind—praised the pork chops with blueberry salsa and the crab cakes without filler. Because I also cleaned up the kitchen, Betty faced no competition from me in either the pre-dinner cocktail chatter or the after-dinner conversation.

My greatest difficulty was helping Betty without damaging her spirit by infringing on her independence. As she had said numerous times, "if you are going to do that for me, I might as well give up." Even when it snowed, she wanted to drive alone the twenty miles into downtown Boston for chemotherapy and radiation treatments at Massachusetts General Hospital. I devised excuses to accompany her, knowing that she was often too tired to drive back. Unless I was with her she had to trudge blocks from the parking garage to the doctor's office and back. Gradually she let me do the driving, conserving her energy for swimming and weight training at our health club.

Nevertheless, the cancer's unrelenting attrition wore her down, forcing her to cut back and eventually to give up trips to the health club. Frustrated by her deteriorating handwriting, she finally turned one of her last remaining chores, check writing and bank account reconciling, over to me.

Previously a heavy sleeper, I began to awaken at slight clues of Betty's distress. In the middle of the night of March 27, 2002, severe pains wracked her intestines. I rushed her to the emergency room at Massachusetts General Hospital where, at 3 A.M. Dr. Charles M. Ferguson removed eight inches of Betty's lower intestine to relieve a bowel obstruction. Grittily she lived on for another year.

Reluctant to travel for fear of a medical emergency, Betty had to be coaxed to take even short trips. To limit fatigue on our drives to Providence to attend Trinity Theatre, I parked the car in a space for the handicapped at the entrance, where we ate soup and sandwiches. We did make the eight-hour trip to Harrisburg a few times, and Betty drove much of the way, an accomplishment that buoyed her spirits, particularly when I asked her to slow down because she was going 80. Stopping at a favorite donut shop in Wilkes-Barre made the trips seem like old times. Although she was exhausted on our return, the visits to her sister Kathleen, her brother Richard and others in the extended King family always raised her morale.

Activities at Sacred Heart Church in Lexington kept her busy; its parishioners had become her family. Despite her illness she visited nursing homes to give communion to the sick. She was one of the regular lectors, reading biblical passages at Mass. She took the job seriously, practicing them at home with the aid of a tape recorder and, sometimes, with the annoyance of my kibitzing. She was equally serious about the choir. Despite her illness, she took lessons to strengthen and improve the quality of her voice.

I encouraged Betty in her efforts to seek reform of the Catholic Church. Inspired by Pope John XXIII and the Vatican II Council, she had become a liberal Catholic in Washington. When we moved to Massachusetts she reinforced those views by auditing courses taught by the Rev. George W. MacRae, a Jesuit at the Harvard Divinity School. Despite reactionary doctrinal moves by Pope John Paul II and by American bishops, Betty remained a Catholic. Inevitably she ran into conflicts.

When Boston Cardinal Bernard Law issued his annual appeal for funds, she wrote him that she wouldn't donate until he treated women justly. Outraged when the cardinal tried to force a conservative priest on her parish, she called a *Boston Globe* reporter, who wrote a story about the controversy. Although shy in public, Betty joined others in speaking at a protest meeting. Cardinal Law withdrew the priest.

As the lector at a Mass she substituted inclusive language for the exclusive male wording in reading scripture. The Rev. James O'Donohoe, the celebrant, admonished her before the congregation for including women in the passage. Standing next to the altar, she told the congregation that church authorities had sanctioned the substitution in guidebooks for lectors. The parishioners applauded.

Betty had lost much of her strength in 2002 when the *Globe* exposed widespread abuse of children by priests in the Boston Archdiocese and the subsequent cover-up of the scandal by Cardinal Law. She joined Voice of the Faithful, a new organization seeking wider participation in the governance of the church. Climbing the stairs at local meetings of the new group taxed her strength but she continued to attend.

The big event of 2002 was the national founding convention of Voice of the Faithful in July. Betty doubted that she had the strength for the trip to and from Boston, the long walks to meetings in the hotel, and lengthy sessions in the auditorium. "You can make it," I said. "We'll go the night before and stay in the hotel." The convention exhilarated her. She applauded, she cried, she cheered, she sang, she laughed, she prayed. She even remembered my birthday and insisted on celebrating at a Legal Seafoods restaurant in the hotel complex.

In January 2003, Dr. Donald S. Kaufman, her oncologist at Massachusetts General Hospital, shattered Betty and me when he said that there was nothing more he could do to retard the cancer and that we should prepare for hospice. I asked about trying Iressa, an experimental drug approved in Japan and Australia, which had shown remarkable results in about 15 percent of cases. Each time I had mentioned it earlier he said it was too early to consider it. This time he adamantly refused. "You don't want to hurt her, do you?" he said.

I did not understand why Dr. Kaufman, whose skills had extended Betty's life, blocked use of Iressa. As he later conceded, he knew almost nothing about the drug, merely classifying it with other experimental medicines. I had been following reports on the drug for two years and knew it was available on a compassionate use basis in the United States for cases like Betty's. Iressa posed little danger to patients; side effects from taking the pill had been mild.

"I guess this is it," Betty said as we left Dr. Kaufman's office. She did not want to go to a hospice, preferring to stay at home as long as possible, and I was confident I could keep her active and comfortable.

As the weeks went by, however, her breathing became more difficult, and, with Betty's agreement, I decided to go around Dr. Kaufman to seek a second doctor's opinion about Iressa. When Dr. Kaufman heard of my effort he called Betty and me to his office. There he reluctantly agreed to set up a meeting with Dr. Thomas J. Lynch, another oncologist at MGH, who had been prescribing Iressa. In mid-April Dr. Lynch examined Betty and said she was "a good candidate" for the new drug. However, the manufacturer, Astra-Zeneca, had recently stopped providing the drug for new experimental cases because it was about to be approved by the Food and Drug Administration. We had to wait, but we were elated; Betty would get another chance.

She never got that chance.

On Saturday, April 26, Betty said she didn't think she could attend Mass, but she summoned her strength and, wearing a favorite red dress with lace collar, sat in a side pew. When the Mass ended, friends crowded around and embraced her. She told them that it was going to be her last Mass. Four days later, early in the morning, I called 911 to rush Betty to the hospital again. She was struggling to breathe. On Sunday, May 4, after two days on oxygen and morphine, she died. The next day the FDA approved Iressa.

Articles I had read warned me of the exaggerated sense of guilt caregivers often feel on the death of a loved one. I was no exception. I berated myself for not moving faster to get a second opinion on Iressa. The chance it would work was slim, but it might have given her a few more months of life. I faulted Kaufman for his intransigence, but blamed myself even more. (In 2005 the FDA advised doctors not to prescribe Iressa because in trials it did not prolong the life of patients.)

My guilt extended even deeper, to my decades of putting my job ahead of her, a transgression worse than the delay over Iressa and to me far worse than transitory sexual infidelities. Looking back, I remembered incidents decades before that a sensitive husband would have recognized as a cry for affirmation.

In Saddle River, New Jersey, she came home one day proudly wearing for the first time her uniform as a "pink lady" volunteer at Valley Hospital in nearby Ridgewood. My mind elsewhere, I didn't notice until she asked if I liked her uniform. A minor transgression, common in marriages and understandable when infrequent, but when a husband's disregard becomes a pattern it demonstrates a second-class status for the wife. Unquestionably, there had been such a pattern.

The *Times* offer to send me to Paris demonstrated the contrast between Betty's willingness to give up a chance to expand her life and my focus on my career. Her first question about a Paris transfer was: "What is best for you?" I confined my reply to an explanation of the routine daily editing involved. I did not ask what was best for her. The discussion focused completely on my career.

As a man who had devoted so much thought and energy to his search for spiritual and philosophical truth I should have discussed the pros and cons for her and not just for me. As a man who talked about fairness and social justice I should have rejected the subordinate role of the wife commonly accepted in the middle of the twentieth century. The fact that I had a professional life and Betty did not was irrelevant. She did not have to study at the Sorbonne or seek to follow Julia Child into French cuisine. The experience of living in Paris and traveling throughout Europe would have expanded Betty's life enormously, especially in art. We were supposed to be equal partners. Why had I not given her a chance to fly, too? Why did I not spend more time with her even after I retired, instead of studying acting and editing *Nieman Reports?*

In one of our early morning conversations in Washington, Scotty Reston had talked about the sacrifice that wives of journalists made. I had not picked up on his observation, perhaps, in part, because I realized that Scotty had done something that I could not do. He had persuaded the Sulzbergers to put his wife, Sally, on the *Times* payroll.

One explanation of my blindness was the fact that Betty enjoyed her role as my life partner. She often said that she wouldn't trade her life for any other. I once asked her what her proudest accomplishment had been. She did not say it was her recognition as an accomplished birder or her efforts to reform the Catholic Church. Her greatest achievement, she said, was helping research court cases for my libel book at the Columbia University Law Library, putting together the index, proofreading the text and providing the title: *Libel: Rights, Risks, Responsibilities.*

Relatives and friends thought our marriage ideal. More often than not, we—well, I (I cannot speak for Betty)—thought so, too. Nephews and nieces called us by one name—BettyBob. Every year we traveled—around the country, to Europe, to Latin America, to Asia, to Alaska, to Hawaii. *Times* correspondents guided us to places she never dreamed we would visit. She and the publisher greeted each other with a kiss. She was a gentle member of the *Times* family.

Betty accepted as her contribution to my job the evenings I spent with colleagues facing professional or personal crises. She never complained of my long hours with Ben Welles as he struggled with the biography of his father or with Richard Halloran as we worked out a new assignment for him after his removal as a foreign affairs reporter. I had taken interns' stories home to work on them and had spent mornings, nights and weekends for months editing and rewriting Charles Bohlen's memoirs. Her compassion for such people helped make me an effective editor.

Nevertheless, my thoughts always came back to the realization that much of this extra time could have been devoted to widening Betty's life. She could have moped and protested, but she didn't. These thoughts counterbalanced to some extent the self-reproach that set in after her death. But there was no escaping the fact that Betty had paid a heavy price in lonely days and nights, in lost weekends, in interruptions of vacations, in opportunities to develop personally and professionally.

Just, as a child, I had accepted the sacrifices my parents had made for me as well as the favoritism of my sister and brothers, I accepted Betty's offering of herself. Instead of learning to give, I had conditioned myself only to take.

Fortunately, when the severity of Betty's illness became clear I did what countless husbands have done. I made the fight against Betty's cancer my only priority. I was late, but I found more satisfaction in caring for her than in any achievement as a journalist. As the months passed I realized that the role of caregiver offered an opportunity for personal fulfillment that I had been blind to in my unrelenting drive for journalistic success. In my new life I didn't mind cleaning up after bouts of diarrhea and vomiting—washing her body, changing sheets and bedclothes, scrubbing the bathroom in the middle of the night. Each little lifting of the burden from her generated a quiet joy in me.

After Betty died, when guilt engulfed me, friends told me I should not judge myself by standards stemming from the campaign for equal rights for women but by the pervasive culture of male dominance into which I had been born. That perception comforted me somewhat but religion had left its mark on me. I had failed to grasp the real meaning of love, of its simple message of putting someone else first.

This was not a religious conversion, certainly not in the evangelical sense. My soul did not cry to be saved. Saved from what? From Satan? I did not believe in Satan. I felt no anxiety about death and the hereafter. Yes, I suffered despair but it sprang from the fact that after all my searching I knew nothing about religious truth. Journalism, while rewarding, had left me spiritually bankrupt, with an emptiness of heart.

Still not a believer in the Christianity that nourished Betty, I was startled one night in the week after her death to see Jesus outside my bedroom window. As I sat on the bed, looking into the back yard, Jesus stood on the lawn in the classic long white robe of funeral-director calendars. I could not believe what I was seeing. I lay down, closed my eyes, opened them and he was still there. Each time I awakened in the night he was standing there, never moving, never speaking.

These visions continued for days. I began to say "Good night, Jesus" to the white sentinel outside my window. Then, one night, on turning over, I noticed that a light from the hall cast its rays into the room and out the window. I closed the door and Jesus disappeared from the lawn. Why wasn't he there before? Because Betty had kept the blinds closed at night.

I told the story to Molly Marsh, a former co-worker at *Nieman Reports* and dear friend. Molly was somewhat of a rarity; she graduated from Harvard Divinity School with her faith intact. She is now an editor-writer at *Sojourners* magazine in Washington.

"What does it mean to you?" she asked.

"It was an illusion, of course," I laughed.

"So?"

I dismissed Molly's provocative reply as an evasion of the truth. I had not seen Jesus. I could turn him on or off with a click of a light switch.

A month or so after the memorial service for Betty at Sacred Heart Church, still bitter over the doctor's delay in trying the drug Iressa, I wept as I looked at the tulips blossoming around our birdbath. Why could Betty not have lived just a little longer, to see the red and white tulips standing tall and the weeping cherry tree in full pink bloom in the background? A few weeks later, with the faded tulips hanging limp, four or five birds fluttered down from the birch tree hanging over the bath. They were fledging orioles. One of them turned and looked up directly at me—or so I thought—splashed, turned around, splashed, turned back toward me, stared at me again, splashed once more, and flew away with the others.

"Is that Betty," I asked myself, "telling me everything's all right?"

Yes, mourners report receiving word from the dead in many forms, symbolically through animals, butterflies, and pets, through dreams, ghosts, and even e-mail messages. What better way for an expert birder like Betty to communicate with her husband than through a favorite bird frolicking at a site where she knew he would be?

My imagination ran wild, but my defenses were heightened because of the Jesus illusion. Despite assurances from friends and relatives, I could not agree the birds had sent me a real message from Betty. As much as I was tempted, I was not going to let a few baby orioles deceive me.

In early fall I remembered Betty's custom of cutting branches of wild firethorn in a woods near our house. The orange-red berries added color to our living areas over the winter. In a half-hour I snipped enough branches for three or four vases. As I started home I noticed a firethorn across a clearing. Loaded with berries, it was the tallest firethorn I had ever seen.

I stood entranced for a few minutes. Then I saw something moving at the top of the big firethorn, something orange and black. A quick check with the binoculars found the bird—yes, yes—an oriole! Another illusion? An adult oriole is an easy bird to identify. What could I say now? Betty had led me there, knowing that I would be clipping firethorn. Imagination or not, the oriole told me again not to worry. In that sense the oriole was real. Everything was going to be all right for Betty and for me, too, for both of us.

I thought again of my backyard Jesus. The question of divinity did not matter. That's what Molly had been saying. Whether divine or an illusion, whether son of God, a perfect reflection of God, or little more than a myth, Jesus was a way-shower, not just to hundreds of millions of Christians but also to nonbelievers—even to me.

This was a decisive moment for me. How far could I go along Betty's path? I knew that as she studied the history of Christianity, particularly the Roman Catholic Church, she had discarded much of the dogma that she had been taught in her youth, such as the Virgin birth, the Christmas story, Jesus's walking on water, the transformation of the communion wine and bread into the actual blood and body of Jesus. For Betty, the two essentials were that God loved her and Jesus was her guide.

Long ago, I had realized that much of my secular faith, journalism, was a myth, but I clung to it because its value far outweighed its imperfections. In view of their claim to ultimate truth I held religions to higher standards. The question for me became this: what was essential to me?

Over the years I had become convinced that because of continued discoveries by scientists and modern biblical scholars, I would never find proof of the Christianity espoused by churches. Betty's faith took her beyond logic to a spiritual assurance of a relationship with God and Jesus. Lacking faith, I could not go all the way with her. I did not possess her conviction in a personal relationship with the divine. I did not feel God's embrace.

Yet messages hinting of the divine had come to me. Must I reject them because there was no scientific proof that they were true? Cannot truth come through the spirit? Isn't that what I told the University of Michigan professor of religion in 1940 in criticizing the Unitarian Church in Ann Arbor?

I was drawn but I hesitated. In the past, every effort to find faith had failed, either because of my blindness to messages or to my stubborn refusal to accept what others, including friends and intellectuals I admired, thought obvious. Or, perhaps, because the skeptic in me had been right all along and faith was a myth. Of one thing I was certain: Betty's death offered a meaning for my life. I determined to find that meaning. My quest was not over.

I would not rush; I preferred to take careful, tentative steps in this renewed search. The first step was to separate the simple core of Jesus's message—loving others—from the trappings of dogma and theology. That meant adopting the forgiveness that Jesus preached and that Betty practiced. Angry for months, I wrote Dr. Kaufman forgiving him for his refusal to give Betty a chance to use the cancer drug Iressa until it was too late. Much more difficult was forgiving myself for putting her life second to mine. I did not forget—that would be impossible—but, applying Christian redemption, I stopped dwelling on this, my greatest of failures.

My main effort beyond redemption is to find the spirit of God that is in me. I have returned to Quaker meetings that I first encountered in Harrisburg sixty years ago. I meditate most every day at home as Betty taught me. So far the goal eludes me. Daily cares always seem to intrude and sometimes I fall asleep (after all, I am almost ninety years old). But I have not given up—nor will I.

A scrap of paper with Betty's scribbling reinforced this resolution. It had sat on a kitchen counter for months untouched after her death until I picked it up. (Another divine message?)

Partly in her shorthand, it was one of the notes that Betty often wrote to herself as a reminder of something important that she had read or heard or thought. This note quoted Michael Hansen's book, *The Land of Walking Trees*. It said that "faith is more about openness of heart to take the journey, to keep moving forward, than it is about reaching any imagined destination."[2]

That was certainly not a new thought, but reading it in the context of Betty's death had special meaning. I remembered our good times together, of getting tipsy on Irish whiskey with her relatives in Limerick, of skinny dipping in Caneel Bay on our twenty-fifth wedding anniversary, of crawling on our bellies in Aransas National Wildlife Refuge in Texas to within inches of a whippoorwill, of her skateboarding in her eighties, of both of us thrown into a cauldron while white-water rafting in Ontario, of a drive in the early morning light in a Vietcong-dominated area of Vietnam. These and other memories kept coming. And they will continue to come and enrich my life—just as will memories of my career as a journalist. The question remains whether these memories will help me discover the spirit of God within that I have never found.

Regardless of the outcome, I have achieved one great advance. Because of Betty's illness and her Christian giving, I have finally learned how to love someone more than myself. I have learned that love is more than deep affection, more than an intimate relationship, more than sharing life's successes and failures. Love is giving of yourself throughout life's journey so others may grow fully. That's what Betty did for me for the fifty-six years of our lives together. As she lay dying on her hospital bed, she whispered, "You were wonderful." I whispered back, "You were the wonderful one."

She deserved the praise for all she did throughout our lives together. I didn't. But, ah! she said it.

# Notes

•

# Index

# Notes

### 1. The Bible (Somewhat Revised) Told Me Who I Was

1. A word about quotations. While my memory is pretty sharp as I march into my tenth decade, I do not lay claim to exactitude in recalling conversations of long ago. Indeed, like many friends far younger, I sometimes forget what I go to the basement to fetch. Thus my use of quotation marks in personal situations recounted throughout this book should not be interpreted as if from an electronic recording. However, I am confident that such quotations do represent the spirit of what was said; in that sense they are as accurate as I can make them and I vouch for their truth. Of course, I cite sources in vital matters.

2. *O Word of God Incarnate* was written by William W. How, an Anglican bishop, about 1867 and has appeared in hymnals since then with harmonization by Felix Mendelssohn.

### 3. Okinawa One: Kamikazes—An African American Hero

1. In 1958, Dr. Walsh obtained President Eisenhower's support to refit a Navy hospital ship as the SS *Hope*, which became a teaching hospital for medical professionals in disadvantaged countries. He died in 1996 after leading Project Hope for thirty-four years.

### 4. Okinawa Two: A *Caine Mutiny* Story

1. Herman Wouk, *The Caine Mutiny* (Garden City, N.Y.: Doubleday, 1951).

2. Robert H. Phelps, "Cupcake Meets America," *Our Navy*, Aug. 1, 1945.

3. After the Pacific war the *Ellyson* served in the Atlantic Ocean and Caribbean Sea. On October 19, 1954, it was decommissioned and transferred to Japan, where it sailed in the Self-Defense Force as the *Asakaze* (morning sea breeze). It was scrapped in 1972.

### 5. Living It Up in Japan, Korea, and China

1. Robert H. Phelps, "Servicemen and Strikes," *Harper's Magazine*, Aug. 1945, 178.

### 6. Two Loves: Betty and Editing

1. Thomas Wolfe, foreword to *Look Homeward, Angel* (New York: Charles Scribner's Sons, 1929).

2. Robert H. Phelps and E. Douglas Hamilton, *Libel: Rights, Risks, Responsibilities* (New York: Macmillan, 1966; rev. ed. New York: Dover Publications, 1978.

### 7. Early Success: A Substitute for Religion

1. Bob Slosser, *Reagan Inside Out* (New York: Word Books, 1984). The book reported that in 1970 at a prayer meeting God had called on Reagan to run for president.

2. Herman H. Dinsmore, *All the News That Fits* (New Rochelle, N.Y.: Arlington House, 1969).

3. John L. Hess, *My Times: A Memoir of Dissent* (New York: Seven Stories Press, 2003).

### 8. Harrison Salisbury: A Flawed Role Model

1. Harrison E. Salisbury, *The Shook-up Generation* (New York: Harper 1958).

2. Warren Commission, *Report of the President's Commission on the Assassination of President John F. Kennedy* (Washington, D.C.: U.S. Government Printing Office, 1964).

3. Michael S. Kramer and Sam Roberts, *I Never Wanted to Be Vice President of Anything* (New York: Basic Books, 1976).

4. Tom Wicker to author, Mar. 14, 1964.

5. Dwight D. Eisenhower, *Waging Peace, 1956–1961: The White House Years* (Garden City, N.Y.: Doubleday, 1965.

6. Wallace Turner, *Gamblers' Money: The New Force in American Life* (Boston: Houghton Mifflin, 1965).

### 9. On to Washington: Gradual Acceptance

1. In 1974 seven women sued the *Times* in a class action case asking for equality with men in pay and assignments. I provided an affidavit in support of the women. The *Times* settled out of court in 1977.

### 10. The *Times* Civil War: My First Setback

1. Daniel Walker, *Rights in Conflict: The Violent Confrontation of Demonstrators and Police* (New York: Bantam Books, 1968).

2. E. Clifton Daniel to author, Aug. 16, 1968.

### 11. Losing a Big Beat on the Vietnam War

1. Max Frankel, *The Times of My Life and My Life with The Times* (New York: Random House, 1999).

2. Ibid.

3. A. M. Rosenthal to author, Aug. 10, 1970.

### 12. The Pentagon Papers: Never Trust the Government

1. Neil Sheehan, *The Arnheiter Affair* (New York: Random House, 1971).

2. Daniel Ellsberg, *Secrets: A Memoir of Vietnam and the Pentagon Papers* (New York: Penguin Putnam Viking, 2002.

3. Ellsberg, 363.

4. Neil Sheehan et al., *Pentagon Papers: Secret History of the Vietnam War* (New York Times, 1971).

5. The National Security Archive: Audio Tapes from the Nixon White House June 14, 1971. http://www.gwu.edu/~nsarchiv/NSAEBB/NSAEBB48/nixon.html

### 13. Watergate One: How the *Post* Beat the *Times*

1. Unless otherwise noted, all quotations attributed to Howard Simons are from the transcript of an interview he gave to Bob Woodward and Carl Bernstein in 1973 for their book, *All the President's Men*. The Simons transcript is among the papers the two reporters sold to the University of Texas Library for $5 million. The papers, open to the public, are held in the Harry Ransom Research Center at the university's Austin campus.

2. Carl Bernstein and Bob Woodward, *All the President's Men* (New York: Simon and Schuster, 1974), 36 .

3. Contract in Woodward-Bernstein Collection at Ransom Research Center, Univ. of Texas at Austin.

4. Bob Woodward, *The Secret Man: The Story of Watergate's Deep Throat* (New York: Simon and Schuster, 2005), 60.

5. The notes on this meeting with "Deep Throat" are the most extensive filed in the Ransom Research Center collection by Woodward regarding his talks with Mark Felt, the FBI source known as "Deep Throat." Notes of only five of the seventeen contacts are included in the Ransom collection. Under terms of the agreement, Woodward and Bernstein have the right to withhold notes of interviews with living confidential sources. Stephen Mielke, the Woodward-Bernstein archivist, estimates that the library has opened about 85 percent of the files. Thus there may be Woodward notes quoting multiple sources, including Felt, in the unopened papers. Also, Woodward has said he did not make notes for every meeting with or phone call to Felt.

The absence of notes of most of the meetings and phone calls raises questions about Woodward's working habits and the precise accuracy of quotations used in the *Post* stories based on them, as well as sections of *All the President's Men* and Woodward's later book *The Secret Man*. On the surface, Woodward seemed to have built long quotations from phrases in his notes, a practice followed by reporters in Washington and elsewhere.

For example, *All the President's Men* devotes nearly three pages to Woodward's meeting with Felt in a Prince George's county bar in February 1973. His single-spaced notes run about 900 words, but a lot more is added in the book, making for easier reading. The notes say Nixon voiced "rage" about leaks. The book leads up to the quotation with a jocular exact-quote exchange (not in the notes) about why the meeting was in the bar and a question about subpoenas issued to the *Post*. Then the book provides "Deep Throat" a transition quote, also not in the notes: "That's only the first step," followed by a rewrite of the notes on Nixon's anger. Instead of just "rage," Felt is quoted as saying: "Our President has gone on a rampage about news leaks on Watergate. He's told the appropriate people, 'Go to any lengths' to stop them. When he says that he really means business."

The quotation continues without interruption for a few hundred words with Felt supplying background material not usually included by sources talking to reporters. In this case Felt says Nixon planned to use money left over from his campaign, "about $5 million or so," against the *Post*. That "5 million or so" is not in his notes.

Are such changes important if the thrust of the writing is correct? Here are two examples of misleading the reader from that interview.

One, Felt is quoted on Page 269 of *All the President's Men* as telling Woodward: "So the White House wants to eat the Washington Post." The notes attribute this quote to FBI Director L. Patrick Gray's report of the meeting as relayed by Felt.

Two, on the same page Felt is quoted as saying "Nixon was wild, shouting and hollering that 'we can't have it and we're going to stop it. I don't care how much it costs.' His theory is that the news media have gone way too far and the trend has to be stopped—almost like he was talking about federal spending." Again, Woodward's notes attribute these quotes, in slightly altered form, to Gray. Thus Woodward passed up two chances to cast a more favorable light on the unfortunate Gray.

Last, the Woodward notes of the February interview are dated "the night of March 5." Woodward does not explain the discrepancy in his references to the meeting. Did he type his notes within a few hours or the day following the meeting and just use the wrong date? Perhaps he waited until March 5 or 6 to prepare them, in which case his memory might not have been sharp. Is there, perhaps, an earlier version of these notes?

Another example, this from that important October 10, 1972, article about a vast plan to disrupt the Democratic campaign. It cited information in FBI and Department of Justice files as sources of its charges. The notes, however, were based on what Felt told Woodward was in the files. Woodward never saw the files. The *Post* also took that extra step in saying that "according to FBI reports, at least 50 undercover Nixon operatives traveled throughout the country" trying to disrupt the Democratic campaign. Again, Woodward did not see the FBI reports. He pressed Felt hard on the number of Republican saboteurs, and got this response: "You can safely say more than 50." Even then, according to Woodward's notes, Felt added this qualification: "from what I conclude" and reports are divided and never put together "except on Gray's desk—and that we don't like." Woodward does not use these qualifications in *All the President's Men*, obviously willing to accept Felt's statements as fact.

6. L. Patrick Gray III, with Ed Gray, *In Nixon's Web: A Year in the Crosshairs of Watergate* (New York: Times Books, 2008), 42.

### 14. Watergate Two: How the *Times* Beat the *Post*

1. As in the previous chapter, all quotations attributed to Howard Simons are from his 1973 interview with Woodward and Bernstein. The transcript is in the Woodward-Bernstein collection at the Harry Ransom Research Center, Univ. of Texas in Austin.

2. Bernstein and Woodward, 207.

3. Bernstein and Woodward, 235.

4. The undated letter is in the Woodward-Bernstein Collection at the Ransom Research Center, Univ. of Texas in Austin.

5. Bernstein and Woodward, 332.

6. Barbara Raskin, *Washington Monthly*, Feb. 1973.

7. Arthur Gelb, *City Room* (New York: G. P. Putnam's Sons, 2003), 573.

8. James Reston, *Deadline: A Memoir* (New York: Random House, 1991), 343.

9. Ibid., 344.

### 15. Imperial Editor—Or Partner Editor?

1. Gelb, 512.

2. David K. Shipler, *Arab and Jew: Wounded Spirits in a Promised Land* (New York: Penguin Books, 2002).

3. Frankel, 427.

4. Baker, Russell. *Growing Up* (New York: Congdon and Weed, 1982).

### 16. Clifton Daniel: Luring Sally Quinn

1. E. Clifton Daniel, *Lords, Ladies and Gentlemen: A Memoir* (Westminster, Md.: Arbor House, 1984).

2. James Naughton, interview, About Poynter. http://www.poynter.org/column. asp?id=62.

3. James Sterba, *Frankie's Place: A Love Story* (New York: Grove, 2005).

4. John Crewdson, *Science Fictions: A Scientific Mystery, A Massive Coverup and the Dark Legacy of Robert Gallo* (Boston: Little, Brown, 2002).

5. Charles E. Bohlen, *Witness to History,* with Robert H. Phelps (New York: Norton, 1974).

### 17. *Boston Globe* Offer: Quitting the *Times*

1. Ellsberg, 368.

2. Christopher Lydon to Davis Taylor, Feb. 24, 1974. Copy in author's files.

3. Tom Wicker to author, 1974.

### 18. School Integration: Pulitzer Gold Medal

1. "Who Holds the Power in Boston?" *Boston Phoenix*, Mar. 25, 1975.

2. "The First Year: An Account of Boston School Desegregation—The Students, the Officials and the Public," *Boston Globe*, May 25, 1975.

3. J. Anthony Lukas, *Common Ground: A Turbulent Decade in the Lives of Three American Families* (New York: Alfred A. Knopf, 1985).

4. Bob Woodward and Carl Bernstein, *Final Days* (New York: Simon and Schuster, 1987).

5. Ibid.

6. Katharine Graham, undated letter in Woodward-Bernstein Collection Ransom Research Center, Univ. of Texas at Austin, 1987.

7. Seymour Hersh, note in Woodward-Bernstein Collection.

**19. End of Journalism: Transcendence—A Love Story**

1. Hans Küng, *On Being Christian* (Garden City, N.Y.: Doubleday, 1976); Hans Küng, *Does God Exist: An Answer for Today* (Garden City, N.Y.: Doubleday, 1980).

2. Michael Hansen, *The Land of Walking Trees: Reflections for the Chronically Ill*(New York: Harper Collins/Dove, 1993), 3.

# Index